The Later Poetry
of
WALLACE STEVENS

The Later Poetry
of
WALLACE STEVENS

**Phenomenological Parallels
with
Husserl and Heidegger**

THOMAS J. HINES

**Lewisburg
Bucknell University Press
London: Associated University Presses**

Associated University Presses, Inc.
Cranbury, New Jersey 08512

Associated University Presses
108 New Bond Street
London W1Y OQX, England

Library of Congress Cataloging in Publication Data

Hines, Thomas J 1940–
    The later poetry of Wallace Stevens.

    Bibliography: p. 277
    Includes index.
    1. Stevens, Wallace, 1879–1955—Criticism and interpretation.
2. Stevens, Wallace, 1879–1955—Philosophy. 3. Husserl, Edmund,
1859–1938. 4. Heidegger, Martin, 1889–   I. Title.
PS3537.T4753Z66   811'.5'2   74-6773
ISBN 0-8387-1613-X

c c

    Acknowledgment is extended to Alfred A. Knopf, Inc. for
permission to quote from the following copyrighted works of Wallace
Stevens: OPUS POSTHUMOUS, edited by Samuel French Morse,
THE NECESSARY ANGEL, LETTERS OF WALLACE STEVENS,
edited by Holly Stevens, and THE COLLECTED POEMS OF
WALLACE STEVENS.

6001453797

for
MY MOTHER
MY FATHER
MY WIFE

"I am one of you and being one of you
Is being and knowing what I am and know."
(CP,496)

Contents

Preface

Acknowledgments

1 Introduction 17
2 Phenomenology and Poetry 29
3 The Self-Description of the Blue Guitar 59
4 From Perception to Disclosure 85
5 A Gaiety That Is Being 115
6 An Outline of the Poetry of Being 138
7 After the Outlines of Being: Its Expressions 213

Selected Bibliography 275

Index of Subjects and Titles 293

Preface

In reading the later poetry of Wallace Stevens, certain questions come to mind that have as much to do with the function of art works as with the powers and possibilities of poetry. In a poem "To an Old Philosopher in Rome," the poet imagines the perfected final work of George Santayana as a "threshold" mediating between earthly and celestial existence and Being where it is "as if the design of all his words takes form/And frame from thinking and is realized" (CP, 511). One of the roles of both poet and philosopher was that of questioner, "an inquisitor of structures/For himself." Yet Stevens does not limit himself to traditional philosophical questions, and the structures that he outlines in his poems turn upon his own continuing meditations of the life of the mind and its relation to "reality" as well as of the epistemological and ontological problems implicit in such thought. How can one express one's sense of the ground of things? What is the structure of Being itself, that "ultimate reality" of which Stevens wrote ". . . it is not in the premise that reality/is a solid. It may be a shade that traverses/A dust, a force that traverses a shade" (CP, 489)? To the visionary, the lover, and the saint, a commonplace reality, those ordinary evenings in New Haven, and the everyday appearances thereof take on a wholly new meaning as the poet's perception (as well as his "sense of things") began to include a visionary, almost mystical understanding of Being itself.

Thus, at the height of his power and in full control of his gift for the seemingly casual cadences of the meditative process, the poet formulates a questioning of Being itself and temporality. Yet, his mode of asking is neither that of the sage ("the old man standing on the tower" in "Credences of Summer," CP, 374) nor that of the philosopher (Santayana questioning the structure of eternity). The poems treat no subject other than the particulars of observation, which include the process of observing as well as the fullness of the world seen. Within the chosen world— the backyard, the park, the landscape limited by one's sense of the particulars both of place and of the observing mind—the poet rehearsed in language the motion of his mind, producing fictions that sufficed to allow the continuation of the process of repeated creation. For meditation is repetition of the same questions, with a kind of confidence that if one's answers, one's fictions, one's acts of mind do not suffice for long, at least the center of one's acts, one's questions, does endure. As Stevens continued, his mastery of the form permitted both an intense duration of meditation (using that *"ungeheures a priori"* that Jean Wahl spoke to him about) and the flashing instants of vision.

In the later poems, both of these elements are necessary to an understanding of the works. And while several kinds of approaches would be adequate to understand this kind of poetry, I have chosen an approach that attempts to clarify the questions that I think Stevens was asking. They are not unfamiliar to readers of Stevens's works. What will seem unfamiliar at first glance will be the works I choose for parallels and analogies in order to understand Stevens. Edmund Husserl and Martin Heidegger represent (and originated) currents in European thought that are considered foreign to the American grain. Husserl is rarely connected in any way with discussions of poetry. Yet, there is much in the meditations of the founder of phenomenology that allows for a full investigation of the acts of the mind as well as numerous insights into the nature and necessity of the creative imagination. In a different way, the entire work of Martin Heidegger points in distinct steps away from traditional views of philosophy and philosophizing toward original visions of thinking and poeticizing that speak directly to Stevens's own development. In both cases the parallels are fortuitous, yet both German philosophers concentrate on problems that are central to Stevens's modes of questioning as well as to his meditations on the function and possibility of poetry as a quest for the full sense of Being itself.

I hope to make Stevens's later work more accessible by showing, through Husserl and Heidegger, some of the meditational processes and, later, some of the visionary forms that Stevens incorporates in his poems. The reader should not imagine that this book will contain a complete account either of Husserl's phenomenology or of Heidegger's complex and fascinating thought, for both tasks are well beyond my immediate purpose. The primary aim is to explain the poetry of Wallace Stevens, and my method is mainly that of explication of particular, whole poems that are demonstrably central to Stevens's opus. I limit my discussion of the philosophers to the precise points of analogy that are useful in clarifying Stevens's practices and in understanding his development. I have tried to make my accounts of both Husserl and Heidegger accurate and clear to the layman and have included quotations from the original texts wherever possible so that the reader can examine the philosophical material that I select. I would hope that the more one is familiar with the works of Husserl and Heidegger, the more easily he will be able to follow the main points of the book. For readers of Stevens, I quote wherever necessary from Stevens's poems. Nonetheless, one's sense of the full context of many passages can be sharpened only by having *The Collected Poems of Wallace Stevens* at hand.

Acknowledgments

I am grateful to the libraries of the University of Oregon and of Kent State University for finding works of Wallace Stevens, Edmund Husserl, and Martin Heidegger that would otherwise have been difficult to consult. I am also indebted to the librarians at the Husserl Archives at the University of Louvain for their gracious assistance. My reading of Stevens has benefited from conversations with Chandler B. Beall, A. Kingsley Weatherhead, and Robert J. Bertholf, all of whom were kind enough to give me critical readings of portions of the manuscript. I would also like to thank the Research Council at Kent State University for grants to assist in the preparation of this manuscript and Joanne Brady and Barbara Burner for fast and accurate typing.

I am grateful to the many commentators on the works of Husserl and Heidegger, both those I have cited in the text and those not mentioned. In particular, I would like to acknowledge the valuable interpretations contained in each of the translations and to thank those who have completed the somewhat thankless task of rendering the works of both German thinkers into English, French, and, sometimes, into German. The last of my personal acknowledgments may very well be to the man responsible for much of my preparation for this work: a *hommage* to René Char whose conversations about poetry, philosophy, and *la Prés-*

ence of Martin Heidegger proved to be the spring from which my study flowed.

1
Introduction

Wallace Stevens was a poet whose consuming interest from the beginning to the end of his career was in the poetic uses of ideas. It should not be surprising then that many of the recent full-length studies of his poetry have attempted to trace the sources and possible influences that philosophers may have had on a poet who was admittedly interested in philosophers and philosophical ideas.[1] But Stevens's interest in philosophical ideas and his eclectic reading habits in contemporary intellectual history do not suffice to earn for him the title of philosopher. Any attempt to make Stevens into a thinker in his own right not only misrepresents the poet's use of philosophical ideas

---

1. For examples of critics who study philosophical influences, see James Baird, "Transvaluation in the Poetics of Wallace Stevens," *Tennessee Studies in Literature, Special Number: Studies in Honor of John C. Hodges and Alwin Thaler* (Knoxville, Tenn., 1961), pp. 163–73; Frank Doggett, *Stevens' Poetry of Thought* (Baltimore, Md., 1966; paperback ed., 1966), esp. pp. 199–216; Richard A. Macksey, "The Climates of Wallace Stevens," in *The Act of the Mind: Essays on the Poetry of Wallace Stevens,* ed. Roy Harvey Pearce and J. Hillis Miller (Baltimore, Md., 1965), pp. 185–223; J. Hillis Miller, "Wallace Stevens," in his *Poets of Reality: Six Twentieth Century Writers* (Cambridge, Mass., 1966), 217–84; Roy Harvey Pearce, *The Continuity of American Poetry* (Princeton, N.J., 1961; paperback ed., 1965), pp. 376–419; Joseph N. Riddel, *The Clairvoyant Eye: The Poetry and Poetics of Wallace Stevens* (Baton Rouge, La., 1965; paperback ed., 1967); Newton P. Stallknecht, "Absence in Reality: A Study in the Epistemology of the Blue Guitar," *The Kenyon Review,* 21 (Autumn 1959): 545–62.

but also contradicts his pointed declaration in a late essay that he was not a philosopher.[2] Suffice it to say at the beginning that he was simply interested in the poetry of ideas and to remark that this is a different kind of interest from that usually associated with philosophers. For Stevens consistently demanded aesthetic sufficiency rather than epistemological certainty or ontological order.

Where the epistemological concerns of philosophers do coincide with Stevens's poetic interests, several critics have made enlightening comparisons.[3] But, unfortunately, where these critics have concentrated too rigorously on the philosophical sources of the ideas in the poems, they have tended to make Stevens sound like "G. E. Moore at the spinet."[4] Frank Doggett shows that Stevens's use of philosophical ideas radically transforms the ideas that are used.[5] Thus, to suspect, as several critics do, that Stevens is secretly a philosopher hiding in poet's laurels is to confuse philosophy with poetry. For even though Stevens suggests that his role might be philosophical when he writes that "a poem in which the poet has chosen for his subject a philosophic theme should result in the poem of poems,"[6] he is nevertheless fully aware that "to define poetry as an unofficial view of being places it in contrast with philosophy. . . ."[7] And the contrast is as important for Stevens as the potential comparison.

Thus, while it may be interesting and profitable to follow up, as Doggett does, the many possible sources of Stevens's ideas, unless the critic pays close attention to the

---

2. In "A Collect of Philosophy," *Opus Posthumous,* ed. Samuel French Morse (New York, 1957), p. 195, Stevens wrote that his friend the French philosopher Jean Wahl "made many suggestions which I am happy to acknowledge for there is no one, what with his immense reading, to whom I could be more easily or more willingly indebted. I am not a philosopher."

3. The best discussions of Stevens's philosophical sources, influences, and affinities are Doggett's *Stevens' Poetry of Thought* and Riddel's *The Clairvoyant Eye.*

4. Randall Jarrell, "Reflections on Wallace Stevens," *Partisan Review* 17 (May–June 1951): 341–42.

5. *Stevens' Poetry of Thought,* pp. 199–209.

6. "A Collect of Philosophy," *Opus Posthumous,* p. 187.

7. *The Necessary Angel: Essays on Reality and the Imagination* (New York, 1951; paperback ed., 1951), p. 41.

whole poem as a particular work of art, he runs the risk of making a few lines of the poet's verse sound like paraphrases of Santayana or Whitehead while ignoring the complexities of the idea as it is contained within a whole work of art. Such practices often lead to violations of the poet and the philosopher by quoting both out of context. James Baird complains in his recent book that all such attempts to explain Stevens by use of philosophical analogues "seem an imposition of the critic's will [rather] than an exposition of the poet at hand."[8] But to condemn "all attempts" because of the sins of the few seems too harsh, particularly when the poet at hand uses ideas that are by nature philosophical. Hence, it is difficult to understand Baird's opinion that "one must question the exclusiveness [of the philosophical approach] despite the sophistication and the ardor with which its adherents proceed."[9] It is surely no more of an imposition to use parallels with philosophers to explain the development and meaning of Stevens's later poetry than it is to use architectural structures to explain the structure and meaning of Stevens's poetry as Baird does.

There are, then, two general groups of critics who have concentrated on Stevens's poetry in the last decade. Both the philosophical and the structural groups have had the same general limitations. Both have failed to account adequately for the changes in the later poetry of Wallace Stevens. Either there is an insistence on the continuity of Stevens's interest in the conflict between imagination and reality or else there is a professed lack of interest in the later poems.[10] Neither approach makes possible a reading of the poetry of *Transport to Summer, The Auroras of Autumn,*

---

8. *The Dome and the Rock: Structure in the Poetry of Wallace Stevens* (Baltimore, 1968), p. xii.

9. *Ibid.*

10. For a complete survey of recent criticism, see Riddel, "The Contours of Stevens Criticism," in *Journal of English Literary History* 31 (March 1964): 106–38. For a complete listing of the Stevens criticism up to 1963, see Jackson Bryer and Joseph N. Riddel, "A Checklist of Stevens Criticism," *Twentieth Century Literature* 8 (October 1962–January 1963): 124–42.

and *The Rock*. Two issues create the present lack of adequate critical discussion of the later poetry. First, the two major subjects of the later poetry are difficult to discuss because they are indefinite, metaphysical ideas rather than concrete facts or everyday concerns. Second, the structure of the later poetry is essentially temporal and, while the importance of the seasonal sequence from summer to fall to winter has been discussed, the cyclic nature of the later poems has received almost no mention.

I take the two major subjects of the later poetry to be Being and time.[11] Both of these subjects are as common and evident as the air, yet considered philosophically both subjects are among the most difficult and evasive of metaphysical topics. These two subjects leave a critic as astute as J. Hillis Miller at something of a loss for words when he attempts to deal with both Being and time in an essay on Stevens's poetry. Miller recognizes the first problem when he complains of a lack of terminology as he attempts to approach the most important concept of the later poetry. The concept very nearly evades him as he writes that "there is one more aspect of Stevens' thought, however, and this is the most difficult to see or to say."[12] The aspect that Miller finds difficult to express is the poet's sense of Being. While he was clearly the first critic to examine Stevens's intuitive sense of Being in the late poems, he writes of the poetry in ways that approximate

---

11. I want to make it clear that Being, being, and existence are going to have different senses in my study. Being with a capital *B* will stand for the ground or source of both the mind and the world. It is that by virtue of which the things that exist are present. It is a difficult term to define in a brief footnote, but it is used in a sense that is distinct from "being," which (as in the term *human being*) simply means existent or something that exists, and from "beings," which are things that exist (objects, animals, humans, etc.). However, I have not changed quoted material to fit these distinctions and as a result, when I quote Stevens, Doggett, or Miller as they talk about the sense of the term, it will be necessary to derive from the context just what each is talking about. For Husserl, *being* usually means existence and thus will not cause any confusion. For Heidegger, *Being* is the translation for *Sein* when used as a noun whereas *being* and *existent* are used here to translate *das Seiende*.

12. Miller, "Wallace Stevens," p. 277.

the difficulty of the subject at hand. Thus, the originality of his insight into the later poetry is somewhat covered over by the extreme reductiveness of his critical approach. Miller's most direct statements about Stevens's late poetry are brilliant evocations:

> This apparent defeat is the supreme victory, for the nothing is not nothing. It is. It is Being. Being is a pervasive power, visible nowhere in itself and yet present and visible in all things. It is what things share through the fact that they are. Being is not a thing like other things and therefore can only appear to man as nothing, but it is what all things must participate in if they are to exist at all. Stevens' later poetry has as its goal the releasing of that evanescent glimpse of being which is as close as man can come to a possession of the ground of things. The paradoxical appearance of being in the form of nothing causes the ambiguity of his poetry. Man's inability to see being as being causes Stevens to say of it "It is and it / Is not and therefore, is" (CP, 440), and yet in supreme moments of insight he can speak directly of it.[13]

Yet, in the brief discussion that follows this passage, Miller merely suggests Stevens's sense of Being by linking some snatches of the last poems together. While he was the first critic to observe the importance of the subject of Being itself in the late poems, he does not expand his suggestive insight into a reading of the later poetry. But, before condemning the critic, an attempt must be made to understand the nature of his problem. When Miller announces that the subject of Being is a difficult subject to talk about, both for the critic and for the poet, he is describing a problem of terminology that has baffled philosophers since Plato. The subject is as evasive as he implies. But this does not mean that the critic has no recourse but silence. Rather, the critic must find a new approach that will make intelligible the subject to be discussed. The poet's attempt to write a poetry that would achieve "the outlines of being and its

---

13. *Ibid.*, p. 279.

expressings"[14] in the later poems demands explanation. And where Miller's explanation fails to clarify the development and meaning of Stevens's "poetry of Being," the use of Martin Heidegger's ontological investigations provides a way of explaining both the development and the meaning of the later poetry. For Heidegger treats the question of Being and the difficulties inherent in such a question in nearly all of his philosophical works. Not only does Stevens simulate in his poems some of the phenomenological methods that Heidegger describes in *Sein und Zeit*,[15] he also describes processes of disclosure and preconceptual awareness of Being that are similar to Heidegger's descriptions of the same processes.

While this study is not the first to suggest that there are important affinities between Heidegger and Stevens, it is the first study that demonstrates the affinities through a comparison of the philosopher's ideas and the poet's use of those ideas in the poems. Furthermore, where Richard A. Macksey, Glauco Cambon, and Marjorie Buhr all suggest fleeting comparisons between some of Heidegger's concepts and a few of Stevens's poems, none of these critics attempts to use the comparisons to explain the development of the later poetry.[16]

---

14. *The Collected Poems of Wallace Stevens* (New York, 1954), p. 424. Hereafter this volume will be cited in the text as CP followed by the appropriate page number or numbers.

15. *Sein und Zeit* (Halle a. d. S., 1929), pp. 27–38.

16. Macksey, pp. 198–99, 201–2, 206, 215–16; Glauco Cambon, "Wallace Stevens: 'Notes Toward a Supreme Fiction,'" in his *The Inclusive Flame: Studies in Modern American Poetry* (Bloomington, Ind., 1963; paperback ed., 1965), pp. 238–39; Marjorie Buhr, "The Impossible Possible Philosopher's Man: Wallace Stevens," *The Carrell* 6, no. 1 (June 1965): 9–12. Even James Baird, who explicitly questions the whole concept of comparing Stevens's poetry to philosopher's ideas, suggests that "phenomenology, being much in the critical mode of present literary studies, would seem to be the next phase. To a degree Mr. Miller has already applied it. So has Richard A. Macksey, in a searching essay of recent date. His study provides some impressive affinities between Stevens and Husserl" (p. xii). Apparently Baird, in spite of the argument that he attempts to build in support of his own critical approach, recognizes the affinities between phenomenology and Stevens as well as the need for further study of these affinities.

My thesis is that the development of the middle and later poetry of Stevens can be profitably explained through comparisons with the phenomenological methods and concepts of Edmund Husserl and Martin Heidegger. Each of the chapters will analyze one segment of Stevens's poetry in terms of the methods and concepts of phenomenology as these were developed and explained by the two German philosophers. However, in stating this thesis, there are several implicit assumptions that must be clarified.

First, the study concerns elective affinities of thought wherein both the philosophers and the poet were concerned with similar problems that are usually considered the province of philosophy. I am not claiming that either Husserl or Heidegger influenced or was influenced by Stevens. Although it is evident that Stevens was aware of both philosophers during his career and was perhaps familiar with the general directions of their respective philosophies, the available evidence seems to make clear that his awareness of both Husserl and Heidegger came toward the end of his career. The only mention of Husserl in Stevens's published writings is an indirect reference to one of Husserl's ideas that was suggested to him by his friend Jean Wahl, the French philosopher and poet. Stevens writes in "A Collect of Philosophy" (1951) that "Jean Wahl wrote to me, saying"

"I am just now reading the *Méditations Cartésiennes* by Husserl. Very dry. But he affirms that there is an enormous *(ungeheures)* a priori in our minds, an inexhaustible infinity of a priori. He speaks of the approach to the unapproachable."[17]

Stevens found this idea, as expressed by Wahl, suggestive and refers to it several times in the essay. However, in terms of influence, there seems to be little chance of Ste-

---

17. *Opus Posthumous,* p. 194.

vens's having even read Husserl much less having been influenced by him.

Stevens's interest in Heidegger also occurs rather late in life. In a letter to his Paris bookseller, he wrote that:

> Heidegger, the Swiss philosopher, has written a little work dealing with the poetry of the German poet, Holderlin [sic]. I have no idea of the title and there is no place here in Hartford where I can find out. I am extremely eager to have a copy of this, particularly if there is a French translation. But I should rather have it even in German than not have it at all.[18]

The reference to the "Swiss philosopher" would seem to negate any possible ideas of influence, particularly since this letter was written three years before Stevens's death. The fact that the first English translations of Heidegger were not published until 1949 also decreases considerably any chance of Stevens's having read Heidegger. While conclusive evidence about the philosophers who influenced Stevens must await the publication of a full biography, all indications seem to disprove any chance of direct influence.[19]

Second, each comparison of philosopher with poet will be used to illuminate the stages of Stevens's development after the publication of *Harmonium* (1923) and to explain the important poems of each stage. In this sense the organization of the study will be chronological, for each chapter will discuss one stage of Stevens's development. It is not the purpose of this study to force Stevens's ideas or his poetic practices into either a Husserlian or Heideggerian mold by treating the poetry thematically. As I have said, the idea of comparing Stevens's thought with the methods and concepts of Husserl's phenomenology and

---

18. A letter to Mlle Paule Vidal, July 29, 1952. *Letters of Wallace Stevens*, selected and ed. Holly Stevens (New York, 1966), p. 758. (Hereafter cited as *Letters.*)

19. The publication of the authorized biography, which has been completed by Morse, is being held up indefinitely by the Stevens family.

Heidegger's phenomenological ontology is not wholly original. A number of surface similarities have been noticed several times in discussions of the middle and later poetry, both in terms of the philosophers' methods and in terms of the particular kinds of problems that both philosophers and poet treat. But each of the critics who suggest Stevens's affinities with either Husserl or Heidegger does little more than quote a phrase or technical term, as if that, by itself, demonstrated the affinity and thus explained both the philosopher's idea and the poet's use of a similar concept. No one has attempted to carry out a full analysis of the affinities in a detailed study of Stevens's poetry. Thus, in one sense, this study will be the first to explain what the affinities are between the philosophers and the poet, as well as the limitations of those affinities. Furthermore it will show how both the uses and limitations of the comparisons help to explain Stevens's poems.

The specific problems that this study will treat can be divided into two general stages. First, there are the poems of *Ideas of Order* (1935) and *The Man with the Blue Guitar* (1937), which are more directly concerned with the problems of epistemology. During this period, Stevens's interest is in the acts of the mind as it confronts and is related to the world around it. As Stevens experiments in the poems with the various possibilities of a new kind of poetry, he simulates several parts of Husserl's phenomenology. In both *Ideas of Order* and *The Man with the Blue Guitar* there are numerous processes evolved which can be illuminated by comparison with Husserl's concepts of intentionality, his idea of the adequacy of original intuitions, and his methods of reduction. Through each of these methods a new beginning is posited from which both the philosopher and the poet hoped to achieve a new understanding of the process of the mind as it is related to the world around it.

During this period, the explicit problem in Stevens's poetry was the separation of the mind (imagination) and

the world (reality). Many of the poems of these two volumes explore what both the mind and the world can do. In
these poems, Stevens meditates the possible relations that
exist between the imagination and reality. He incorporates
methods that reduce both the exterior world of "things as
they are" and the interior world of mental things (preconceptions, old ideas, and old constructs of the imagination)
to minimal levels. Each reductive process that is described
in the poetry tends to equalize both the interior and exterior, both imagination and reality, so that interaction can
occur between the two opposing poles. In *The Man with the
Blue Guitar* Stevens incorporates the processes of reduction into the poem as he explores the possibility of a poetry
that is about the processes of the mind. As he discovers
that the imagination can create and sustain itself within its
own creations, he also discovers the necessity of maintaining a balance between the imagination and reality. Like
Husserl's methods of reduction and intuition, Stevens's
poems that describe reductive and decreative[20] processes
are discovered as acts of the mind describing itself. Each of
these acts makes a poem and thus Stevens develops a new
definition of modern poetry. Philosophically considered,
each of the problems that Stevens treats in the poetry of
this period is epistemological and many of the methods
that he develops are surprisingly similar to Husserl's
phenomenological methods. These developments are discussed in chapters 2 and 3.

The change from the first stage and its related epistemological problems to the second stage and its related
ontological problems is discussed in chapters 4 and 5. As
Stevens rejects the division between mind and world, he
also finds that the clear perceptions that were available
through the processes of reduction that he had developed

---

20. *Decreation* is a term that I will explain more fully in the next chapter. It is
part of Stevens's creative cycle, which moves from the destruction of old constructs to creation of new ones. See Roy Harvey Pearce, pp. 412–19, for another
discussion of this aspect of Stevens's poetry.

in *Ideas of Order* and *The Man with the Blue Guitar* were inadequate for his aesthetic purposes. As the gap between subject and object is closed in several of the poems of *Parts of a World* (1942), the poet discovers a new relation of self and world. This relation is most easily explained by comparing each step described in the poems with Heidegger's analysis of *Dasein's* relation to Being. Using Heidegger's concept of the difference between Being and beings provides a way of explaining Stevens's poems that describe the disclosure of Being as the center and source of both the mind and the world.

Each of the poems that describe the poet's sense of Being includes concepts of time and the relation of time to the experience of disclosure. Both of these concepts are incorporated into Stevens's major aesthetic proposal, *Notes Toward a Supreme Fiction* (1942), which is discussed in chapter 6. Stevens's concern in the poems after *Notes* revolves around his sense of Being and his concept of temporality. As I have pointed out, these two subjects cause numerous difficulties and obscurities in the poetry and the criticism. Using Heidegger's analysis of the question of Being, the ontological function of language, and the relation of ontology and poetry, the last chapter explains the temporal and ontological development of the late poems.

When Stevens wrote that poetry was to have a role that was at least the equal of philosophy, he included a concept of Being in his aesthetic. Thus, where he writes of the nature of poetry, he defines it "as an unofficial view of being" and adds that "this is a much larger definition of poetry than it is usual to make."[21] But, as I have insisted, this definition did not equate poetry and philosophy.

To define poetry as an unofficial view of being places it in contrast with philosophy and at the same time establishes the relationship between the two. In philosophy we attempt to approach truth through the reason. Obviously this is a state-

21. "The Noble Rider and the Sound of Words," in *The Necessary Angel*, p. 40.

ment of convenience. If we say that in poetry we attempt to
approach truth through the imagination, this, too, is a statement of convenience. We must conceive of poetry as at least
the equal of philosophy.[22]

Thus, when Stevens declares that poetry and philosophy
are related, he is talking, as most poets are prone to do in
their prose and criticism, directly about his own practice as
a poet. To conceive of poetry as the equal of philosophy is
not to make the two identical endeavors. They are equal in
importance and related because they both deal with the
same kinds of problems. Yet, where the philosopher seeks
epistemological certainty, the poet seeks aesthetic adequacy. Where the philosopher seeks an ontological system,
the poet seeks only to express his sense of Being. The
crucial difference for Stevens between the poet and the
philosopher is outlined in the same essay. This difference
could be called a difference in purposes and ends. For "if
the end of the philosopher is despair, the end of the poet is
fulfillment, since the poet finds a sanction for life in poetry
that satisfies the imagination."[23] For the poet, the fulfillments and satisfactions are the essential results of his fictions. For it is only in the fictive durations that the poet
creates and in turn decreates those fulfillments and satisfactions which are available at the end.

---

22. *Ibid.*, pp. 41–42.
23. *Ibid.*, p. 43.

2
Phenomenology and Poetry

i

Stevens's first volume, *Harmonium* (1923), provided a polished and uproarious beginning for many of the themes and approaches he explored in the later poetry. But the prevalent style, tone, and language of *Harmonium* were soon rejected along with the dominant view of a reality whose violence can only be matched by the violence of the imagination. The flashy and highly colorful combat of Stevens's vocabulary with a gaudy, but recalcitrant reality could only end in a draw.[1] *Harmonium* is a fascinating experiment or group of experiments that create a remarkably diverse world of the imagination. And taken in the

---

1. For other evaluations of *Harmonium,* see particularly Joseph N. Riddel, *The Clairvoyant Eye: The Poetry and Poetics of Wallace Stevens* (Baton Rouge, La., 1965; paperback edition, 1967), pp. 52–56, 102–3; Frank Kermode, *Wallace Stevens* (Edinburgh, 1960; paperback edition, New York, 1961), pp. 24–52; Daniel Fuchs, *The Comic Spirit of Wallace Stevens* (Durham, N. C., 1963), pp. 3–4, p. 15; Herbert J. Stern, *Wallace Stevens: Art of Uncertainty* (Ann Arbor, Mich., 1966), *passim;* Robert Buttel, *Wallace Stevens: The Making of Harmonium* (Princeton, N. J., 1967), *passim;* Yvor Winters, *"Wallace Stevens, or the Hedonist's Progress," In Defense of Reason* (Denver, Colo., 1943), pp. 431–59; Frank Lentricchia, *The Gaiety of Language: An Essay on the Radical Poetics of W. B. Yeats and Wallace Stevens* (Berkeley, Calif., 1968), pp. 119–86.

context of the thirty years that were to make up the rest of Stevens's creative development, *Harmonium* stands as both beginning and end. It is a beginning in the sense that a number of ideas that are developed in the later poems are initially suggested or implied in the first volume. It is an end in the sense that Stevens explicitly rejected the kind of poetry that *Harmonium* came to represent to him. The first poem of the next volume that Stevens published was "Farewell to Florida" (CP, 117),[2] and this poem represents not only a repudiation of Florida but also a rejection of what Stevens called the reality of "light and warmth" that much of the poetry of *Harmonium* represented.[3] I begin then not at the beginning, but rather at a point of renewal, *in medias res*, when the poet began to search for a new understanding of what poetry could be. The nature of this search is expressed in the poems that initiate and carry through Stevens's ideas about poetry and the imagination. The revitalized search is, in one sense, an investigation of the power of the mind itself and the relation of the mind to reality.

But unlike the philosopher, whose investigations of con-

---

2. *The Collected Poems of Wallace Stevens* (New York, 1954), p. 117. I use here the method of citation of passages from Stevens followed by recent commentators: CP for *Collected Poems;* OP for *Opus Posthumous,* ed. Samuel French Morse (New York, 1957); NA for *The Necessary Angel* (New York, 1951). Arabic numerals following the letters indicate page numbers. The abbreviated title *Letters* represents *Letters of Wallace Stevens,* ed. Holly Stevens (New York, 1966). The first edition of *Ideas of Order* (Alcestis Press, 1935) began with the poem "Sailing After Lunch" (CP, 120). The second edition (Knopf, 1936), and all subsequent editions including that published in *Collected Poems* are begun by "Farewell to Florida."

3. "Two or Three Ideas," OP, 210. I am indebted to Louis Martz, who calls this poem ("Farewell to Florida") a renunciation of "all that 'Florida' has symbolized in his [Stevens's] earlier poetry: that world of vivid physical apprehension, where man created within the bounds of the natural order," in his essay "Wallace Stevens: The World as Meditation," in *Literature and Belief: The English Institute Essays for 1957,* ed. M. H. Abrams (New York, 1958), pp. 139–65; also printed in *Yale Review,* n.s. 47 (Summer 1958): 517–36. Reprinted in *Wallace Stevens: A Collection of Critical Essays,* ed. Marie Borroff (Englewood Cliffs, N.J., 1963), pp. 133–50, esp. p. 138. Although Daniel Fuchs takes Martz to task for this view, Fuchs's argument is based on the implications of some of the poems of *Harmonium* and not on the meaning of "Farewell to Florida." See Daniel Fuchs, p. 42.

sciousness and the relation of subject and object are directed toward the discovery of a system or theory of knowledge, Stevens directs his investigations toward a better understanding of the processes of the mind that lead to a new poetry. In other words, Stevens's interests are philosophical in nature but the intended result is aesthetic, not philosophical. Thus, while I shall show that Stevens's methods in the poetry of *Ideas of Order* through *Parts of a World* are very similar to Husserl's description of the methods of phenomenology, the importance of this comparison is the extent to which it explains Stevens's development.

Both poet and philosopher begin by proposing an approach that will avoid the errors of the idealist philosophers and logical positivists. All notions of transcendant or absolute ideas that exist beyond or behind reality as it is observed are rejected. The formula or slogan of Husserl's phenomenology was *zu den Sachen selbst* (or, in Stevens's terms, "Let's see the very thing and nothing else" [CP, 373]). The return to the things themselves meant that the only basis of certainty was the objects that were perceived by the mind. For Husserl, the rejection of all presuppositions was the only way to assure that perception could take place without the distortions of previous conceptions of reality.[4] To reject all universal ideas, all transcendant systems of thought, all beliefs in absolute or eternal values or ideas was, for Husserl, to eliminate the intellectual preconceptions that had plagued philosophical investigation since Plato's ideal. The same kind of rejection of all "idealism" that takes place in the phenomenological method is frequently suggested in Stevens's verse where the archetypal idealist philosopher, Plato, is called "the reddened flower, the erotic bird" (CP, 253). In fact, the anti-idealist stance of Stevens begins in *Harmonium* where the famous reference to "the ultimate Plato," which occurs

---

4. Husserl, "Philosophie als strenge Wissenshaft," *Logos* 1 (1910–11): 340.

in "Homunculus et la Belle Etoile" (CP, 27), appears in a context that suggests poetry as the "ultimate Plato," which is beyond and in all senses better than the dry ideals of Plato's philosophy.

On the other hand, neither Husserl nor Stevens would uphold the principal foundations of realist philosophers. Husserl contended that the initial assumptions of realism were naively based on a kind of unquestioning acceptance of the natural world. For Husserl, the idea of a rational or logical order within the mind of each observer was a fiction that took as much for granted as the assumptions of later German idealists. Pure logic was as suspect as idealism because both extremes of philosophy refused to establish the absolute certainty of their respective assumptions. Whereas Husserl rejects the basis of pure logic, Stevens frequently makes fun of the limits of logic as well as all manners of rational (realist) thought: "Rationalists, wearing square hats, / Think, in square rooms . . . They confine themselves / To right-angled triangles" (CP, 75).

Only by rejecting both the idealist and the realist assumptions could philosophy and poetry return to the origins of consciousness. Husserl's hope was to provide an absolutely certain and presuppositionless basis for all knowledge. Stevens thought that modern poetry was to be "The poem of the act of the mind finding / What will suffice . . . "(CP, 239). To record the mind's acts in the poetry, Stevens proposes certain steps that allow the poem to represent the mind's encounter with "things as they are." Phenomenology was organized around several kinds of "reductions" that were intended to clear of all complications both the mind and the world of objects, so that the thinker could receive original perceptions of the phenomena.

Husserl's objective was to fulfill "Descartes's demand that all philosophical knowledge be founded in an absolutely certain insight, raised above every possibility of doubt."[5] Husserl sought the ultimate foundation of all rational assertions in an immediate vision, that is, an original intuition of the things themselves about which one wishes to make statements.[6] The motto of Husserl's technique, "to the things themselves," meant that we, the thinkers, must return to the immediate original data of our consciousness. The basis of Husserl's phenomenological method was that all consciousness was intentional.[7] Another way of expressing this assumption would be to say that all consciousness is directed toward an object and that, as a result, each act of the consciousness has as its object a thing other than itself. The objects of consciousness were self-evidently there only if the mind in the act of perception was stripped of all possible preconceptions and preconditions. The starting point of philosophical inquiry was then the field of original experiences rather than merely one intuition or fundamental principle. The single "cogito" upon which Descartes based his whole philosophy was expanded to an unlimited field of intuitions. Starting with a field of primordial phenomena rather than with one intuition (as Descartes had done), Husserl denied the validity of logical induction or deduction in favor of a pure intuition that was based on exact analysis and description.[8] What was needed was a way to see the thing itself without cognitive distortions.

To achieve this goal, Husserl suggests two general steps that are calculated to assure a certain foundation for the investigation of consciousness. The steps are both decreative because both reduce the necessary components of

5. Joseph J. Kockelmans, *Phenomenology and Physical Science,* trans. Henry J. Koren (Pittsburgh, Pa., 1966), p. 31.

6. Husserl, *Ideen zu einer reinen Phänomenologie und phänomenologischen Philosophie,* ed. Walter Biemel, in *Husserliana* (The Hague, 1950), 3: 42–44, 50–53. Hereafter, this work will be cited as *Ideen* I.

7. Husserl, *Die Idee der Phänomenologie,* ed. Walter Biemel, in *Husserliana* (The Hague, 1950) 2: 29–32. Also see *Ideen* I: 79–81.

8. "Philosophie als strenge Wissenschaft," p. 341.

perception (subject and object) to a minimal level of complexity so that an original perception can occur. The first step toward achieving "original intuition" is the simplification of reality itself. The whole of reality must be reduced to a field of possibility within which separable objects can be perceived. The intuition that Husserl desires necessitates an equality of the perceiver and the perceived. When the subject and the object are present to each other on the same level, the intuition of "origins and beginnings" is possible.[9] Hence, the first step is the discrimination of the things themselves, which Husserl calls "original intuition."[10] The philosopher must seek the lowest common level at which subject and object are present to each other. Original intuition calls for a simplified reality of separable, individual elements (*Ding an sich*).

The second step leads to this intuition at the lowest common level from the other side of the dialectic. Husserl calls this second step "reduction" and means, by this term, a procedure by which one places oneself in the "transcendental sphere" where he can perceive things as they are in themselves without distortion or preconception. Reductions provide means of eliminating the errors and preconceptions of past methods of perceiving. Most simply stated, reduction is, as Joseph J. Kockelmans writes, "a change of attitude, by virtue of which we learn to see things we previously thought to perceive, in a different way, i.e. in an original and radical way."[11] By the processes of reduction, the thinker is taught to see more of the object of his consciousness. He can "penetrate deeper into things and learn to see more profound 'layers' behind what we first thought to see."[12]

9. Husserl, *Ideen* I: 52–53.
10. *Ibid.*, p. 52. Husserl's phrase is "jede originär gebende Anschauung eine Rechtsquelle der Erkenntnis sei, dass alles, was sich uns in der 'Intuition' originär, (sozusagen in seiner leibhaften Wirklichkeit) darbietit, einfach hinzunehman sei, als was es bibt. . . ." (p. 52).
11. Kockelmans, *Phenomenology and Physical Science*, p. 35.
12. *Ibid.*, p. 37.

While Stevens's approach to the problem of consciousness (mind) and reality is scarcely as rigorous, consistent,
or well-defined as Husserl's, the initial concern of many of
his poems is the problem of the difference between the
mind and what the mind perceives. In Stevens's terms, this
problem is stated as the relation between the imagination
and reality. Through an intuitive process that is developed
in the early poems of *Ideas of Order* (1935), and then tried
out in *The Man with the Blue Guitar* (1937) and *Parts of a
World* (1942), Stevens approximates these two steps of
Husserl's phenomenology. For Stevens, this process was
evolved gradually and each step in his approach to a
poetry of the mind tends to be a development of what
preceded it. While the similarities between some of Stevens's methods and those of Husserl's phenomenology
have been suggested by several critics, none of these writers has attempted to compare Stevens's approach to the
outlines and main aspects of phenomenology. Glauco
Cambon implies that an analogy exists between the
methods of the philosopher and the poet when he writes:

> Whether Stevens was acquainted with the philosophy of Hus-
> serl or not, the parallelism between his poetry as a process of
> dialectical discovery and Husserl's phenomenology as an
> exercise in objective awareness of the quality of reality is too
> striking to be overlooked.[13]

However, Cambon goes no further than this statement in
defining the relationship in his study of Stevens. Richard
A. Macksey comes closer to suggesting a definite affinity:

> One development of twentieth-century philosophy which
> "brackets" systematic metaphysical speculation, does in its
> point of departure and its method suggest a means of looking
> at [Stevens's] poetics. Enmeshed in the world, open to the

---

13. "Wallace Stevens: 'Notes Toward a Supreme Fiction,'" in *The Inclusive
Flame: Studies in Modern American Poetry* (Bloomington, Ind., 1963; paperback
edition, 1965), p. 237.

future, and the concreteness of experience, the phenomenologist chooses Husserl's "third way" between the dangers of absolute realism and idealism. His cry of "to the things themselves" and his insistence that all consciousness is intentional, that every *cogito* is an act, reveal fundamental aspects of Stevens's approach to writing poetry; the poems, ultimately, have to reveal themselves.[14]

But Macksey, like Cambon, does little more than suggest that there is a fundamental and very important similarity between the German philosopher and the poet. I am not only suggesting that there is a similarity in approach, but also that both the poet and the philosopher tend to push their techniques toward similar goals. The first part of my discussion will show how the specific steps that Stevens takes in his poetic explorations are similar to Husserl's steps that I have outlined. As Stevens accomplishes these steps of rejection (a process that is analogous to Husserl's original intuition), reduction (a process that is similar to Husserl's demand for perception without preconceptions), and decreation (which is similar to Husserl's demand for minimal level of interaction between perceiver and the object of perception), he proceeds toward an apprehension of reality that is similar to Husserl's goal of the "essence of the thing itself." However, as I point out these similarities, I want to stress that Stevens was not following Husserl's formula. There is no evidence that Stevens was influenced by or even aware of Husserl's investigations.[15] Rather, my point is that if we understand how Stevens's procedures in the poems were often parallel to the procedures of phenomenology, I think we can more easily understand the complex issues involved in his poetic development. I think we can also gain insights into Stevens's poetry that will suggest why he later evolved an interest in

---

14. "The Climates of Wallace Stevens," in *The Act of the Mind: Essays on the Poetry of Wallace Stevens*, ed. Roy Harvey Pearce and J. Hillis Miller (Baltimore, Md., 1965), p. 192.
15. See n16 in introduction.

Being. The similarities are, as Cambon declares, "strik-
ing," but the comparisons are valuable only inasmuch as
they permit insights into Stevens's poetry and poetics.

ii

For the present, I will turn to Stevens's poems of the
thirties to show how the parallels with Husserl illuminate
his poetic procedures. The first step in the renewed poetry
of the thirties is signaled in the first poem of *Ideas of Order*.
"Farewell to Florida" (CP, 117) initiates a search for new
ideas of order that will replace the stale ideas of the past.
But, before starting the search, the experiences of the past
must be purged from the mind. "Farewell to Florida" is
explicitly a rejection of the tropics where the experience of
an overabundant reality had overwhelmed the powers of
the imagination and left it powerless.[16] A similar process of
rejection has been suggested in *Harmonium* where Stevens
had sent Crispin on a voyage to seek a fitting relation to
reality in "The Comedian as the Letter C" (CP, 27–46),
but the reality of the tropics was too much for the realist of
the imagination. In balmy Yucatan, Crispin, the poet
figure, had found not the essence of reality, but "the
fabulous and its intrinsic verse" (CP, 31). In a similar way,
the poet in "Farewell to Florida" finds that the South is
detrimental to the imagination. The ever-present power of
reality is represented as a female mind, which had
threatened the poet and his imagination with a kind of
oppression that is similar to the oppressive reality that

---

16. In the following discussion, I am indebted to John Finch's early article
"North and South in Stevens' America," *Harvard Advocate* 127, no. 3. (December
1940): 23–26, where he writes that "the movement of Stevens' poetry has been a
movement away from the imagination's south. *Harmonium* is a book of the south
predominantly" (p. 25). Finch implies that the following volume of verse, *Ideas of
Order*, is predicated on a "renunciation" of the south of the individual imagination and a settling in the north of the common imagination. For an account of
these figures (North and South) which takes all of Stevens's poetry into account,
see Eugene Paul Nasser, *Wallace Stevens: An Anatomy of Figuration* (Philadelphia,
Pa., 1965), pp. 39–41.

Crispin found in Yucatan. For Crispin, the fantastic colors and sensations of the tropics were

> So intertwined with serpent-kin encoiled
> Among the purple tufts, the scarlet crowns,
> Scenting the jungle in their refuges,
> So streaked with yellow, blue and green and red
> In beak and bud and fruity gobbet-skins,
> That earth was like a jostling festival
> Of seeds grown fat, too juicily opulent,
> Expanding in the gold's maternal warmth.
>
> (CP, 32)

For the speaker in "Farewell to Florida," the rich and never-changing reality of Florida was like a tyrant:

> Her mind had bound me round. The palms were hot
> As if I lived in ashen ground, as if
> The leaves in which the wind kept up its sound
> From my North of cold whistled in a sepulchral South,
> Her South of pine and coral and coraline sea,
> Her home, not mine, in the ever-freshened Keys,
> Her days, her oceanic nights, calling
> For music, for whisperings from the reefs.
>
> (CP, 117)

The speaker emphasizes that the South is where the female figure of reality had exposed him to a world that was not his own. He had been controlled by the "mind" of this mindless chaos. The possibility of interaction between the poet and his surroundings was taken away, and the poet feels alien and out of place. Florida is a possession of the figure of reality; it is "her South," "her home," "Her days, her oceanic nights." Like Crispin, the speaker finds the opulent landscape of the tropics dominated by a reality that is too oppressive, and he must leave to find a land more congenial to the imagination.

The poem calls for a sparser, less opulent world where the imagination can begin to deal with a reality that is more equal to its power. The poet describes the geography of his mind when he begins to extol the qualities of his announced destination:

My North is leafless and lies in a wintry slime
Both of men and clouds, a slime of men in crowds.
The men are moving as the water moves,
This darkened water cloven by sullen swells
Against your sides, then shoving and slithering,
The darkness shattered, turbulent with foam.
To be free again, to return to the violent mind
That is their mind, these men, and that will bind
Me round, carry me, misty deck, carry me
To the cold, go on, high ship, go on, plunge on.

                                                      (CP, 118)

The poem had begun with an address to the ship that is
carrying him away from the South to the cold and barren
North, a land that, unlike Florida, is "leafless." As the
poem describes the unfriendly and unaccommodating reality of the northern world, the images of "wintry slime"
are transferred to the "men in crowds." Stevens's "north"
is both a literal place and a symbol of a new relation between mind and world. The north of the imagination is
protrayed as a place where the slime of modern reality
affects both "men and clouds." In other words, it is a reality that is unattractive both in terms of the natural landscape (leafless, wintry, cold, barren) and in terms of the
human condition. The movement of the men in crowds is
compared in a simile to the movement of the sea. The
repetition of the sea image (a figure for the chaos of reality
in Stevens's early poems) and the accompanying alliteration of the sibilants reinforces the effect of a slime of apprehension that the speaker feels about entering into an
unknown area of the mind where the comfortable warmth
of the oppressive female reality will no longer be available.
But, the movement toward the wintry climate represents a
movement toward freedom. The domination by the
female reality of the South, which had stifled creativity, is
to be exchanged for a raw world of the North where there
is a promise of freedom.

The new landscape implies that a certain violence of the
imagination will be required to match the "violent mind /

that is their mind, these men." The freedom that is asserted is part of the release of the imagination that is implied by the rejection of Florida and all that Florida (the
"venereal soil" [CP, 47]) had represented in the geography
of Stevens's mind. The vital confrontation of the mind and
reality requires, then, as is stated in this poem, the rejection of an overabundant reality in favor of a simplified and
less complex reality of the North. Here, Stevens achieves a
simplification of reality through a spatial movement from
South to North. In later poems, this simplification will be
symbolized by a seasonal change from summer to winter,
for as Stevens comes to realize, it is in time, not in space,
that both the mind and reality change.

The movement in space from South to North, which
represents a movement from a complex and dominant
reality to a simplified and sterile reality, sets the tone for
the rest of the poems in *Ideas of Order*. It forms the first
step toward the stripping of a complicated and powerful
concept of reality to the thing itself, a step that is similar to
Husserl's procedure in phenomenology. The second step
in Stevens's progress toward a confrontation with "things
as they are" is also analogous to the processes of
phenomenology in the sense that it repeats Husserl's call
for consciousness without presupposition.

In *Harmonium,* Stevens had occasionally demonstrated a
demand that all preconceptions, all beliefs, and all order
be destroyed. But in the early poems of the first volume,
this demand is not consistent. A poem like "The Snow
Man" (CP, 10) illustrates a kind of absolute decreation of
mental sets while, on the other hand, "Sea Surface Full of
Clouds" illustrates the enormous potential of the mind to
add from its store of images, feelings, and ideas, "fresh
transfigurings of freshest blue" (CP, 102). In "Sunday
Morning," the woman is urged to forget the balm of Chris-
tianity and to reject the old beliefs that stood as barriers to
an appreciation of the natural world where

> Deer walk upon our mountains, and the quail
> Whistle about us their spontaneous cries;

> Sweet berries ripen in the wilderness;
> And, in the isolation of the sky,
> At evening, casual flocks of pigeons make
> Ambiguous undulations as they sink,
> Downward to darkness, on extended wings.
>
> (CP, 70)

But, in "The Comedian as the Letter C," Crispin's voyage to the new world resulted in an ironic deflation of his creative capability. The poet figure in "The Comedian . . ." finds only disappointment in the world without belief. Thus, where the decreative process of the imagination is only occasionally successful in *Harmonium,* in *Ideas of Order* the search for possible ideas of order is predicated upon the decreation of all preconceived ideas, all beliefs, and all imaginative or rational orders. The shift in emphasis that takes place between the poems of *Harmonium* (1923) and those of *Ideas of Order* (1935) manifests itself in the frequent demand for a new beginning wherein the poet can begin to build a poetry of perception.

In "Academic Discourse at Havana" (CP, 142), Stevens demonstrates the process of decreation first by a series of substitutions that replace the images of old mythologies in Section I, which I quote in full:

> Canaries in the morning, orchestras
> In the afternoon, balloons at night. That is
> A difference, at least, from nightingales,
> Jehovah and the great sea-worm. The air
> Is not so elemental nor the earth
> So near.
>   But the sustenance of the wilderness
> Does not sustain us in the metropoles.
>
> (CP, 142)

Beginning at the bottom, the modern life is no longer the simple life of nature and mythology. The "wilderness" of earlier history has been replaced by "urban" reality ("the metropoles"). As a result, the explicit statement in the last line of this passage provides a starting point for understanding the process of replacement that is demonstrated in the first four lines. The speaker of the "academic discourse" substitutes canaries for the romantic nightingale, orchestras for the Judaic-Christian Jehovah, and finally balloons for the "great sea-worm" of the mythologies of the past. The preferred images are all nonreferential, nonsymbolic objects of common reality. As replacements, each of these images deflates the symbolic meanings inherent in the nightingale, Jehovah, and the "great sea-worm." As Daniel Fuchs comments: "the natural is valued as the real; the sundry of our lives takes the place of the miraculous and the ineffable."[17] Keats's famous nightingale, which was a symbol of poetic inspiration, is replaced by an ordinary Cuban bird. The canary carries none of the traditional, referential value of the nightingale and stands for none of the possible meanings that Keats's bird calls to mind.

The second substitution, "orchestras" for "Jehovah," involves the same process of rejecting the symbol for past orders and myths and introducing in its place a mundane feature of the park. The mythology that Jehovah symbolizes is the order that is rejected in "Sunday Morning" and elsewhere. It is Stevens's most frequently used example of old, outworn orders and beliefs that are no longer vital to the modern imagination. Faith in myth or religion ("the sustenance of the wilderness") is not adequate in modern reality. The third substitution, the balloons instead of the "great sea-worm" is perhaps a little more obscure. This replacement, like the first two, is again a deflation, of a symbol of romantic poetry of the nineteenth century where it had stood for an entire realm of mythological creatures that existed beyond the domain of reality.[18] To Stevens, the myths created by poets are no different from the poetic myths of God. All of these are

---

17. Fuchs, p. 66.
18. I suspect that this symbol is an allusion to the Old English *wyrms,* which were the mythological sea monsters of ancient legends.

examples of orders that were created by the imagination and all must be decreated so that the mind (the imagination) can begin again. But the process of substitution is not enough. Even though the old myths created a sense of order, reality was falsified. "The air / is not so elemental nor the earth / so near" as they were when myths were credible.

It is within this context of an urban, antiromantic, and antipoetic reality of "metropoles" that life becomes "an old casino in the park," where the symbols of the majesty and beauty of past orders are envisioned:

> The bills of the swans are flat upon the ground.
> A most desolate wind has chilled Rouge-Fatima
> And a grand decadence settles down like cold.
> (CP, 142)

The swans in this passage, like the swans in "Invective Against Swans" (CP, 94), represent a system of belief that is no longer credible. Hence, instead of swimming majestically, they are described as having fallen flat like deflated balloons.[19] The "Rouge-Fatima" is a symbol of ideal beauty that is deflated. Like the swans, she is chilled by "a most desolate wind" of the cold, northern reality that destroys old ideals. But where section II of the poem simply describes the present state of these symbols, swans and "Rouge-Fatima," section III relates two parables that are, in effect, accounts of the respective ages of the swans and ideal beauty. The life described in both of these examples is treated ironically. Stevens evokes comic images, but his

---

19. Fuchs, writing of the swans in the poem "Invective Against Swans" (CP, 94), observes that "the tone of the old sovereign images bothers Stevens—the purity, the aloofness, the pomp—as typified by swans. They arouse his genteel invective" (p. 65). Fuchs's comment also applies to "Academic Discourse at Havana," where the swans represent the same kind of figures. However, I suspect that Eugene Paul Nasser, who asserts without a doubt that the swans are "symbols of Christian myths" (p. 89), has imposed his own symbolic structure on the poem. The context of the poem does not support such a definitive identification.

point is serious. In each age, the belief that held the age
together was false. In the age when the swans stood for a
world order that was credible, they ". . . arrayed / The
twilights of the mythy goober khan."

> The centuries of excellence to be
> Rose out of promise and became the sooth
> Of trombones floating in the trees.
>
> The toil
> Of thought evoked a peace eccentric to
> The eye and tinkling to the ear. Gruff drums
> Could beat, yet not alarm the populace.
> The indolent progressions of the swans
> Made earth come right; a peanut parody
> For peanut people.
>
> (CP, 142–43)

The pun on Coleridge's "Kubla Khan" (Stevens's "goober
khan") suggests the poet's attitude toward such romantic
visions of ideal order. The aura of unreality undercuts this
vision in which any "thought" based on the beliefs of this
period evoked a "peace" that was not in accord with reality. It is "eccentric to the eye" because it contradicts what
the eye sees. It is "tinkling to the ear" because it is hollow.
The "gruff drums" of violence made ominous sounds, but
the people who believed ("the populace") could ignore the
violence of reality that did not agree with their illusions.
The "earth came right" in much the same way the perfor-
mance of a circus illusion comes right: "a peanut parody
for peanut people."

The second age, composed of an even "serener myth"
than that represented by the swans, appeared to appease
the mind:

> Conceiving from its perfect plenitude,
> Lusty as June, more fruitful than the weeks
> Of ripest summer, always lingering
> To touch again the hottest bloom, to strike
> Once more the longest resonance, to cap

> The clearest woman with apt weed, to mount
> The thickest man on thickest stallion-back,
> This urgent, competent, serener myth
> Passed like a circus.
>
> (CP, 143)

Superlatives abound in this "serener myth" because it is the idealist's myth of perfectability. In the belief of idealists, things are absolute and without comparison; hence "ripest, hottest," "longest," "clearest," "thickest." But the perfection implicit in the idealist's world view is, like that of the age of swans, an example of illusion that resembles a spectacle with circus performers and peanut galleries who, for that moment, are content with illusion. Stevens's point is not simply that these examples are no longer sufficient for contemporary life. As both of the parables imply, the basis of belief was groundless, even at the time when it was in effect. Thus, the believers are mocked along with their beliefs.

Even recent thinkers, who have supposedly ordained "imagination as the fateful sin" (CP, 143), are prone to the same illusions. "Politic man" declares

> The world is not
> The bauble of the sleepless nor a word
> That should import a universal pith
> To Cuba. Jot these milky matters down.
> They nourish Jupiters. Their casual pap
> Will drop like sweetness in the empty nights
> When too great rhapsody is left annulled
> And liquorish prayer provokes new sweats: so, so:
> Life is an old casino in a wood.
>
> (CP, 144)

Yet, even these pronouncements of what "the world is not" imply an illusion, for these pompous pronouncements ("milky matters") are every bit as mythical as the beliefs of the past. "They nourish Jupiters" in the sense that they encourage the same myth-making capacity that is exem-

plified by the nightingale, the Jehovah figure, and the
"great sea-worm." The politician's theories ("casual pap")
will replace the orders that have been destroyed ("the too
great rhapsody . . . left annulled"), but the tone of this section leaves no doubt that this is not to be considered an
improvement. The emergence of "politic man" with all his
antipoetic qualities suggests that he is a cause of, as well as
an effect of, the "grand decadence" of section II.

Having deliberately debunked the old systems of order
as well as the myths of religion and political theory, the
poem has effectively taken away the possibility of the
poet's resuming his role as myth-maker. However, Stevens
does not end the poem on a totally negative note. Instead,
he begins to consider the question of the function of the
poet in the age of disbelief that he has evoked when, in
section IV, he asks:

> Is the function of the poet here mere sound,
> Sublter than the ornatest prophecy,
> To stuff the ear?
>
> (CP, 144)

This question functions as both the conclusion to and a
comment on the preceding three parts of the poem. The
movement of the poem returns to the function of poetry
which, in this case, has commenced in section I with a
process of destruction. The ridicule and removal of old
orders is one of the steps that Stevens takes toward clearing the mind of preconceived ideas. In this sense, the poetic procedure in this poem is like the process of
phenomenological reduction. In the passage cited above,
the question that is asked then is somewhat rhetorical since
the poem has obviously been doing more than making
"mere sound." However, at this point in the poem, a re-
definition of poetry and the function of the poet is re-
quested. The "infinite repetition" of myths from "ebon"
and "halcyon" must be rejected (CP, 144).

As part of nature he is part of us.
His rarities are ours: may they be fit
And reconcile us to our selves in those
True reconcilings, dark, pacific words,
And the adroiter harmonies of their fall.
                                                            (CP, 144)

The speaker proposes that the poet should concern himself with the present and the real, rather than the myths.
The poet's "rarities" should be appropriate to mankind's
needs in a decadent world. He should "reconcile" what is
human to the reality of the "metropole." In the wasteland
that is evoked in the poem, it is the poet's task to suggest
ways of living with the destructive forces of modern life.
One such way is suggested in the process of this poem. It is
a process of destruction wherein the ancient orders are
reduced to nothing. By example, parable, and ridicule, the
poem clears away preconceptions and then moves toward
a hymn to the imagination, implying a faith in the powers
of the mind to match and overcome the decadence of
modern reality. The old songs must be stopped: "Close the
Cantina" (CP, 144). The false light of modern science must
be turned off: "Hood the chandeliers," so that moonlight,
"a white that silences the ever faithful town" (CP, 144),
may function. The imagination (moonlight) creates most
effectively when all order is decreated. The quality of the
imagination is such that it "silences" the town, which is
composed of the "everfaithful" who have not yet rejected
belief. Once the mind is made free, a new perception of
reality appears that suggests an authentic interaction between the mind and the world:

How pale and how possessed a night it is,
How full of exhaltations of the sea . . .
                                                            (CP, 144)

This fresh perception of reality ("the sea") is proclaimed as
a possible value of poetry. That the perception is "older

than its oldest hymns" is not a detracting statement. It
suggests rather that these are original intuitions of reality
that were valid when man had no ideal orders or preconceived beliefs. Like the primordial perception that Husserl
proposes, these experiences of the sea are ageless, yet original. This passage proposes that poetry has the ability to
give a constant sense of the renewal of these experiences.
These exclamations have "no more meaning than tomorrow's bread" (CP, 144). Yesterday's bread has no meaning,
but mankind lives in his projection toward the future. In a
world without the possibility of belief, "tomorrow's bread"
is all that is meaningful. The essential reality, as Stevens
will say in *The Man with the Blue Guitar,* is "The book and
bread, things as they are" (CP, 172).

Thus, the fresh perceptions of reality will take the place
of the ideas of order that have been thrown out. They will
form part of the "epic of disbelief" (CP, 122) which, the
poet predicts,

> Blares oftener and soon, will soon be constant.
> Some harmonious skeptic soon in a skeptical music
> Will unite these figures of men and their shapes
> Will glisten again with motion, the music
> Will be motion and full of shadows.
>
> (CP, 122)

The skeptic of this passage (it is from "Sad Strains of a Gay
Waltz") is the figure of the poet. As "Academic Discourse"
has made abundantly clear, the possibility of belief has
passed. Thus, when the poet speaks, he will create a "skeptical music" which will nonetheless be of value. Stevens
concludes "Academic Discourse" with a restricted statement: "Let the poet on his balcony / Speak" and he will be
heard by the "sleepers in their sleep" (CP, 144–45).

> This may be benediction, sepulcher,
> And epitaph. It may, however, be
> An incantation that the moon defines
> By mere example opulently clear.
>
> (CP, 145)

The process of poetry may take the place of belief as the newest example of what the imagination can do. However, Stevens carefully qualifies his conclusion with a conditional clause. It *may* be an adequate replacement. It *may*, on the other hand, simply be another illusion, another "incantation that the moon defines." The possibilities of the momentary perception of reality that were praised are not fully realized at this point. Stevens expresses a skepticism in the last section of "Academic Discourse" that is characteristic of his later poetry. In the later volumes he will be less ambivalent about the value of poetry, but he will continue to qualify his assertions and to consider multiple points of view. One critic has remarked that the one aspect of Stevens that makes him "unique in English poetry is the frequency with which he closes his poems on a tentative note. He resorts repeatedly to some of the modal auxiliaries—may, might, and must, could, should, and would—to conclude his statement."[20] In "Academic Discourse" the assertion is tentative, to be sure, but it nevertheless posits one result of the process of decreation that will become the center of Stevens's search for a vital poetry. The necessity of fresh perceptions of reality, "the exhalations of the sea," is part of Stevens's new poetic.

From this discovery, Stevens proceeds toward some notions of possible orders. "Academic Discourse" represents the reduction of all old orders and it is fully representative of many of the poems of *Ideas of Order*. The same method is repeated in most of the poems, and whether the old order is music as in "Sad Strains of a Gay Waltz" (CP, 121), romantic poetry as in "Sailing After Lunch" (CP, 120), art as in "Dance of the Macabre Mice" (CP, 123), or religion as in "Evening without Angels" (CP, 136), the preconceptions that preclude original intuition are to be cleared away. The world of "Academic Discourse at Havana" is also typi-

---

20. See Vendler, "The Qualified Assertions of Wallace Stevens," in *The Act of the Mind,* p. 164, for an interesting discussion of Stevens's modes of expression.

cal of the cold northern world that was predicted in
"Farewell to Florida." *Ideas of Order,* as a volume, proposes
a chaotic universe where

> Day after day, throughout the winter
> We hardened ourselves to live by bluest reason
> In a world of wind and frost.
>
> (CP, 124)

In a cold and barren atmosphere even the sublime "comes
down./ to the spirit itself, / The spirit and space / The
empty spirit / In vacant space" (CP, 131). These passages
(they are from "Meditations Celestial and Terrestial" and
"The American Sublime") described the world that is left
after the old ideas of order have been tossed out, thus
clearing the mind and the world, reducing both subject
and object to simpler, more barren, and, finally, more accessible levels.

Throughout *Ideas of Order,* Stevens emphasizes these
two steps that incorporate a kind of mental clearing or
reduction, but the process of decreation has left a dark,
uncertain world in which the role of poetry and the function of the poet are both in question. Even the most positive poem of the volume asserts the power of poetry in a
carefully qualified fashion. "The Idea of Order at Key
West" is not the great poem of order that some critics have
made it out to be.[21] The poem describes the impressions of
the speaker as he listens to a woman singing by the sea in
Florida. The woman is a figure for the imagination who

---

21. For example, Joseph N. Riddel, in *The Clairvoyant Eye,* writes that "there is
a suggestion here [in "The Idea of Order at Key West"] of three realities, sea,
song, and the higher synthesis of the two, another repetition of Stevens' secular
trinity" (p. 119). He also comments that the "song is the lyric modulation of the
sea's impersonal, even cosmic rhythms, a modulation which allows the sea its
immensity and vitality, but nevertheless brings it within sensible proportions"
and implies that reality was somehow brought under control (p. 118). Riddel says
all this in spite of the careful qualification in the poem which guards against the
idea that reality is changed except in the mind of the singer. However, there are
contrasting readings of the poem. At the opposite extreme from Riddel's poem
of order is Frank Lentricchia, who claims in *The Gaiety of Language,* p. 179, that

sings "beyond the genius of the sea" (CP, 128) and in so doing, creates an idea of order. The title of the poem suggests that the order that is observed is ideational rather than factual. The order that is suggested to the observer by the woman's song is not part of or in unison with the surrounding reality represented by the sea. In fact, the poem describes the process of the ordering imagination in terms that continually stress the difference between the idea (the created song) and the sea (physical reality). In a series of negations, the speaker describes not the song itself, but what the song was not. The order that is created is not transcendent or public. After describing what the song did not do, the speaker then asserts some possible effects of the singer's act before implicitly defining the creative process, which he finally calls the "Blessed rage for order" (CP, 130). This "rage for order" is both a desire of the poet and something that has been described by the speaker's commentary on the effects of the singing.

The poem begins by establishing the essential separation of the acts of the mind from the objects that provide the background for those acts:

> She sang beyond the genius of the sea.
> The water never formed to mind or voice,
> Like a body wholly body, fluttering
> Its empty sleeves; and yet its mimic motion
> Made constant cry, caused constantly a cry,
> That was not ours although we understood,
> Inhuman, of the veritable ocean.
>
> (CP, 128)

---

the poem is "painfully ambivalent" and wrought with ironies and levels of irony. Lentricchia refuses to accept even simple statements without imposing levels of ambiguity that leave the poem without meaning. For other readings of this poem, see particularly Marius Bewley, "Romanticism Reconsidered," *Hudson Review,* 17 (Spring 1964): 127; M. J. Collie, "The Rhetoric of Accurate Speech: A Note on the Poetry of Wallace Stevens," *EIS,* 12 (January 1962): 54–66; Daniel Fuchs, pp. 111–12; Kermode, pp. 55–58; Louis L. Martz, "Wallace Stevens: The World as Meditation," in *Wallace Stevens: A Collection of Critical Essays,* p. 137; Ronald Sukenick, *Wallace Stevens: Musing the Obscure* (New York, 1967; paperback ed., 1967), pp. 78–80; and Henry W. Wells, *Introduction to Wallace Stevens* (Bloomington, 1964), pp. 128–29.

The singer "sang beyond" the capacity of the sea because she is of a different kind of intelligence. The vital difference between mind and reality is asserted and there can be no harmony of voices human and inhuman. The "cry" of the sea is vaguely understood by the listeners, but it is finally "inhuman" ("not ours," i.e., not part of humanity). The "mimic motion" of the waves creates the rhythmic sounds that the speaker calls a "cry." But as he listens to the song, he realizes that he must discern between human song and the pathetic fallacy it might engender. Stevens's process of reduction is again at work as the speaker separates mind and world. Finally, the "cry" must be rejected as an imposition of the mind of the observer on the real. In other words, it is a "cry" only in the mind of the listeners who have begun to project human qualities into the sea. But this effort is denied, since "water never formed to mind or voice." The "body" of water is "wholly body" in the sense that it has no limbs ("empty sleeves") and no head, thus no mind or feeling.

The poem continues to define the relation between the singer (imagination) and the sea (reality).

> The sea was not a mask. No more was she.
> The song and water were not medleyed sound
> Even if what she sang was what she heard,
> Since what she sang was uttered word by word.
> It may be that in all her phrases stirred
> The grinding water and the gasping wind;
> But it was she and not the sea we heard.
>
> For she was the maker of the song she sang.
>
> (CP, 128–29)

Neither the sea nor the singer is a mystery for the poet. They are what they appear to be: inhuman and human respectively. Because of this, there is no union of sea and the girl's mind in the song, "even if" the singer was trying to imitate the sound of the sea.

As the speaker rejects any idea of union or fusion of the "maker" (or poet, in the root sense) and the sea, he also refuses to admit any of the traditional notions about the sea:

> The ever-hooded, tragic-gestured sea
> Was merely a place by which she walked to sing.
>
> (CP, 129)

Stevens felt that the sea was considered something of a mystery by poets of the past. Its essence remained undisclosed ("ever-hooded") and was frequently imputed to have human attributes ("tragic-gestured"). All such preconceived ideas of the reality that is present are to be rejected. The sea was "merely" a place. It simply provided a setting for a song and neither its mystery nor the human qualities attributed to it are applicable.

Having prepared for the essential question by this series of decreative statements, all of which negate old ideas about self and imagination, the speaker then asks his companion "Whose spirit is this?" (CP, 129). Two possible answers to this question are immediately rejected. Both answers would have been typical of romantic idealists. The two conditional clauses ("If it was") suggest that if it were either sea or sky, then the song would have been "sound alone" without sense or significance.

> But it was more than that,
> More even than her voice, and ours, among
> The meaningless plungings of water and the wind,
> Theatrical distances, bronze shadows heaped
> On high horizons, mountainous atmospheres
> Of sky and sea.
>
> (CP, 129)

The spirit of the song is the imagination, which is more than the "voices" of those present. This passage is frequently misread by critics, who think that the spirit is "more than," but part of, voices merged with the "plungings" of the sea and the wind.[22] I take the last three lines of this passage to be images of the sea and wind that are placed in apposition to suggest poetic ideas about nature that must be rejected. Stevens uses these phrases in much the same way that he uses the phrase "ever-hooded, tragic-gestured sea." The poem effectively deflates these images because they all suggest the preconceived notions that act as barriers to fresh perception. All these images are like the "plungings" in the sense that they are meaningless in the context of the poem, and the poem is clearly not ambivalent about this matter, Frank Lentricchia to the contrary.[23]

The poem then makes two statements about the positive value of the song (and by extension, the value of the creative act of the imagination that is the spirit of her song):

> It was her voice that made
> The sky acutest at its vanishing.
> She measured to the hour its solitude.
>   (CP, 129)

She has given meaning to the scene through her song and, in doing so, she has given the scene an order. The song

---

22. An example of this tendency is found in Helen Hennessy Vendler's essay where she writes that "the complicated progressions ('even if . . . since . . . it may be . . . if . . . or . . .') simply serve to implicate the various alternatives ever more deeply with each other so that the sea, the girl, the water, the song, the wind, the air, the sky and cloud, the voices of the spectators, all become indistinguishable from each other, as Stevens wants them to be" (p. 175).

23. Lentricchia, p. 179. On p. 184 he writes that "the middle section of the poem offers more irony before revealing the identity of the 'spirit.' It was neither the sound of the sea, sky or cloud, nor the singer's voice or the poet's interacting with nature which composed spirit." Here Lentricchia seems to be on the right track until he decides that what the whole poem has demonstrated is wrong for Stevens: "Stevens feels that the woman had become too much an escapist of the imagination, as she focuses at the horizon where the world seems to end, too willingly a solipsist who disregards the hard particulars of experience" (p. 185). If the woman represents the creative imagination, as Lentricchia has claimed, this interpretation would imply that Stevens is criticizing the very power of the imagination that he is celebrating. The result of Lentricchia's multiplying levels of irony is that he contradicts nearly every positive statement that he makes about the poem.

adds meaning (makes the sky "acutest") to the meaningless sunset. The creator adds feeling to a senseless sky and thus, without changing, altering, or unifying her relation with reality, she makes that reality part of her imagined world for "she was the single artificer of the world / In which she sang" (CP, 129). She alone becomes the measurer of the time, not by clocks but by its emotional content:

> And when she sang, the sea,
> Whatever self it had, became the self
> That was her song, for she was the maker. Then we,
> As we beheld her striding there alone,
> Knew that there never was a world for her
> Except the one she sang and, singing, made.
>
> (CP, 129–30)

Many of Stevens's critics have cited this passage as proof of the poet's tendency to dissolve the imagination and reality into a unified whole. Joseph Riddel writes, for example, that the poem "is an impressionistic marriage of subject and object. . . ."[24] But to take this passage out of context to prove a point, as Riddel does, is to misread it. The context has asserted that the singer (self) and the sea (reality) are different in kind and not degree. The qualifying phrase "whatever self it had" undercuts any sense of cosmic fusion of subject and object. The only possible "self" for the sea (which "never formed to mind or voice") is in the human imagination. Hence, this passage means, as Ronald Sukenick succinctly comments, that "when she sang, the sea took on the identity that her song gave it."[25] The singer creates a sea in the world of her song.

Hence she creates an ordered world, but it is a unique world shaped in a work of art and not an inclusive world that subjugates, alters, or unifies reality. After the song has ended, there is a moment of expanded vision in which it

---

24. Riddel, p. 119.
25. Sukenick, p. 79.

appears to the speaker as if the "glassy lights" of the
fishing boats in the harbor had

> Mastered the night and portioned out the sea,
> Fixing emblazoned zones and fiery poles,
> Arranging, deepening, enchanting night.
> (CP, 130)

The experience of observing the singer create her own
world has the effect of momentarily carrying over into the
observer's perception. But, as the concluding stanza
suggests, the appearance of order in the universe is part of
the spirit of the song rather than a fact. Instead of asserting that the universe was given order, the speaker asks his
companion a question and implies, through the question,
that the sea and the sky seemed to have been arranged,
deepened, and enchanted. This is another example of Stevens's use of the qualified assertion; in this case a question
takes the place of a declarative statement. He answers his
own question with further qualification:

> Oh! Blessed rage for order, pale Ramon,
> The maker's rage to order words of the sea,
> Words of the fragrant portals, dimly-starred,
> And of ourselves and of our origins,
> In ghostlier demarcations, keener sounds.
> (CP, 130)

He realizes that he has been affected by what he has seen.
It was the desire for order ("Blessed rage") rather than
order itself that caused the mastering of the night and the
portioning out of the sea. This desire is "blessed" because
it is the poet's "rage" to create ("to order words of the sea")
and, by creating, to give order to a chaotic reality. Here, as
before with the girl's song, it is "words" rather than the sea
that are to be ordered. The creation of order is finally an
idea that must be achieved in words. These words must be
concerned with reality ("of the sea") as well as with the
openings to reality through which perception is to take

place ("fragrant portals, dimly-starred"). The words must also be concerned with the self ("of ourselves and of our origins"). The poem, in short, must deal with both subject and object.

At the same time, the spirit of the song is the same spirit of the "maker's rage": the imagination, which mediates between self and reality, subject and object, as a spiritual limitation ("ghostlier") and yet as a concrete work of art ("keener sounds" of actual poems). The creative act is then both example of the desire for order and an achievement of a momentary order in the world of the imagination. "The Idea of Order at Key West," like the song that is described therein, is both an example of its title and a definition of itself as *Kunstwerk*. It is composed of "keener sounds" that prescribe the "ghostlier demarcations" of the spirit of the imagination. As a poem that both prescribes and exemplifies the poetic process, it provides a tentative answer to the question ("Is the function of the poet here mere sound?") that was posed in section IV of "Academic Discourse at Havana" (CP, 144). It is but a short step from this poem to section XXII of "The Man with the Blue Guitar," where Stevens proposes explicitly that "Poetry is the subject of the poem" (CP, 176). Yet, characteristically, Stevens qualifies his view of poetry and the role of the imagination in "The Idea of Order at Key West." A thorough reading of the poem in context makes clear what the poem means not only in terms of itself, but also in terms of Stevens's development. The idea of order that is discovered is the idea of the imagination, and once this is revealed, Stevens will proceed to find out what the imagination can do.

The poems of *Ideas of Order* have introduced first the idea of a simplified reality. Even at Key West, the images evoked are of a reality that no longer resembles the lush tropical world of the South as it appeared in *Harmonium*. Instead there is simply the sea, the wind, and the sky. Stevens begins consistently to reduce the "a priori" of the mind by throwing out all orders, beliefs, and myths. In the next volume, *The Man with the Blue Guitar,* Stevens explores the further possibilities of the imagination as mediator between the self and reality. As he proceeds to propose different roles for the imagination he will again choose methods that are similar to Husserl's.

3
The Self-Description
of the Blue Guitar

In the volume *The Man with the Blue Guitar and Other Poems*, which Stevens published in 1937, the poet begins to apply the lessons that he had projected in *Ideas of Order* and reaches several tentative conclusions about the processes of the imagination that will add to his developing concept of poetry. Immediately before the writing of *The Man with the Blue Guitar*, Stevens had written his only long polemical poem, *Owl's Clover* (1935, 1936). In this poem, he attempted to defend the role of the poet in a time of political unrest and social revolution. In the long and (as he was later to remark) overly "rhetorical" poem, Stevens argued for the necessity of the artist to remain above political concerns, socialist critics, and social problems.[1] Part of *Owl's Clover* was specifically an answer to the criticism of a leftist writer who had roasted Stevens, in a review of *Ideas of Order*, for failing to come to terms with the social upheaval of the thirties.[2]

---

1. Stevens's attitude about "Owl's Clover" and several other poems is recorded by Samuel French Morse in *OP*, p. xxiii.
2. See Stanley Burnshaw, "Turmoil in the Middle Ground," *New Masses*, 17

The Man with the Blue Guitar also expresses Stevens's realization that the modern reality of the depression must be confronted in poetry, but his confrontation with that reality is as a poet, not as a social prophet. As Stevens wrote later, the thirty-three short poems that make up "The Man with the Blue Guitar" would "say a few things that I felt impelled to say 1) about reality 2) about the imagination 3) their interrelations; and 4) principally, my attitude toward each of these things. This is the general scope of the poem, which is confined to the area of poetry and makes no pretense of going beyond that area."[3] Stevens knew, better than his critics, that his poems were about poetry and it is his description of the process of poetry that is important in these poems.[4] Each of the thirty-three poems is related to the possible ways a new poetry might fit the contemporary situation. Each poem (played upon the blue guitar, a symbol of the imagination) is a variation on a single theme which, as section XXII announces, is simply the process of poetry itself: "Poetry is the subject of the poem" (CP, 176). The rest of the poems move around this proposition. However, this statement is hardly a confession of the self-centeredness of the poet or the solipsistic quality of his thought. The first twenty sections are all attempts to define what poetry is and once a tentative definition of poetry is reached Stevens (in section

---

(October 1935): 42. See also Stanley Burnshaw, "Wallace Stevens and the Statue," *Sewanee Review* 69 (July–September 1961): 355–66, in which Burnshaw changes his mind about Stevens's poetry and decides that he had been somewhat overly critical in his earlier review of *Ideas of Order*.

3. *Mattino Domenicale ed Altre Poesie*, trans. Renato Poggioli (Torino, 1954), p. 174. Stevens provided an interesting, albeit untrustworthy, commentary on a number of his poems for Poggioli, who was translating a selection of Stevens's poems into Italian in the early 1950s. Poggioli published the commentary along with his translations.

4. For other readings of this poem, see especially Kermode, pp. 66–71; Riddel, pp. 136–48; Sukenick, pp. 82–104; Merle E. Brown, "Concordia Discours in the Poetry of Wallace Stevens," *AL* 24 (May 1962): 247–54; J. V. Cunningham, "The Styles and Procedures of Wallace Stevens," *The Denver Quarterly* 1 (Spring 1966): 8–28; and Newton Stallknecht, "Absence in Reality: A Study in the Epistemology of the Blue Guitar," *The Kenyon Review* 21 (Autumn 1959): 545–62.

XXII) can then expound one of the postulates upon which he bases his poetic. Within the context of the entire series of poems in "The Man with the Blue Guitar," this statement is the climax of a number of important proposals that Stevens makes in individual sections.

Throughout the series, the blue guitar has provided both a means of interacting with the things as they are (reality) and a means of distorting these things in the poems. In the first six sections of "The Man with the Blue Guitar," the guitarist is confronted by an audience that presents an ideal program for poetry. Having heard that "things as they are / Are changed upon the blue guitar," the audience demands a song that transcends them and yet is faithful to their reality as it is:

> And they said then, "But play, you must,
> A tune beyond us, yet ourselves,
>
> A tune upon the blue guitar
> Of things exactly as they are."
>
> (CP, 165)

The essential demand is for a return, like Husserl's original intuition, to the things themselves ("exactly as they are"). Yet, the imagination does not present reality as it is: "Things as they are are changed upon the blue guitar" (CP, 165). There is a vital difference between reality as it is and the poem's version of reality. This difference is pointed out in section II, where the poet answers the audience.

> I cannot bring a world quite round,
> Although I patch it as I can.
>
> I sing a hero's head, large eye
> And bearded bronze, but not a man,
>
> Although I patch him as I can
> And reach through him almost to man.

> If to serenade almost to man
> Is to miss, by that, things as they are,
>
> Say that it is the serenade
> Of a man that plays a blue guitar.
>   (CP, 165–66)

He complains that he can only *approach* the world of things in the poem. Each approach is a version of reality, not reality. Each attempt to present the reality of human existence (and thus, reality itself) is a near-miss because the poem must remain a poem. It will not transcend itself. One attempt to represent man in the poem is a song of parts where "a hero's head, large eye / And bearded bronze" are evoked as symbols of man. But synecdoche in this case is still a partial version of the thing and not the thing itself. Each part remains a fragment rather than the whole. The speaker in this section describes one of the limitations of imaginative activity. His admission is effectively that the poem cannot be reality even though the poet approaches things as they are in the poem.

Beginning the series with two poems that prescribe one of the limits of poetry, Stevens then proceeds to analyze both the audience's demand and the poet's potential. The following sections are trials, all of which present ideas about what poetry can and cannot do. In section II, the poet cannot form a sufficient version of man (and by extension, reality). In section III, the poem expands the idea that was first suggested by the audience in section I. The third section is a series of infinitive phrases that expresses the desire "to play man number one" (CP, 166). In other words, the goal is to concentrate on making man the center of the poem's concern. Each of the infinitive phrases stresses the violent activity of the imagination as it concentrates on man: "to drive," "to lay," "to pick," "to nail," "to strike," "to tick it, tock it, turn" and finally "to bang it from a savage blue" (CP, 166). The violence evoked by the verbs suggests the necessary violence of the imagination that concentrates on defending man. The imagination is a force for self-preservation. As Stevens says elsewhere, "it is a violence from within that protects us from a violence without. It is the imagination pressing back against the pressure of reality."[5] But even with the violence of the infinitives, the series of verbal phrases leads to no result, merely another statement of what is wanted, but cannot yet be achieved.

In section XIX, the poet expands the idea of the necessary violence of the imagination as a prerequisite to authentic poetry:

> That I may reduce the monster to
> Myself, and then may be myself
>
> In face of the monster, be more than part
> Of it, more than the monstrous player of
>
> One of its monstrous lutes, not be
> Alone, but reduce the monster and be,
>
> Two things, the two together as one,
> And play of the monster and of myself
>
> Or better not of myself at all,
> But of that as its intelligence,
>
> Being the lion in the lute
> Before the lion locked in stone.
>   (CP, 175)

The monster in this passage is reality. The process described in this poem is the reduction of reality to a simplified state. With the mind and reality facing each other after the reduction of the monstrous reality, the poet will then use his imagination ("play") to mediate between the self and the monster. Stevens commented on this section that he wanted "man's imagination to be completely

---

5. *NA,* p. 36.

adequate in the face of reality."[6] His sense of this equality
is necessary for any kind of original intuition to occur. For
Stevens, equalizing imagination and its counterpart requires two different acts. First, he must reduce reality
(which, like Husserl's step toward original intuition, reduces the universe of perceptions to a single perception).
Second, he must make the imagination equal the violence
of the reality that it faces. Stevens represents this step
through animal metaphor. The violent beast ("lion") of the
imagination ("in the lute") confronts the violent beast
("lion") of reality ("locked in stone"). This is an extremely
compressed image of both the reduction to equality (lion
vs. lion) and the necessary violence of both mind and object. When this equality is achieved, the interaction of the
imagination and reality results in valid perceptions expressed as poems.

Section IV returns to exactly the kind of process that has
been denied in section II. But, in this case, the poem does
not achieve any more than a bare statement:

> And that's life, then: things as they are,
> This buzzing of the blue guitar.
> (CP, 167)

The statement is that reality (things as they are) is the same
as the sound of the imagination ("buzzing of the blue
guitar"). In spite of what Stevens writes about the poem,
bare statement does not effect a metamorphosis.[7]

In section V, the audience speaks again to the player:

---

6. *Letters,* p. 790. Stevens adds "I want, as a man of the imagination, to write
poetry with all the power of a monster equal in strength to that of the monster
about whom I write" (Letter to Poggioli).

7. Stevens writes of this poem: "In this poem, reality changes into the imagination (under one's very eyes) as one experiences it, by reason of one's feelings about
it" (*Letters,* p. 793). While it is always interesting to find out what Stevens might
have intended, this example might serve to illustrate the difference between
intention and achievement. It might also serve to show that poets are seldom their
own best critics.

> Do not speak to us of the greatness of poetry,
> Of the torches wisping in the underground,
>
> Of the structure of vaults upon a point of light.
> (CP, 167)

Here, the demand of the audience is for a poetry of ordinary modern reality. With the rejection of an overabundant reality (as in "Farewell to Florida"), there can no longer be a poetry "of the torches wisping in the underground." Since the vitality of myths and mystical orders has been consistently denied by the progressive decreative power of the imagination, poetic visions of "structures of vaults upon a point of light" are no longer acceptable. The heavens and hells of past poetry are explicitly ruled out as a fit subject of modern poetry. Instead, the poet must begin again to perceive reality at its simplest level. Part of this demand coincides with Husserl's demand for a return to the first level of perception. The audience describes the common reality as a simplified world of objects where beliefs and preconceptions are absent. Things as they are (the things themselves) remain; hence:

> There are no shadows in our sun,
>
> Day is desire and night is sleep.
> There are no shadows anywhere.
>
> The earth, for us, is flat and bare.
> There are no shadows.
> (CP, 167)

The finer modulations of the "vaults upon a point of light" suggest an absolute reality beyond the visible, present world. The modern world of the audience is without the shades of light and "shadows" with which the idealist imagination used to embroider reality. A "flat and bare" earth is now the central fact and poetry must deal with this present world and no other. Since all orders, all fixed ideas, and all preconceptions are denied,

> Poetry
>
> Exceeding music must take the place
> Of empty heaven and its hymns,
>
> Ourselves in poetry must take their place,
> Even in the chattering of your guitar.
>   (CP, 167)

While this may seem to be a considerable demand upon poetry, it is only so if one still thinks of "empty heaven and its hymns" as things that actually existed in the past. For Stevens (or, more accurately, for the audience who declares this to be the ideal role of poetry), the point of this passage is not that poetry shall be the new religion.[8] Rather, the passage affirms that poetry is part of the same imaginative capability of man that once created and sustained the gods and heaven.[9] The audience is demanding that poetry, stripped of religious and mythological import, must create a vision of man: "Ourselves in poetry must take their place." This demand, even though it is not so evangelical as several of Stevens's critics have taken it to be, is nonetheless an important part of his view of poetry.[10] However, once the poetic imagination is conceived as the

---

8. When Sukenick, for example, insists that poetry (for Stevens) "can take the place of faith" (p. 85), he seems to imply that a new religion is in the making and that this is Stevens talking. I am suggesting that the audience does not necessarily represent the poet's point of view.

9. Stevens paraphrases this section: "We live in a world plainly plain. Everything is as you see it. There is no other world. Poetry is the only possible heaven. It must necessarily be the poetry of ourselves; its source is the imagination" (*Letters*, p. 360).

10. See, for example, J. Hillis Miller, *Poets of Reality: Six Twentieth Century Writers* (Cambridge, Mass., 1966), p. 224, who confuses poetry and religion several times when he quotes Stevens's "adagia" out of context in order to prove that the death of God generates much of Stevens's poetry. He writes, "in defining poetry as a substitute for religion Sevens is joining himself to a tradition extending from the romantics through Matthew Arnold down to our own day."

creative force that had formerly provided credible myths, the potential of poetry in Stevens's poetic becomes fully evident.

The poet can no longer be myth-maker. He must face the demands of a particularly desolate reality that has been reduced to the things themselves and is no longer (in *Ideas of Order* and thereafter) lush, productive, and dominant. From the audience's demand for a poetry of man as a replacement for the poetry of God and mythology, Stevens will develop the idea of the "supreme fiction." This notion is brought up again in sections XVIII and XX and will, in later volumes, become one of the central theories of Stevens's poetry. I will save a full discussion of the "credible fiction" for the sixth chapter, but I do want to point out the early manifestations of this idea to show how the idea of a "supreme fiction" develops as the poet works his way toward resolving the aesthetic problems that are the center of his concern in this poem.

In section VI, the audience continues to outline its needs to the guitar player. These demands only expand those of sections I and V that poetry become a secular equivalent of the desire for belief and order. The great demand is for the "credible fiction" that will present reality, without distortion, by means of the imagination. Or, as Sukenick writes, "an adequate fiction [that] will not distort the nature of reality."[11] Hence, the request is:

> A tune beyond us as we are,
> Yet nothing changed by the blue guitar;
>
> Ourselves in the tune as if in space,
> Yet nothing changed, except the place
>
> Of things as they are and only the place
> As you play them, on the blue guitar
> (CP, 167)

---

11. Sukenick, p. 85.

This section more clearly articulates the desire of the audience to be represented in the poem without any change from what they are. The impossible request of the audience is to exist in an imaginative construct (the tune) just as they are in reality (space), with only the location changed. If it were possible to achieve this ideal in art, then the result would be as follows:

> Placed, so, beyond the compass of change,
> Perceived in a final atmosphere;
>
> For a moment final, in the way
> The thinking of art seems final when
>
> The thinking of god is smoky dew.
> The tune is space. The blue guitar
>
> Becomes the place of things as they are,
> A composing of senses of the guitar.
>   (CP, 168)

Once things as they are are transferred to the work of art without change, they are removed from the flux of reality and made permanent for a moment ("for a moment final"). This achievement is compared to the conceptualization in art that "seems" final when the concepts of God are disintegrated ("smoky dew"). Imagination would become the place of reality ("the tune is space") and, if this were possible, then the constant opposition of imagination and reality would be shattered, since, ideally, the imagination would then be reality. At any rate, that is the fully explicated desire of the audience. But, in "The Man with the Blue Guitar," this desire is an idealist's view of what is possible in a poem.

The realist's view is that of the guitar player/poet, who declares in the opening section that "Things as they are / Are changed upon the blue guitar." The desire of the audience is beyond the capacity of the poet figure. Even though Stevens carefully controls the narrative voices of his personae, several of his critics declare that this passage is an example of the unity of the imagination and reality and, therefore, a victory.[12] This passage is hardly an affirmation by the poet, since the argument of this section is voiced by the audience and is an expression of their desire rather than an assertion of what is possible for the guitar player. It is almost as if Stevens placed a conditional "if" clause at the beginning of the passage and then proceeded to express the possible results of a conditional premise. If such a union of the imagined and the real were possible, then the expression (song, work of art, poem, all are metaphorically involved) would be "for a moment final." But, as with all art, the moment only "seems" final and Stevens is as fully aware of the difference between "seems" and "is" as he is of the difference between art and reality.

After this section, the form of the poem changes as the narrative device of the dialogue between the player and his audience is dropped.[13] For, after the audience has expressed its desire in sections V and VI, the remaining twenty-seven sections examine the possibility that poetry could become what the audience has proposed. The rest of the poem proceeds almost as if the guitar player had moved off by himself to play the possible improvisations and variations that might lead to this achievement. However, there is a considerable difference between the desired function of poetry expressed in section VI and the actual functions of poetry that are proposed in the rest of the poem. Stevens's interest in the rest of the sections is mainly in what poetry can actually do.

---

12. See Sukenick, for example, who writes that "the process described is like one of contemplation at the end of which reality is brought into intense rapport with the mind . . . ," which, he then claims, "bridges" the subject-object opposition (p. 86).

13. Riddel mistakenly sees this change as an arbitrary and unrelated act on the poet's part and does not see any purpose or design in including a dialogue in the poem. The absence of the audience in the remaining sections of the poem is a sign, he writes, "of the casualness of Stevens' organization . . ." (p. 137).

First, the guitar player examines the possible relations between the imagination and reality in poetry. Poetry cannot depend purely on the imagination without reality (sections VII and XIII), nor can the poem represent reality without the imagination (section VIII). Imagination without reality (when "The sun no longer shares our works" [CP, 168]) makes the strings "cold on the blue guitar" (CP, 168).

This idea is expanded in section XIII, where reality becomes only "pale intrusions into blue" of imagination. When reality is devalued to this degree, what is left is the pure imagination. Divorced from reality, the poet must then be "content to be / The unspotted imbecile revery" (CP, 172). He becomes thoughtless ("imbecile"), pure ("unspotted"), and lost to a dreamlike world of illusion ("revery"). At "The heraldic center of the world / Of blue" (CP, 172), the poet is no longer capable of the clear perception that is essential to poetry. Hence, the world of the pure imagination, the world where "blue" becomes "Amorist adjective aflame. . . ," is rejected.[14]

The world of the pure imagination is an intense world where the incandescent power is unleashed to the detriment of both reality and the self. Reality is effectively dis-

---

14. Frank Doggett, on the other hand, in *Stevens' Poetry of Thought* (Baltimore, Md., 1966; paperback ed., 1966), sees this passage as a positive rendering of the "pure knowing self." He writes that "the self as pure knowing subject then becomes a point or center of conception for all its world" (p. 77). If taken out of the context of the poem, this reading would make sense. For other readings of this section of "The Man with the Blue Guitar," see Mac Hammond, "On the Grammar of Wallace Stevens," in *The Act of the Mind: Essays on the Poetry of Wallace Stevens*, ed. J. Hillis Miller and Roy Harvey Pearce (Baltimore, Md., 1965), pp. 179–84, esp. pp. 181–84, where Hammond gives a full word-by-word analysis of the syntax, grammar, and semantics of this passage and concludes, rightly I think, that for Stevens the imagination is not a thing, but "a quality or an action," even though "Stanza XIII of 'The Man with the Blue Guitar' entertains, through a kind of linguistic trickery, the notion that the imagination is an entity. Such hypostatization is a typical result of metalanguage or of metapoetry—speech about speech" (p. 184); as well as Joseph N. Riddel, *The Clairvoyant Eye: The Poetry and Poetics of Wallace Stevens* (Baton Rouge, La., 1965; paperback ed., 1967), pp. 141–42; and Merle E. Brown, "Concordia Discors in the Poetry of Wallace Stevens," *American Literature* 34 (May 1962): 246–69.

counted and the self reduced to "imbecile revery." However, the implicit rejection that is involved in this section is
aimed at the idea of purity and not at the imagination
itself. In fact, the next section presents the strongest
statement concerning the potential value of the imagination that can be found in "The Man with the Blue Guitar."

> A candle is enough to light in the world.
>
> It makes it clear. Even at noon
> It glistens in essential dark.
>
> At night, it lights the fruit and wine,
> The book and bread, things as they are,
>
> In a chiaroscuro where
> One sits and plays the blue guitar.
>   (CP, 172)

There are two symbols for the imagination in this passage.
First, there is the candle (as opposed to the over-elaborate
German chandelier, which represents scientific knowledge, i.e., reason). It provides clear sight, "even at noon."
The function of the imagination is to make clear perception possible ("it lights the fruit and wine . . . things as they
are . . ."). Second, the established symbol of the blue
guitar, which is being played throughout, provides a
means of expressing the definition of the imagination as
the power of clear sight. In this passage, the imagination
(blue guitar) defines itself and its potential (the candle),
and, in doing so, proves that it can generate a definition of
itself within its own constructs.

By backtracking to the steps that Stevens achieves in
Ideas of Order, I can explain this a little more clearly. The
rejection of an over-complex reality was accomplished by
the imagination. The subsequent decreation of all assumptions (all orders, all old myths, all old beliefs) was also a
function of the imagination. Hence, when the poem at this
point announces that the imagination makes clear percep-

tions of reality possible, it is with reference to what the imagination has done in previous poems, since both the rejection of the first step and the reduction of the second step are vital stages in Stevens's procedure and in his concept of the imagination.

Within the conflict between the imagination and reality that is posed here, there must be a balance between the two. In section XIII, there is too much imagination. In section VIII, there is too much reality. When reality is too powerful, "the vivid, florid, turgid sky, / The drenching thunder rolling by" (CP, 169), the effect is equally detrimental to creativity. The brute reality of nature in section VIII dominates the mind, thus destroying the possibility of a fruitful interaction between the imagination and the world. The creative impulse is reduced, leaving, for the guitarist, "the feeling heavy in cold chords / Struggling toward impassioned choirs" (CP, 169).

The poem must include both imagination and reality without destroying the essential separateness of the two. In section XI, the poet proposes the possibility of a metamorphosis of self with environment where "slowly the ivy on the stones / Becomes the stones. Women become / The cities, children become the fields" (CP, 170–71). This proposed fusion won't work, though, because it denies the essential individuality of the objects. Metamorphosis is as deadly to clear perception as extremes of either imagination or reality. A poem that proposes such a union in metamorphosis is "a chord that falsifies" (CP, 171). The rest of this section proposes the opposite extreme, wherein it is the environment that overwhelms the self rather than vice versa:

> The sea returns upon the men,
>
> The fields entrap the children, brick
> Is a weed and all the flies are caught,
>
> Wingless and withered, but living alive,
> The discord merely magnifies.
>   (CP, 171)

When the "discord" between man and his environment is emphasized, the result is an exaggeration rather than falsification. Nonetheless, if the imagination presents this possibility, it is again distorting the uniqueness of "things as they are." Living things become "flies" that are impotent though alive, suggesting the death within life that occurs when reality (the sea) dominates the man of imagination.

With both extremes of metamorphosis rejected, the final couplet suggests hopefuly that there will come an era when

> Deeper within the belly's dark
> Of time, time grows upon the rock.
> (CP, 171)

Stevens comments that this passage looks forward "to an era when there will exist the supreme balance between [imagination and reality]."[15] The era is in the future, where within the process of gestation ("in the belly's dark / Of time"), there will emerge a vision of a reality (the rock) that will nourish human life (time).[16] This vision does not predicate a change in reality or in man. Rather, it seems to be a prediction of a possible "balance" that will be achieved in poetry. The idea of a balance between the forces of reality and the forces of the mind will be an essential part of the "supreme fiction" that Stevens will later develop.

The poet returns to the idea of the "credible fiction" in section XVII, where he proposes the possibility of

> A dream (to call it a dream) in which
> I can believe, in face of the object.
> (CP, 174)

---

15. *Letters*, p. 363.
16. I am indebted in my reading of this section to the suggestion of Frank Doggett, who writes that "the poet places this concept of growth metaphorically within the all-encompassing flux and concludes his poem with an image of time as a pregnancy, deep in the dark of its own mystery of process . . ." (p. 74). While Dogget fails to explain this dense passage, he does suggest one way in which Stevens treats the concept of time in the poetry. In my sixth chapter, I will expand this suggestion of Stevens's concepts of time.

Within the poem, this dream becomes transformed into a thing of reality. It becomes "a dream no longer a dream, a thing, / Of things as they are" (CP, 174). Like the fiction in which the poet can believe, this dream is credible and like the desire expressed by the audience in sections I and V, this fiction becomes a thing itself, part of reality, and hence will not distort reality. But, like "light in a mirroring of cliffs, / Rising upward from a sea of ex" (CP, 175), the dream is a vision that is only possible in the imagination. It can be a thing itself only in the sense of an imagined thing. The return to the confrontation with reality (the monster) in section XIX completes the poet's rejection of the believable dream, but Stevens's rejections of this possibility are never permanent. The idea of the "fiction" that will combine imagination and reality (be both "dream" and "thing") returns in the following volumes for reconsideration.

After the reduction of the monster of reality in section XIX, the poet reaffirms his goal of reduction in section XXI where he proposes that the self, reduced, stripped, and laid open at its core, is to be both the subject and the object of the poem.

> A substitute for all the gods:
> This self, not that gold self aloft,
>
> Alone, one's shadow magnified,
> Lord of the body, looking down,
>
> As now and called most high. . . .
>   (CP, 176)

The simplified "self" of the present must replace the majestic visions of gods, myths, and giants. Those figures of the myths of past imaginations ("gold self aloft," "one's shadow magnified" and "Lord of the body") must be forgotten. In preparation for the new poetry, the poet must concentrate on:

> One's self and the mountains of one's land,
>
> Without shadows, without magnificence,
> The flesh, the bone, the dirt, the stone.
>   (CP, 176)

This passage reiterates the dual nature of the reduction that Stevens has incorporated into his poetic procedure. Like many of the other passages in *Ideas of Order* and "The Man with the Blue Guitar" that describe the desire to reduce both the imagination and reality to an equal basis, the images in this passage that represent the self are stripped to barren, essential figures ("the flesh, the bone") that match the images of reality ("the dirt, the stone").

For each movement thus far, the phenomenological method of Edmund Husserl has provided an analogue from philosophy that helps clarify the direction of Stevens's poetic development. Both the process of original intuition and the specific reductions of both the mind and the world are vital parts of the phenomenological method. Husserl's theory helps to explain the steps Stevens takes toward a "poetry of perception" (a poetic that reaches its fullest statement in the early poems of *Parts of a World*). Stevens's implicit idea that there must be a balance between the imagination and reality becomes most clearly evident when the reader has in mind the epistemological goals of such an idea. Furthermore, the crucial roles of the processes of the imagination (which for Husserl make possible the phenomenological method)[17] are more easily understood when Husserl's methods are invoked.

---

17. See Husserl's *Ideen* I: 163, where he posits the value of both the imagination and the concept of fiction as essential elements that form the basis of the phenomenological method. About the use of the imagination and its resultant fiction, Husserl writes "if anyone loves a paradox, he can really say, and say with strict truth if he will allow for the ambiguity, that the element which makes up the life of phenomenology as of all eidetical science is the concept of 'fiction' (*die Fiktion*), that fiction is the source whence the knowledge of 'eternal truths' draws its sustenance" (*Ideas: A General Introduction to Pure Phenomenology*, trans. W. R. Boyce Gibson [London, 1931], p. 201). Although Husserl doesn't push this suggestion very far, it is a telling sign of his honesty about his endeavors to conceive of a pure ego and pure intuition, both of which would seem to be results of what Stevens would call "the power of the imagination."

Following the description of the process in section XXI
which, like Husserl's phenomenological reductions, decreates the images of both reality and the mind to the
simplest level of equality, Stevens then formulates the
central thesis of "The Man with the Blue Guitar." It is not
necessarily a logical step, because the argument of the
whole poem does not follow a logical pattern. Rather, it is a
form of ellipsis that leaves out intermediate steps. The
previous sections have proposed various ways in which the
mind and reality interact, including several ways that are
either not possible or not desirable. The poet, at this point,
concludes that what he has been doing all along is valid
and that the process of the imagination as it carries out the
interactions beween the self and reality is poetry. In other
words, the subject of poetry is not man or reality, but the
process of the imagination itself. Or, as Stevens writes:

> Poetry is the subject of the poem,
> From this the poem issues and
>
> To this returns. Between the two,
> Between issue and return, there is
>
> An absence in reality,
> Things as they are. Or so we say.
>
> But are these separate? Is it
> An absence for the poem, which acquires
>
> Its true appearances there, sun's green,
> Cloud's red, earth feeling, sky that thinks?
>
> From these it takes. Perhaps it gives,
> In the universal intercourse.
>   (CP, 176–77)

This section is frequently misread by critics who have
taken the lines (particularly the first three lines) out of the
context of "The Man with the Blue Guitar." At this point
in the larger context of the whole poem, Stevens consoli-

dates what he has been attempting all along. But, the act of consolidation is less complex than many of his critics have tried to make it.[18] The process of the imagination has been exemplified by frequent repetition in preceding sections. Once the decreation has occurred, a fresh perception takes place through the imagination's power to "light the world" and make "it clear" (CP, 172). This cycle of reduction and perception forms the cycle of "issue and return" of the poem. During this cycle, there is a lack of ("absence in") reality. Or, as section I declares, "Things as they are / Are changed upon the blue guitar" (CP, 165). The poem is neither reality nor things as they are, even though it begins with the objects of perception. Reality is the source, but, in the poem, the particulars of reality (the smell and feel of things as they are) are absent.

It is just this absence that the poet wants to question. He asks if "these" are separable, referring to poem and reality by asking if the fact that the poem is of the mind and not of matter is really an absence, since the poem has its origins in reality? The poem begins with sun, cloud, earth, and sky (all figures of reality) and adds the imagination's distortions, which turn the sun green, the clouds red, and then personifies the earth and the sky. The imagination's distortions take away the sense of reality while adding meaning. Hence, in "the universal intercourse" between mind and reality, the poem not only takes its source from reality, it also gives back a meaning to a world of objects without inherent significance. The absence is thus corrected by an exchange between reality and the imagination in the poem: "From these it takes. Perhaps it gives . . ." (CP, 177).

---

18. Among the more complicated readings of this section are those of Sukenick and Riddel. Sukenick writes that "the poem's absence in reality is its perception of reality," obscurely hinting at a concept of "esthetic integration" that he does not explain (p. 95). Riddel gets several chapters ahead of his argument when he suggests mysteriously that "the absence in reality is the unperceived, the nothingness we can know of, but never know" (p. 144).

However, in terms of the entire poem, the poet has not succeeded in resolving the difficulty that was posed in the opening sections. The audience's demand that reality be transposed into the poem without change is not answered. Instead, two compromises are offered: first, that poetry is not about reality; it is about its own process; and second, that instead of the simple transfer from world to poem there is an active interchange between the two.

The following sections add "A few final solutions" (CP, 177), with which Stevens returns to the issues of the earlier sections. In sections XXV–XXVII Stevens treats the first issue, the concept of change or flux. In the poetry of *Harmonium*, Stevens was aware of a law of change that was constant. For example, "Sea Surface Full of Clouds" (CP, 98) demonstrates the power of the imagination to change its perspective. It is, in short, a poem whose subject is not the seascape that is envisioned in six different ways, but rather the process of the imagination changing its perspective. Another example in the early poetry of the same phenomenon is the frequently explicated poem, "Thirteen Ways of Looking at a Blackbird" (CP, 92). The subject of this poem is hardly the blackbird of the title. The bird is the source in reality where the poem begins, but the poem is about the imagination's power of association. It is a poem that demonstrates the process of change as it is manifested by the imagination. These and other examples in *Harmonium* illustrate the poet's preoccupation with change as it occurs in the mind.

In "The Man with the Blue Guitar," the idea of flux is first associated with the imagination in the guitar player's complaint in section II. But in the final sections of the poem, the concept of change is observed to be part of reality. The clown figure in section XXV watches the world turn upon his nose and rejoices not only in his ability to "fling" the world in his mind but also in his ability to perceive reality changing by itself. The inevitable cycles of change in nature are symbolized: birth and death, the seasons, and daily cycles of the cosmos ("cats had cats and the grass turned gray / And the world had worlds" [CP, 178]). The figure of the poet (the nose) is called "eternal" because, in relation to the instability of the world, he is a constant.

The following section (XXVI) proposes another kind of change. It adds the fluctuating world that the clown watches to the changing integrations of the mind and the world that the imagination creates. The world is the ever-changing shore "to which his imagination returned, / From which it sped" (CP, 179). It changes form ("whether sound or form / Or light") and becomes both the source and the antagonist for the poet. First, like a "rock" providing a foundation, it then becomes the "giant that fought / Against the murderous alphabet" (CP, 179), the symbols and sounds the poet must use. The integrations of the mind and the world reflect the constant change in both and the poetry thus becomes "a mountainous music" that "always seemed / To be falling and to be passing away" (CP, 179). Realization of the full meaning of change necessitates a never-ending renewal for the poet whose "music" is always becoming obsolete as soon as it is heard.

One answer to the frustrations inherent in the instability of both mind and world is self-knowledge. A full awareness of oneself is what is lacking in the man who would travel to see changes in reality. For this man "The sea is a form of ridicule" (CP, 180). Change is present in the snow in New England if one is aware of the process of change that is implicit in the weather. If not, then "the iceberg settings" of winter "satirize / The demon that cannot be himself, / That tours to shift the shifting scene" (CP, 180). Any man who is unable to attain a stability of self amid the constant change is the "demon" who must wander in search of change when change is taking place in front of his eyes. To the man, conversely, who has self-knowledge (i.e., who has attained a use of the imagination's power to see reality clearly and who, as a result, knows himself), the constant flux that is symbolized by the weather can be observed sitting in Hartford, Connecticut.

This kind of self-knowledge is further explained in the following sections (XXVIII and XXXII) where the issue is no longer change, but self-identity.

> I am a native in this world
> And think in it as a native thinks,
>
> Gesu, not native of a mind
> Thinking the thoughts I call my own,
>
> Native, a native in the world
> And like a native think in it.
>
> It could not be a mind, the wave
> In which the watery grasses flow
>
> And yet are fixed as a photograph,
> The wind in which the dead leaves blow.
>
> Here I inhale profounder strength
> And as I am, I speak and move
>
> And things are as I think they are
> And say they are on the blue guitar.
>   (CP, 180)

A kind of self-discovery is implied in this section and it is one possible solution to the problem of the conflict between the mind and reality. The speaker proposes a kind of familiarity with his world that precludes questioning. It is the expression of one who is fully at home in his world and does not question the appearances of the things themselves. Things-as-seen *are* as they are in the world. His claim is based on the premise that he does not live in the mind, but rather in the world. He stands out of himself, projecting himself into a world that is always clear and unambiguous for him. The full realization of this possibility would break down the dualism that has formed the basis of almost all of the previous sections of "The Man with the Blue Guitar." As a possible mode of existence, this state of mind is similar to Husserl's "natural standpoint."[19] For Husserl as for Stevens, this mode of existence is characterized by a kind of simple confidence that excludes doubts about the possibility of subjective distortions. Husserl's description of this state of mind accurately explains Stevens's passage:

> Ich bin mir einer Welt bewusst, endlos ausgebreitet im Raum, endlos werdend und geworden in der Zeit. Ich bin mir ihrer bewusst, das sagt vor allem: ich finde sie unmittelbar anschaulich vor, als daseiende, ich erfahre sie. Durch Sehen, Tasten, Hören usw., in den verschiedenen Weisen sinnlicher Wahrnehmung sind körperliche Dinge in irgendeiner räumlichen Verteilung für mich einfach da, im wörtlichen oder bildlichen Sinne "vorhanden", ob ich auf sie besonders achtsam und mit ihnen betrachtend, denkend, fühlend, wollend beschäftigt bin oder nicht. . . .[20]
>
> Für mich da sind wirkliche objekte, als bestimmte, mehr oder minder bekannte, in eins mit den aktuell wahrgenommenen, ohne dass sie selbst wahrgenommen, ja selbst anschaulich gegenwärtig sind.[21]

The phenomenologist's description of the world from the *natürlichen Einstellung* displays the same kind of confidence as Stevens's spokesman for the "native" stance.

For a moment, then, in this section, Stevens proposes a new relation of self and world. It would seem to be an

---

19. Husserl, *Ideen,* I: 57–65.

20. *Ibid.,* p. 57. Boyce Gibson translates this passage in *Ideas,* p. 101: "I am aware of the world, spread out in space endlessly, and in time becoming and become, without end. I am aware of it, that means, first of all, I discover it immediately, intuitively, I experience it. Through sight, touch, hearing, etc., in the different ways of sensory perception, corporeal things somehow spatially distributed are for me simply there, in verbal or figurative sense 'present,' whether or not I pay them special attention by busying myself with them, considering, thinking, feeling, willing."

21. Husserl, *Ideen,* I: 58. In *Ideas,* p. 101, this passage is translated as follows: "For me real objects are there, definite, more or less familiar, agreeing with what is actually perceived without being themselves perceived or even intuitively present."

intuitive realization of a possible way of solving the Cartesian duality between mind and world that has been the
center of concern throughout Stevens's verse. Instead of
discovering the self in the mind, the speaker has discovered the self in the world. Strangely enough, this possibility is not expanded in "The Man with the Blue Guitar."
The subsequent sections of the poem return to the
imagination-reality dichotomy. However, this mode of
existence will become more pronounced in the later volumes. It is a mood of confidence that leads Stevens toward
an apprehension of Being as the center of his poetry. But,
before the poet begins to express an interest in Being itself, he returns to the problem of man in the abstract: first,
in the final sections of this poem, then in the poems of
Parts of a World.

This is the third issue with which the last dozen poems
of "The Man with the Blue Guitar" are involved. In section
XXX, the poem returns to the problem that was first presented in section II. But at this point the poet has discovered what the imagination can do and, as a result, the
confidence that is implicit in section XXVIII is made
explicit:

> From this I shall evolve a man.
> This is his essence: the old fantoche
>
> Hanging his shawl upon the wind,
> Like something on the stage, puffed out,
>
> His strutting studied through centuries.
>   (CP, 181)

The essence of man that could not be found in section II is
here evolved by the imagination. He is like the figure of
the "fantoccini," which is abstracted to an essence.[22] He

---

22. Stevens suggests the "fantoche"—"fantoccini" relationship (*Letters*, p. 791).
He denies, though, in the same letter, any "conscious reference to Shakespeare"
(p. 791), even though Poggioli had apparently recognized the similarity.

resembles Shakespeare's "walking shadow, a poor player / That struts and frets his hour upon the stage." But the essence is not defined except by metaphor. The figure of man is an abstract idea of man that must be placed among the factories and housing tracts of "Oxidia," the "banal suburb" of contemporary America. These are the conditions under which a man will be evolved in poetry. He must confront the workaday world that was first posited in "Academic Discourse at Havana." Faced with that world, he must know that "there is no place, / Here, for the lark fixed in the mind, / In the museum of the sky" (CP, 182). The sky that the romantic poets knew (the "lark" is perhaps Shelley's skylark) as a museum of nature is replaced by the lifeless, smoggy sky of Oxidia.

> It must be this rhapsody or none,
> The rhapsody of things as they are.
>
> (CP, 183)

Out of these conditions, which are prescribed by the poet, a modern poetry will re-create an idea of man.

At the end of "The Man with the Blue Guitar," Stevens has still not evolved a man in the abstract, unless the idea of the self as part of the idea of man is to be accepted. Yet, the lack of an expressible idea of man is not a total failure, because the poet has set up the conditions under which the idea of man may be evolved. He has explored the possibilities of poetry in the contemporary reality and has shown what poetry can do. He has also affirmed that poetry is able to evolve the essence of man, even though this affirmation remains unproven. According to Stevens, this essence will be an abstract idea that will take form in the imagination. However, the subject of poetry is not this essence, it is the process of the imagination as it interacts with reality.

As section XIV suggests, the imagination "is enough to light the world" (CP, 172). It not only provides clear perception through its processes of reduction and decreation, it also can produce an idea of the self as creator. Through one's own creations, one comes to know one's self and one's identity. The task that remains is that of attempting to describe the essence of man. This task, along with its corollary the "credible fiction," will provide two major concerns of the next two volumes.

The importance of the steps that Stevens puts to work in "The Man with the Blue Guitar" cannot be overestimated for they begin to form the basis of his poetic procedure. The methods I have described in this discussion become fully integrated into Stevens's poetic and, as the following discussions will indicate, they lead Stevens from a profound interest in "things as they are" to a concern for the Being of the things that are.

The parallels between Husserl's methods and Stevens's will continue to be important to a full understanding of the latter's development, but as Stevens turns his interest from the idea of a conceptual essence to the possibility of a nonconceptual essence, his poetic investigations will take on interesting affinities with the investigations of Martin Heidegger. The techniques are still basically like those of phenomenology, but Stevens's use of those techniques will more closely approximate Heidegger's interpretation of phenomenology than Husserl's. This development is the subject of the next chapter.

4

From Perception to Disclosure

In *Parts of a World* Stevens collected the poems he had written between 1936 and 1941 (for publication).[1] Most of Stevens's critics agree with Frank Kermode, who writes that this volume "is nobody's favorite."[2] But this judgment is of the separate volume of poems without the qualifying context of the whole of the *Collected Poems*. Within this larger context, there are several important directions in Stevens's development that are explored in these poems. Kermode cites one direction. But he has only partially understood Stevens's development when he describes these poems as a group whose "main topic is the exteriority of things, but it is philosophically considered; the thought is revolved, not transmuted into those images which wake in the poet's blood for *Notes Toward a Supreme Fiction*."[3]

In the previous volumes, the poet had developed methods that are, as I have shown in the last two chapters, curiously parallel to the methods of Edmund Husserl's phenomenology. The processes of reduction and decrea-

---

1. *Parts of a World* (New York, 1942) is reprinted in *The Collected Poems of Wallace Stevens* (New York, 1954).
2. *Wallace Stevens* (Edinburgh, 1960; paperback ed., New York, 1961), p. 71.
3. Kermode, p. 71.

tion that Stevens had incorporated into his verse had
brought about the contemplation of a confrontation with
the thing itself, the object in reality that otherwise had
seemed inaccessible. But I want to note, at this point, that
neither Stevens nor Husserl was interested in the "thing"
for its own sake. Both are involved, not with describing
things for the sake of description or listing the concrete,
physical properties of objects, but with describing the
mind in the act of perceiving the thing. For both the poet
and the philosopher, the important issue is the act of consciousness and not the "thing" itself that is perceived. Because of this interest, Stevens is scarcely to be called an
imagist poet, as some critics have attempted. I suspect that
those who claim Stevens as a poet of reality or of things are
misled by some of his statements or titles, like "Not Ideas
About the Thing But the Thing Itself" (CP, 534), which
purport to be doctrine or, at least, are taken as such by the
unwary reader. While the later poetry of Stevens may take
its point of origin from an object perceived, the poetry
moves, as James Baird observes, from "object to idea."[4]
From this point the idea then takes shape as something invented or created. In a similar way, Husserl's cry of "*zu den
Sachen selbst,*" which is frequently confused with William
Carlos Williams's phrase "no ideas but in things," is not an
expression of a necessity to return to the physical world of
solid objects, but rather a slogan that is used to describe
the phenomenologist's preference for "intuition" over
logic. For Husserl, all certainty must be based on clear
perceptions of the object that is intended by the act of
consciousness, but it is the process of consciousness that is
of interest. The object itself counts for very little because
the *Ding an sich,* the naked object that is stripped of meaning, is only itself.

---

4. *The Dome and the Rock: Structure in the Poetry of Wallace Stevens* (Baltimore,
Md., 1968), p. 14. Baird devotes an extended discussion to this very issue and
concludes that Stevens's poetry moves from "object to idea" and that the idea
then takes shape as a structure that is created.

As the poet discovers the aesthetic inadequacy of the exterior world of things, he also discovers that it is not the thing itself that he is interested in. The subject of the poetry becomes the process of perception through which the objects of the exterior world are grasped. Stevens develops what several critics have called a "poetry of process," in which the processes of the mind provide both the subject matter and the structure of the poetry.[5] But, while Stevens had implied this much in *The Man with the Blue Guitar,* he explicitly announces the nature of his poetry in "Of Modern Poetry" (CP, 239), where he declares that modern poetry will be:

> The poem of the mind in the act of finding
> What will suffice. It has not always had
> To find: the scene was set; it repeated what
> Was in the script.
>
> (CP, 239)

In an age in which belief is no longer possible, the poem can no longer follow the "script" of myth and religion. Hence, modern poetry "has to be living" (CP, 240) in the sense that it must face the problems of existence.

> It has to think about war
> And it has to find what will suffice.
>
> (CP, 240)

The poem then will be "*of* the act of the mind" and will represent the movements of the mind as it searches for whatever will suffice in the modern situation. The poem becomes, as Stevens writes, "an insatiable actor" (CP, 240),

---

5. Miller calls Stevens's poetry a "cycle of decreation followed by a new imagining of reality," which for Miller is a poetry of "process rather than progress." *Poets of Reality: Six Twentieth Century Writers* (Cambridge, Mass., 1965), p. 259, also p. 266. I am also indebted to Robert J. Bertholf, who defines the middle stage of Stevens's verse as "a poetry of process." See his "The Vast Ventriloquism: Wordsworth and Wallace Stevens," Ph.D. diss., University of Oregon, 1968, p. 168 and passim.

who must re-create both the stage and the play of the mind
for an "invisible audience" who will become like the mind
itself. The goal of the poem is not necessarily belief, pleasure, or instruction. Rather, the poet will be content to
represent the processes of the mind. The poem is compared to

> A metaphysician in the dark, twanging
> An instrument, twanging a wiry string that gives
> Sounds passing through sudden rightnesses, wholly
> Containing the mind, below which it cannot descend,
> Beyond which it has no will to rise.
>
> (CP, 240)

These processes of the mind decreating and creating
"sounds" (words) will "wholly contain the mind" in the
sense that they will become the mind's acts. Riddel comments that "throughout 'Of Modern Poetry,' the poet is
metaphorically an actor, in the dual sense of [one] playing
a part (and apart), and one doing; his audience is himself,
for he is the sum of his audience, creating and requiting."[6]
If one extends Riddel's assertion, he can say that both poet
and poem are acting in the mind (of the reader) and that
here one has reached a point where the processes of the
mind have become more important than the goals of these
processes. It would seem to be the logical end of "a poetry
of process." But, as the poet knows, process for its own
sake is as dry as "objects" for their own sake. Finally, the
poem

>   Must
> Be the finding of a satisfaction, and may
> Be of a man skating, a woman dancing, a woman
> Combing. The poem of the act of the mind.
>
> (CP, 240)

----

6. *The Clairvoyant Eye: The Poetry and Poetics of Wallace Stevens* (Baton Rouge,
La., 1965; paperback ed., 1967), p. 159. For other readings of this poem, see
Daniel Fuchs, *The Comic Spirit of Wallace Stevens* (Durham, N.C., 1963), pp.
20–21 and Ronald Sukenick, *Wallace Stevens: Musing the Obscure* (New York,
1967; paperback ed., 1967), pp. 107–8.

While it may be true that it matters little to Stevens what the poem literally treats as its subject, it nevertheless must satisfy the same mind whose act it represents.

Thus, in the middle of *Parts of a World* Stevens explicitly announces the mode of the poetry that he is composing. If the goal of the poet were to record the processes of the imagination as it confronts the object (reality) and to make these processes (as he did in *The Man with the Blue Guitar*) the subject of the poetry, then the first poems of *Parts of a World* could be said to represent this exercise at its purest level. Many of the poems are exercises of the mind in the act of observing its own convolutions, and the descriptions of these reflective processes are recorded in the poems. While several of Stevens's commentators have found them somewhat dry (Joseph Riddel calls them "academic exercises"[7]), the lack of sustained emotional power in many of the poems of *Parts of a World* can probably be attributed to the level of abstraction that Stevens has reached. He is no longer vitally concerned with the real world of buzzing, chaotic life that was so powerfully presented in the verbal fireworks of *Harmonium*. As one might guess from a reading of "Of Modern Poetry," the poet's interests are directed toward the world of his own mind. This leads to a poetry of contemplation, meditation, and to a level of abstractness that is often at one or two removes from the so-called real world. The problem with *Parts of a World* is succinctly summarized by Doggett:

> Now as the stature of Wallace Stevens begins to show itself as above and apart from the disputes of his contemporaries, the place of abstraction in poetry must be sought, and on his terms; for in his work abstraction again becomes a major element in poetry.[8]

The poems of *Parts of a World* are important because they

---

7. Riddel, p. 150.
8. *Stevens' Poetry of Thought* (Baltimore, Md., 1966; paperback ed., 1966), p. 199.

initiate and set the patterns for the major poems that are
to follow in *Transport to Summer*. It is in this volume that the
major concerns and techniques of Stevens's later poetry
are announced and developed.

At the beginning of *Parts of a World,* Stevens begins to
test the value of the thing itself clearly perceived. Characteristically, the doubt is not that the perception is clear
(although the difference beween what is there and what is
perceived is a problem that rarely escaped Stevens's self-
consciousness), but rather whether, if the perception is
clear, the thing itself delivers enough to the poet. Is it
enough to have an original intuition of the thing itself? For
the philosopher, the answers to these kinds of questions
are sufficiently evident. Husserl's methods are all directed
toward the development of a "first philosophy" that will
provide a basis for all other sciences. The idea of
phenomenology is to achieve primordial perceptions upon
which a basis of certainty can be assumed. Husserl proceeds on the assumption that the only apodictic certainty
possible is that which is made available through original
intuitions. Thus, the entire complex of reductions is developed by Husserl to achieve that goal. For the poet, on
the other hand, the philosophical value of his poetic procedures is not important. He is concerned with aesthetic
values. While Stevens does desire certainty, he is aware at
the same time that certainty is no longer possible within
the context of contemporary thought.

"The Poems of Our Climate" is the first poem in *Parts of
a World* to make an issue of the value of "objective reality."
The poem describes a reduced scene with objects clearly
delineated. The field of perception available to the eye is
purified by a single perception.

> Clear water in a brilliant bowl,
> Pink and white carnations. The light
> In the room more like a snowy air,
> Reflecting snow. A newly-fallen snow
> At the end of winter when afternoons return.
>   (CP, 193)

With a painter's eye for the values of light and a philosopher's eye for the nature of the object that is perceived, the poet describes a purified scene before him, only to conclude that "Pink and white carnations—one desires / So much more than that" (CP, 193). The speaker continues to describe the scene as in his mind he reduces it to its simplest level.[9] Only the thing perceived remains to confront the perceiver:

> The day itself
> Is simplified: a bowl of white,
> Cold, a cold porcelain, low and round,
> With nothing more than the carnations there.

> II
> Say even that this complete simplicity
> Stripped one of all one's torments, concealed
> The evilly compounded, vital I
> And made it fresh in a world of white,
> A world of clear water, brilliant-edged,
> Still one would want more, one would need more,
> More than a world of white and snowy scents.
>   (CP, 193–94)

With the concentration upon the single object of perception, the rest of reality has been set aside. The poet perceives "nothing more than the carnations there." Here, the poet emulates the first phase of Husserl's phenomenological reduction. He has temporarily suspended the rest of

---

9. Nasser attempts to read this poem by using the color symbolism, and in doing so confuses the meaning of the poem without adding any significant insight. Attempting to work "The Poems of Our Climate" into his system of symbols, Nasser finds himself asking "Why, for example, does [Stevens] say, "Pink and White carnations—one desires so much more than that?" and resolves his question by commenting that "red being the color of unabstracted reality in all its harshness, we see that the statement, in fact, says that we desire so much more than reality can offer us. Pink is a stronger color than we want, part of a cold astringent scene." One is not quite sure how Nasser's system has had any effect in reaching this conclusion. See *Wallace Stevens: An Anatomy of Figuration* (Philadelphia, Pa., 1965), p. 38. Daniel Fuchs in his *The Comic Spirit of Wallace Stevens* (Durham, N.C., 1963), reaches the exact-opposite conclusion about this poem when he observes that "the still life conceals the struggles within ourselves. It is an evasion of reality" (p. 160). Both critics seem to have missed the point of the reductive processes that are described.

the world just as Husserl proposes to suspend the natural world in brackets (to put the world of things in "brackets" by withholding judgment).[10] Stevens's first step then is comparable to the phenomenologist's ἐποχή.[11]

Then the poet suggests the temporary suspension of subjectivity when he adds the conditional phrase "Say even that this complete simplicity / Stripped one of all one's torments, concealed / The evilly compounded, vital I / And made it fresh in a world of white" (CP, 193). Here, he is emulating the second phase of the phenomenological reduction, wherein Husserl proposes to set aside the complexities of the individual ego in order to reach the pure ego (purified of subjective limits). Among the reductions that Husserl describes, this step is the most purely idealistic since the shift from the individual ego to the transcendental ego presupposes the possibility of self-transcendence.[12] For Stevens, this final reduction is proposed only by a

10. Husserl explains that the ἐποχή (which he derives from the Greek term, ἐποχή) is the fundamental phenomenological reduction wherein one "puts in brackets," and thus suspends judgment on, the validity of the Being (i.e., for Husserl, the existence) of the world that we naturally take for granted in our normal activities. See *Ideen I*, 3:6. Also, see especially the chapter *"Radikale Änderung der natürlichen Einstellung; die Ausschaltung,"* pp. 63–69.

11. *Ideen I:* 110–12. In a later work, Husserl redefines the ἐποχή when he writes that he uses the Greek term to signify the radical alteration of the natural standpoint, wherein "I no longer attach any validity to the natural belief in the existence of what I experience." See *Cartesian Meditations,* trans. Dorion Cairns (Martinus Nijhoff, The Hague, 1960), pp. 20–21.

12. Husserl describes this reduction in several of his works. Essentially, his account goes as follows: After one has completed the phenomenological ἐποχή one assumes the existence of a pure ego (the self), which cannot be experienced like the objects of consciousness and hence cannot be "bracketed" in the same way that the rest of the world can in the method of the ἐποχή. The ego is "the residuum of the phenomenological suspension of the world" and is necessary for each act of the consciousness, yet is purified by the act of reduction. Its psychological processes are stripped so that it is present and pure which, for Husserl, means that it is transcendent, since he calls the "Ich" a "quite peculiar transcendence . . . a transcendence in immanence." ("Verbleibt uns als Residuum der phänomenologischen Ausschaltung der Welt und der ihr zugehörigen empirischen Subjektivität ein reines Ich—wenn wir hier passende Reservationen machen—[und dann für jeden Erlebnisstrom ein prinzipiell verschiedenes], dann bietet sich mit ihm eine eigenartige—in gewissem Sinne nicht konstituierte—Transzendenz, eine Transzendenz in der Immanenz dar" (*Ideen I:* 138).

conditional proposition, as if he were saying "even if this were possible, what would result?"

The result for Stevens is "A world of clear water, brilliant edged" (CP, 194). Having carried out the second phase of Husserl's phenomenological reductions by "suspending" (in Stevens's words: "stripping" and "concealing") the complexities of the individual ego ("the evilly compounded, vital I"), he has cleared away all the barriers of subjectivity that prevent a clear perception of the object. According to Husserl's prescribed methodology, these two reductions should lead to the original intuition. In other words, having simplified the world of objects and suspended the ego, Stevens should arrive at one goal of the phenomenological method: absolute clarity of perception. But at the same moment that this perception is reached and the poet sees the object of his contemplation "brilliant edged," he realizes that this is insufficient:

> Still one would want more, one would need more,
> More than a world of white and snowy scents.
> (CP, 194)

The phenomenologist's process of reduction, by itself, fails for the poet because "There would still remain the never-resting mind" (CP, 194), which "wants" and "needs" more than clarity and purity of perception. The purity of perception does not (in the terms of "Of Modern Poetry") "suffice" because it does not satisfy the whole mind. Second, the clear perception that is imagined is attained only on the condition that the perceiving "I" can be stripped of its complexities. Stevens implies that the assumption of a pure or detached ego is dishonest because the premise of complete detachment contradicts the truth of the human condition. Thus, while it may be the desire of both the poet and the philosopher to transcend the complications and flaws of finite human existence, it is the poet rather than the philosopher who is fully conscious of the difference between what is desired and what is attained. Husserl proceeds to make the desire into a theory of the transcendental ego.[13] Stevens stops in the middle of the process of reducing the "evilly compounded, vital I" and considers the implications of such a theory. By a process of ellipsis, Stevens rejects the idealism implicit in the reduction of the ego in the "transcendental ego" when he denies the possibility of human perfection that any theory of "self-transcendence" implies.[14] Man is finite and there is no ideal existence possible. The poet concludes that his task is to celebrate "the imperfect," which for us, as modern men, "is our paradise" (CP, 194), and not to concoct possible perfections. The ambivalence of the poet of the finite is registered in the final lines:

> Note that, in this bitterness, delight,
> Since the imperfect is so hot in us,
> Lies in flawed words and stubborn sounds.
>   (CP, 194)

The "bitterness" refers to the poet's awareness of the impossibility of transcendence. But that is not all. A further bitterness comes from the uncertainty that is inherent in any expression of the kinds of perceptions that he does have. The poet's words, his medium of expression, add to the difficulty that has already been implied. Yet, ironically for the poet, the ambiguity of language is the source of delight, further emphasizing the crucial difference between phenomenology in philosophical discourse and phenomenology in poetry. The poet can take delight

---

13. *Ideen I:* 174–77. See also n12 above.
14. Stevens's implicit rejection of "self-transcendence" is surprisingly similar to Husserl's critics' rejection of the theory of the transcendental or pure ego which, for many philosophers, is ultimately too much like the idealism that Husserl renounced early in his career. See especially Joseph J. Kockelmans, "Husserl's Transcendental Idealism," in *Phenomenology: The Philosophy of Edmund Husserl and Its Interpretation,* ed. Joseph J. Kockelmans (Garden City, N.Y., 1967), pp. 183–93; and Ludwig Landgrebe, *Phänomenologie und Metaphysik* (Hamburg, 1949), pp. 83–100.

even in the epistemological failure, because his criterion is aesthetic and not philosophical.

Thus, at the end of the poem, the imperfection of the human condition precludes the possibility of certainty. The direct and clear perceptions achieved through the reductive processes fail to sustain the poet. Even though the results are, in principle, sufficient for the philosopher, they are inadequate for the poet. The conditional suspension of the complexity of the mind that corresponds to Husserl's phenomenological reduction is as much a fiction as the other beliefs, whether religious or idealistic, that have been rejected in *Ideas of Order* and *The Man with the Blue Guitar*.

However, Stevens continues his interest in these philosophical speculations and returns to a consideration of the different aspects of the acts of perception in "The Glass of Water" (CP, 197–98):

> That the glass would melt in heat,
> That the water would freeze in cold,
> Shows that this object is merely a state,
> One of the many, between two poles. So,
> In the metaphysical, there are these poles.
> (CP, 197)

Given the perception of the glass of water, the poet through his imagination is able to conceive of the glass and the water in first one, then another possible state of the potentially changing states of existence. As the mind contemplates the object, it gives to the object various possible meanings: not that the object itself reflects or suggests these meanings, but that the mind (imagination) creates meaning out of virtually nothing. The power of the mind that is involved in this process is the imagination.[15] When

---

15. Stevens once defined the imagination as "the power of the mind over the possibilities of things; but if this constitutes a certain single characteristic, it is the source not of a certain single value but of as many values as reside in the possibilities of things." "The Imagination as Value," *NA*, p. 136.

the glass of water (the object perceived) is placed in the
center of perception, the poet discovers one possible relation and then another, each leading to several possible
meanings:

> Here in the centre stands the glass. Light
> Is the lion that comes down to drink. There
> And in that state, the glass is a pool.
> Ruddy are his eyes and ruddy are his claws
> When light comes down to wet his frothy jaws.
>   (CP, 197)

The metaphor for light (that which makes the perception
possible) is the lion—the same beast of violence that stood
for reality in section XIX of *The Man with the Blue Guitar*.[16]
By means of the metaphor, the mind is shown discovering
relationships and meanings through a process of free variation (a process that could probably be called "fancy" if we
were to follow Coleridge's critical definitions). The process
that is developed in this section of the poem is similar to
Husserl's eidetic reduction wherein the object of perception is contemplated in order to arrive at the essence of its
being. In a simplified form, the eidetic reduction seeks to
find the essence (the *eidos*—the ideational essence) of the
thing perceived. Husserl describes the method as follows:

> The *Eidos,* the pure essence, can be exemplified intuitively in
> the data of experience, data of perception, memory, and so
> forth, but just as readily also in the mere data of fancy (*Phan-
> tasie*). Hence, with the aim of grasping an essence itself in this
> primordial form, we can set out from corresponding empiri-
> cal intuitions, but we can also set out just as well from nonem-
> pirical intuitions, intuitions that do not apprehend sensory
> existence, intuitions rather "of a merely imaginative order."
>   . . . In the play of fancy . . . we can through ideation secure
> from this source primordial and even on occasion adequate
> insight into pure essences in manifold variety.[17]

---

16. For other readings of "The Glass of Water," see David Owen, " 'The Glass
of Water,' " *Perspective* 7 (Autumn 1954): 175–83; and Daniel Fuchs, pp. 22–23.
17. Husserl, *Ideas: General Introduction to Pure Phenomenology*, trans. W. R. Boyce
Gibson (London, 1931), p. 57. In the original this passage is as follows: "Das Eidos,

As Husserl develops the method of "eidetic reduction," he emphasizes the privileged role of the imagination as that which can, through free variation, find the "immutable and necessary complex of characteristics" without which the thing that is contemplated cannot be conceived.[18] These characteristics compose the "eidetic" or ideational essence of the thing.

In "The Glass of Water," Stevens's speaker first considers the empirical changes that the glass of water could undergo. The object is then evolved in the mind into one of several possible physical states. Then the poet moves to the metaphysical states and begins imaginatively to evolve another possible way of looking at the object. He concludes his metaphorical extension of the object by quickening the pace of his variations. The expanding metaphor of stanza two stops and the poet returns to a consideration of the process that is being illustrated by metaphor.

> And there and in another state—the refractions,
> The *metaphysica*, the plastic parts of poems
> Crash in the mind—But, fat Jocundus, worrying
> About what stands here in the centre, not the glass,
> But in the centre of our lives, this time, this day. . .
>   (CP, 197–98)

The different states of the object as it is revolved in the mind are placed in apposition to the "refractions, / the *metaphysica* —the plastic parts of poems." All of these are variations of the thing as the poet tries to place the object in the center. But the center that he seeks is not the physical center of his attention. Rather, he is attempting,

---

das reine Wesen, kann sich intuitiv in Erfahrungsgegebenheiten, in solchen der Wahrnehmung, Erinnerung usw., exemplifizieren, ebensogut aber auch in blossen Phantasiegegebenheiten. Demgemäss können wir, ein Wesen selbst und originär zu erfassen, von sowohl aber auch von nicht-erfahrenden, nicht-daseinerfassenden, vielmehr, bloss einbildenden Anschauungen."

"Erzeugen wir in der freien Phantasie . . . so können wir daran durch "Ideation" mannigfache reine Wesen originär erschauen und ev. sogar adäquat. . . ." *(Ideen I:* 16–17).

18. *Ideen I:* 160.

through the process that he displays, to evolve—in much the same way that Husserl proposes—the essence of the object. These versions of the object "crash in the mind" because it is in the mind that these changes occur and it is within the mind that they make their reverberations (crash), both literally colliding and making noise.

Each state is evolved as a variation of the thing itself as the poet's imagination evolves the *"metaphysica"* toward an essence. In the midst of these evolutions, the poem falls apart as the poet discovers that it is not the *eidos* (the essence of the object) that is the "centre." It is his existence. In this case the existential concern momentarily takes precedence over the search for essence. Hence, the process of eidetic reduction that is emulated in the first two stanzas is temporarily dropped. But, the final lines reflect the speaker's return to the principle of "free variation."

> In a village of the indigenes,
> One would have still to discover. Among the dogs and dung,
> One would continue to contend with one's ideas.
>   (CP, 198)

The figure of the poet (the "fat Jocundus") retains his concern for the problems of existence even in the midst of metaphysical speculation. The human mind and its functions (those that are demonstrated in the second stanza and then enumerated in the third) are inescapable. Even in terms of the present moment and its existential contingencies, the mind must still exert its force. The acts of the mind remain to be discovered. If the place and conditions were different, the same kinds of contemplation would occur and the acts of the mind would still take precedence over physical reality.

This conclusion is not resignation. Rather, it is a statement of Stevens's belief in the necessity of the life of the mind. The previous illustrations of the mind's activities have value because they are part of the process of discovery that will play an important part in Stevens's later poems in *Transport to Summer* and *Auroras of Autumn*. Meditation on an object begins the poem, but the object serves to suggest an idea that the imagination evolves in the poem. The poem itself displays each step of this process as it follows the act of the mind. Or, as James Baird succinctly comments, "The poet first receives the world through his senses; his reality, his sense of the world eventuates from the play of the mind upon the data of the senses. Yet more simply . . . with the poet Stevens, *object* proceeds to *idea*."[19]

In both of these poems, the object itself does not suffice. Even though poetry may begin with perception of the thing itself, it must progress beyond that into the mind. What is perceived adds to the world of the mind. The objects of the world may, like the pears of the poem "Study of Two Pears," suggest other forms, analogous colors, and related impressions, but they will, in the end, resist the transformations of metaphor. "The pears are not seen / As the observer wills" (CP, 197). The object perceived may be the origin of the poetic act, but it will not provide poetry.

Like the figure of the sun in "Add This to Rhetoric," the object exists independent of the poet's images. His own efforts are ridiculed since "Tomorrow when the sun, / For all your images, / Comes up as the sun, bull fire, / Your images will have left / No shadow of themselves" (CP, 198). What is wanted? The object of the poet's desire is not the image of the thing. Rather, as the speaker concludes, it is "the sense [that] creates the pose" (CP, 199) in the poem. The poet's sense of his own world is the goal of the poem. In the poem, this sense "moves and speaks" (CP, 199). Ironically poking fun at his own habits, the speaker states that "This is the figure and not / An evading metaphor" (CP, 199). Rejecting for a moment the metaphorical basis of poetry, the poet asserts that the poem will be that which is added to the rhetoric of the language. He concludes: "Add this. It is to add" (CP, 199), almost as if the poem

---

19. *The Dome and the Rock*, p. 19.

were to add to the language a sense of the world that is
essentially more direct than metaphor ("images" at one
remove from the thing).

In "The Man on the Dump" the images that were rejected in "Add This to Rhetoric" become refuse at the gar-
bage pit. Again the poet reflects upon the inadequacy of
the thing itself and upon the shortcomings of the images
that proliferate in the language and become stale versions
of things. In the dump, the false poetic images have become discarded artifacts. The poet must go to the dump in
order to realize the full sense of destruction that precedes
creation. "The dump is full / Of images" (CP, 201). Much
of this poem is full of discarded images, which must be
named in order to be destroyed. Or, as the poet remarks,
"One rejects / The trash" (CP, 202) so that he can experience the present perception of reality without the encum-
brance of previous ways of imagining and conceiving reality. Stevens again expresses his tendency to demonstrate
the reduction processes of the phenomenological method
as he dramatizes the process of stripping the consciousness
to a new nakedness. Having accomplished the desired
purge, the present moment of the poem is that of renewal:

> Now in the time of spring (azaleas, trilliums,
> Myrtle, viburnums, daffodils, blue phlox),
> Between that disgust and this, between the things
> That are on the dump (azaleas and so on)
> And those that will be (azaleas and so on),
> One feels the purifying change.
>
> (CP, 202)

The flowers, all of which bloom in the spring, are the trite
figures of the season of renewal. The poet has already
rejected the attempts of others to emulate the freshness of
nature. The sense of newness suggested by the dew that
"men have copied" and that women "have covered themselves with" (CP, 202) in the first stanza is debunked as
part of man's desire to have "heads / Of the floweriest

flowers dewed with the dewiest dew." Nonetheless, the present moment in spring is suspended between the images of the past springs (things already "on the dump") and the unavoidable images of future springs ("those that will be"). The naked poet recognizes the freshness of the present moment. He calls it a "purifying change" and implies that this change takes place not only in nature where time is always present, but also in the mind where the perception of the instantaneous "now in the time of spring" negates both past and future images.

> That's the moment when the moon creeps up
> To the bubbling of bassoons
>
> (CP, 202)

William Burney perceptively remarks that "only in that explicit poverty and misery do objects come to the senses purified of all their entanglements and encasements in images, works, and categories; and only then is one a man who is similarly purified."[20] The mass of trivial objects that clutter up the real world are disposed of in the dump. Out of the portrait of destruction that is presented, the poet must begin to create, but the destruction must be completed first. Only with the completion of the reductive process can the poet once again perceive the real as it is, stripped of all preconceptions, all orders, and all old representations:

> Everything is shed; and the moon comes up as the moon
> (All its images are on the dump) and you see
> As a man (not like the image of a man),
> You see the moon rise in the empty sky.
>
> (CP, 202)

The moon in these lines does not stand for the imagination. The perception results in "the figure and not / An evading metaphor" (CP, 199). The speaker has announced

---

20. *Wallace Stevens* (New York, 1968), p. 104.

the goal of his decreations and reductions. However, the clear perception that results is not an end in itself. The poet desires "so much more than that" (CP, 193). Even though the speaker declares that "what one wants to get near" (CP, 202) is his belief, the final stanza makes clear that the belief that is desired cannot be achieved.

> Could it after all
> Be merely oneself, as superior as the ear
> To a crow's voice? Did the nightingale torture the ear,
> Pack the heart and scratch the mind? And does the ear
> Solace itself in peevish birds? Is it peace,
> Is it a philosopher's honeymoon, one finds
> On the dump?
>
> (CP, 202–3)

These questions are not answered directly, but the tone of the interrogation as well as the rhetorical device of a series of questions that take the place of assertion both suggest that, for this poem as for "The Poems of our Climate," the perception is not enough. It would be wrong, just as poets in the past have been misled, "to sit among mattresses of the dead, / Bottles, pots, shoes and grass and murmur *aptest eve*" (CP, 203). None of these images, neither the fresh images of the present moment nor the dead images of the past, has brought the poet any nearer to belief. One cannot sit in the dump and listen to the cries of the blackbirds and say *"Invisible priest."* Nor can the poet "pull / The day to pieces and cry *stanza my stone*" (CP, 203). Hence, the answer to the poet's final question is apparent from the context and tone of "The Man on the Dump." The speaker asks a final question: "Where was it one first heard of the truth? The the" (CP, 203). His search has been for a singular truth that would include all others. It would be a definitive truth for which the definite article stands. There are two possible answers. The first reply might well be that he heard of the truth in the pages of past belief that he has destroyed.

However, I suspect that a more accurate answer for Stevens is suggested in the second line of the following poem, "On the Road Home" (CP, 203). Here the speaker writes that "It was when I said, / 'There is no such thing as the truth,' / That the grapes seemed fatter" (CP, 203). I think that critics like Frank Doggett, who insist that "The the," Stevens's equivalent of the absolute truth, is accessible in "the specific experience of the poem," have ignored the irony of the context.[21] When Doggett writes of "The the" as " . . . that certain instant of light that is *this* instant, [which] includes the reflective life of the mind as well as the life of the sense,"[22] he is attempting to imply that there is such a thing as an absolute truth for Stevens. Doggett's view would force affirmative answers to the ironic series of questions that Stevens poses in the final lines of "The Man on the Dump" and would thus result in a misreading of this poem, since it is precisely the notion of absolute truth that Stevens is attacking. The fresh perception of nature that results from the decreations and reductions of this poem may be true for the poet. But, these perceptions are a long way from "The the" or any notion of absolute truth. The narrator of the poem "On the Road Home" further clarifies this point when he records the words of his companion:

> You . . . You said,
> "There are many truths,
> But they are not parts of a truth."
> Then the tree, at night, began to change,
>
> Smoking through green and smoking blue.
> We were two figures in a wood.
> We said we stood alone.
>   (CP, 203)

---

21. Doggett, p. 6.
22. *Ibid.* I also note here that I am somewhat indebted to William Burney who, while he does not give an adequate reading of "The Man on the Dump," does suggest that "On the Road Home" might answer Stevens's question about "the truth" (p. 104).

The speaker and his companion are on the way back to the center of their lives. Their voyage "home" is a metaphor for the movement of the mind toward a more appropriate relation to its own world. Each step in their return takes them closer to the center of their existence. As the companion declares the relativity of truth, nature itself begins to change. The tree "becomes an experience and the real (the green) becomes the blue (the conceived)."[23] The metamorphosis that takes place in this section of the poem illustrates the bare statement of the companion. The world is transformed in their imaginations, thus showing how men establish their own relation to the world that they experience.

> It was when I said,
> "Words are not forms of a single word
> In the sum of the parts, there are only the parts.
> The world must be measured by eye"
>
> (CP, 204)

Here the poet explodes the symbolist's concept of the logos. A vital distinction is made between the word (the absolute or pure word) of the transcendental or symbolist concept of logos and the words that deny any transcendent order.[24] The speaker insists upon the ascendancy of the plurality of words over the single unifying "word." At the

---

23. Doggett, p. 210, discusses "On the Road Home" at some length and perceptively notes that "Stevens, too, finds *the* truth falsely enshrined; and finding reality in the idea of pluralism, like a poet but unlike a philosopher, he turns it into a way of regarding the world, and the idea is dissolved in experience" (p. 211). It is probably because of the way Doggett skips around the *Collected Poems* selecting examples to fit his various philosopher's ideas that he doesn't connect this poem with the preceding poem, "The Man on the Dump."

24. Michel Benamou, "Wallace Stevens and the Symbolist Imagination" in *The Act of the Mind: Essays on the Poetry of Wallace Stevens*, ed. Roy Harvey Pearce and J. Hillis Miller (Baltimore, Md., 1965), pp. 92–120, writes an extended study comparing the symbolist aesthetic and Stevens's poetics in which he distinguishes rather convincingly between the symbolist idea of the word and Stevens's notion of the plurality of words. Benamou concludes that "Stevens' ascetic look resembles the phenomenologist's ἐποχή much more than it does the symbolist's *askesis*" (p. 117).

same time, he shifts from transcendence to immanence, from idea to perception. The qualities of the speaker's relationship with the world must be measured by unique perceptions of the individual observer. The possibility of the fusion or unity of a transcendent truth is denied in favor of the description of the fragmentary parts of the world that are "measured by eye."

The sum of the distinctions made by the two travelers as they proceed toward their "home" brings to both a common feeling of a kind of truth. This feeling is not "the" truth, but rather a state of mind in which both travelers sense that they are closer to an authentic relation to the world and to themselves. This sensation is concretely presented through the images of their surroundings:

> It was at that time, that the silence was largest
> And longest, the night was roundest,
> The fragrance of the autumn warmest,
> Closest and strongest.
>
> (CP, 204)

This new relation to the night and the season is not "The the" that was called for in "The Man on the Dump." Instead, it is a state of mind that precludes absolute truth while affirming the poet's unquestionable relationship to his own world. The superlatives announce a moment of satisfaction that has resulted from their clear perception of the human condition of imperfection where there is no truth, no absolute, no transcendence, and, above all, no belief in the myths that originated these ideals. Stevens's "idols" (the images of the gods) have never seen "the" truth (CP, 204). Hence the missing sense of an absolute truth that is invoked in "The Man on the Dump" is rejected completely in "On the Road Home." The processes of reduction and decreation that have led to fresh perceptions of the world have failed to fulfill the desire for *a* truth. However, Stevens's skepticism, while combating the comforts of belief, does not prevent him from considering the possibilities of belief, even the possibility of transcendence.

In much the same way that the speakers in "The Poems of our Climate" and "On the Way Home" dramatize the possible methods by which one might reach an absolute reality beyond the ordinary reality of appearances, the speaker in "Landscape with Boat" (CP, 241) examines the assumptions of the "floribund ascetic" who carries the processes of abstraction to their logical extensions.[25] The poem tells the story of a man who, like a reductive painter or perhaps the artist of "minimal art" (and, by extension, like a transcendental phenomenologist who wants more than what is), stripped both reality and the mind to a "neutral center."

> He brushed away the thunder, then the clouds,
> Then the colossal illusion of heaven. Yet still
> The sky was blue. He wanted imperceptible air.
> He wanted to see. He wanted the eye to see
> And not be touched by blue. He wanted to know,
> A naked man who regarded himself in the glass
> Of air, who looked for the world beneath the blue,
> Without blue, without any turquoise tint or phase,
> Any azure under-side or after-color.
>
> (CP, 241)

Although I doubt that Stevens has the phenomenologist in mind, he describes a quest for "The the," the absolute truth, which is sought by a systematic reductive process similar to Husserl's phases of phenomenological reduction. The ascetic "brushed away" the real objects in the sky (the thunder and the clouds), then the "colossal illusion" (those things that are believed). He brushes as if he were a painter removing images from a canvas, but also as if he

---

25. Daniel Fuchs observes that the word *floribund* does not occur in the dictionary. It is, as Fuchs writes, "a colorful coinage, implying with the wit of oxymoron, an ornate asceticism which is moribund in being asceticism at all" (p. 144). I think that Fuchs is suggesting that the word seems to be a combination of "florid" with moribund, and hence deriving its "oxymoronic" quality.

were figuratively brushing away, in the sense of a thinker putting to the side or removing from consideration, the existence of the exterior world. He can be seen then to be carrying out the same steps of the phenomenological ἐποχή that were described in "The Poems of Our Climate." All that remains is the basic "blue" of the sky, which the ascetic would also like to eliminate. As a reductive thinker, he is described as desiring absolute clarity ("imperceptible air") so that he may "see" what he is seeking and "not be touched by blue." Both the literal and figurative sense of "blue" apply here: first, the man wants to see beyond ("beneath") the blue of the sky, and second, he wants the perception to be free of the blue of the imagination ("without blue"). In effect, Stevens again describes the ideal of the phenomenological reductions: the suspension of belief in the real world (the bracketing method of the ἐποχή) and then the assumption of a transcendental point of view (again, the image is of "nakedness" and a purified "eye"), where the blue shadings of the imagination ("turquoise tint, azure under-side or after-color") are no longer present.

Achieving such a state, the floribund ascetic is described as

> Nabob
> Of bones, he rejected, he denied, to arrive
> At the neutral center, the ominous element,
> The single colored, colorless, primitive.
>   (CP, 241–2)

The image of a "Nabob of bones" is perfectly appropriate to this character who has rejected life, himself, and Being-in-the-world to arrive at an absolute. He is then like Andersen's proverbial emperor who wore invisible clothes, since his wealth is measured in images of barrenness. He has attempted to transcend himself. But he fails. As the poet explains:

It was not as if the truth lay where he thought,
Like a phantom, in an uncreated night.
It was easier to think it lay there. If
It was nowhere else, it was there and because
It was nowhere else, its place had to be supposed,
Itself had to be supposed, a thing supposed
In a place supposed, a thing that he reached
In a place that he reached, by rejecting what he saw
And denying what he heard.

                                                    (CP, 242)

To the extremist of the reductive process, there is still one presupposition (the truth), and it is the presupposition rather than the process of reduction that Stevens attacks. The whole effort of the "ascetic" is based on the premise that "the" truth, "the single colored, colorless, primitive," existed "in an uncreated night." If that were the case, then the process by which the ascetic attempts to reach this truth would seem to be a fitting way. As if in opposition to the absence of absolutes that Stevens posits in "The Man on the Dump" and "On the Road Home," the ascetic attempts to imagine ("to suppose") the absolute and then to imagine how it might be approached. But, as the speaker points out, the approach to the transcendent absolute necessitates transcendence of the self "by rejecting what he saw / And denying what he heard." More clearly, the ascetic rejects his own senses, thus implicitly rejecting the reality of his own world.

The irony involved in Stevens's flat, matter-of-fact statements that describe the ascetic's progress effectively deflates the desire for transcendence as well as the presupposition of the existence of an absolute truth beyond or behind appearances. The terse statement "He would arrive" (CP, 242) is hardly a positive assertion, since it is in the conditional mood rather than the present indicative. Furthermore, even this carefully qualified statement is undercut by the prescribed conditions of arrival:

> He had only not to live, to walk in the dark,
> To be projected by one void into
> Another.
>
> (CP, 242)

The ascetic's process of reduction has led to a rejection of feeling, imagining, sensing, in short, all the aspects of actual existence. In this sense, the ascetic is "moribund," because he denies life and attempts to use this denial to project himself into a void where the light of consciousness is no longer present. The loss in such an extreme procedure is twofold, since both the world and the self are sacrificed. Just as the multiplication of nothing by nothing gives zero, so the projection of a voided self into a nonexistent world ("the uncreated night") results in another void. Even though "it was his nature to suppose, / To receive what others had supposed, without / Accepting," the extremist of this poem also "received what he denied" (CP, 242). In other words, much like Stevens, the protagonist of this poem withheld his belief and suspended judgment on received ideas. However, there is one vital difference. For Stevens, there was no absolute truth. For the ascetic, there was this *a priori* notion:

> . . . as truth to be accepted, he supposed
> A truth beyond all truths.
>
> (CP, 242)

This is the premise that Stevens attacks.[26] The *a priori* sup-

---

26. Curiously, I am overturning several recent readings of this poem. For example, Baird, p. 274, writes that "the depths of the adjacent 'Landscape with Boat' open perilously. What is the truth of this desolation? Is there some causality 'at the neutral centre . . . / The single-colored colorless primitive'? For it was in this 'primitive,' this 'ominous element,' that human time began. The center is arcane. The poet says only that it may be supposed. On the instant Stevens seems to approach the major inquiry of all theologies. But the darker deep suddenly closes as he turns to himself. Because he is a man, it is 'his nature to suppose / To receive what others had supposed, without / Accepting,' 'He never supposed / That he might be truth . . .' (CP, 242)." My quarrel with Baird is not that his

position of a singular, transcendent truth leads the ascetic
astray. It leads him away from Being, from life, and from
himself. To Stevens, the failure of the protagonist is not
that he thought too much, but rather that he failed to
imagine enough.[27]

> He never supposed
> That he might be truth, himself, or part of it,
> That the things that he rejected might be part
> And the irregular turquoise, part, the perceptible blue
> Grown denser, part, the eye so touched, so played
> Upon by clouds, the ear so magnified
> By thunder, parts, and all these things together
> Parts, and more things, parts.
>
> (CP, 242)

Referring back to the first stanza, the poet names the
things that had been rejected. The clouds, thunder, and
the blue of the sky are all used as examples of what is and,
hence, what might be true. The reference to "the percep-
tible blue" stands, as Daniel Fuchs observes, "in opposition
to the 'imperceptible air' which the protagonist was seeking"[28] in the first stanza. The faulty premise of the ascetic
caused him to neglect what was most obvious. He is lost in
abstraction because he has failed to use his imagination to
visualize the whole truth of his perceptions of the blue
("grown denser" as he observes) and of the clouds that
touch the eye (i.e., both literally come in physical contact
and figuratively make emotional contact). The cause of his
failure to imagine is that

---

argument does not make good sense. Rather, I think that he has confused Stevens
with the "floribund ascetic" who is the protagonist of this poem. While the poem
may very well be read as an implied lesson for the poet as well as an explicit lesson
for the "ascetic," it is not Stevens who has done the supposing and it is not Stevens
who "supposed / a truth beyond all truths" (CP, 242).

27. I am indebted here to Fuchs, who writes that "the failure of the floribund
ascetic is a failure of the imagination. He has failed to see the conceptual power of
a landscape because he has failed to see the landscape itself" (p. 148).

28. Fuchs, p. 147.

> He never supposed divine
> Things might not look divine, nor that if nothing
> Was divine then all things were, the world itself,
> And that if nothing was the truth, then all
> Things were the truth, the world itself was the truth.
>
> (CP, 242)

Within the poet's corrective to the errors of the "floribund ascetic" in these lines, there is a reaffirmation of his doctrine of the necessity of ordinary physical reality. These lines repeat the lesson of "On the Road Home" and are intended not only for the protagonist of this poem, but also as a piece of pedagogy for the reader (and perhaps, by implication, for the poet himself). The natural world and, by extension, "all things" are divine since the idea of the sacred is no longer admissible.[29]

The poem ends with a suggestion of what might have been possible for the protagonist had he not fallen into the trap of presuming "a truth beyond all truths":

> Had he been better able to suppose:
> He might sit on a sofa on a balcony
> Above the Mediterranean, emerald
> Becoming emeralds. He might watch the palms
> Flap green ears in the heat. He might observe
> A yellow wine and follow a steamer's track
> And say, "The thing I hum appears to be
> The rhythm of this celestial pantomime."
>
> (CP, 243)

Being better able to suppose means to have a more capable imagination. It means that if one were capable of imagining no transcendent reality, then he could, through the

---

29. Mircea Eliade in *The Sacred and the Profane: The Nature of Religion,* trans. Willard R. Trask (New York, 1958; paperback ed., 1958), p. 203, writes lucidly of the position implied by Stevens when he observes that "modern nonreligious man assumes a new existential situation; he regards himself solely as the subject and agent of history, and he refuses to appeal to transcendence . . . man makes himself completely in proportion as he desacralizes himself and the world. The idea of an absolute reality, the sacred, is the prime obstacle to his freedom. He will become himself only when he is totally demysticized."

powers of his imagination, achieve a fresh relationship and interaction with the world as it is. This passage is a description of what the man of capable imagination (for Stevens, "the poet or any man of imagination")[30] *might* do with the "Landscape with Boat" that confronts him. The imagination, freely altering what is perceived, makes meaning of what is seen. The process that is described is that of re-creating the world in the mind. Hence, as he watches the sea, it becomes through metaphor an "emerald," which in turn divides into a pluralistic state as the mind creates its own version of the world. To the man of imagination the merest tune "appears" to be that which describes the order of the reality that is observed in much the same way that the song of the woman in "Idea of Order at Key West" (CP, 128–30) ordered the world in her mind. If the earth ("the world itself") is divine, then the appearances of the world are as close to the celestial as we are to get.

In one sense, this poem is perfectly congruent with Stevens's frequently repeated doctrine of "belief in the natural world" that was first announced in the lesson that was taught the woman in "Sunday Morning" (CP, 66–70). In this instance, though, it is not religious belief but philosophical belief that is attacked.

As I have illustrated, the mistaken premise leads the ascetic into a fatal philosophical error wherein the process of suspending belief in the validity of the world of ordinary experience is shown to be misleading. Stevens provides an effective criticism of Husserl's phenomenological ἐποχή by calling into question the aesthetic validity of both the method of phenomenological "bracketing" and the idealistic implications of such a method. I do not think that Stevens is aiming this lesson at Husserl specifically. Rather, I think that the poet's parable of the "floribund ascetic" is directed at any system of philosophy that assumes the pos-

---

30. Quoted by Samuel French Morse from a jacket note on *The Man with the Blue Guitar*, in "The Motive for Metaphor," *Origin 5*, no. 2 (Spring 1952): 16.

sibility of a transcendent "truth beyond all truths," any system that ignores the fragmented world that we know through the senses.

This does not mean that Stevens is rejecting all his reductive and decreative methods. In fact, the same processes of reduction that were begun and then falsified by the floribund ascetic are also the initial impetus of the protagonist of "The Latest Freed Man" (CP, 204). But where the ascetic uses these processes as a means to carry out his quest for a "phantom," the latest freed man is described as one who uses the reductive processes to achieve an entirely new relation with the ordinary world. The protagonist of "Landscape with Boat" is portrayed as mistaken in his rejection of the ordinary things because, as the poem suggests, "all things were the truth, the world itself was the truth" (CP, 242). The protagonist of "The Latest Freed Man," instead of "suspending or bracketing" the *natürlichen Einstellung* as the floribund ascetic does, is shown embracing an attitude that is similar to Husserl's "natural attitude." This attitude was first described in "The Man with the Blue Guitar" (CP, 180) as a state of feeling oneself "a native in the world," where he can say:

> Here I inhale profounder strength
> And as I am, I speak and move
> And things are as I think they are . . . .
> (CP, 180)

Some of the implications of this attitude have already been discussed, but I wish to emphasize the differences that become apparent in Stevens's poetry as he begins to investigate the nature of Being itself. In each of the poems of *Parts of a World* that I have discussed thus far, the underlying assumption that has caused the central tension between mind and world is the notion of the difference between subjectivity and objectivity, that is, plainly speaking, the difference between mind and world, subject and object, imagination and reality. As long as the poet assumed, like Husserl, the notion that consciousness is inescapably different from the object of consciousness, the attempts to resolve this dualism ended in an unresoluble conflict. The poet was forced to choose either the mind of the world, either imagination or reality.[31]

The rejection of the subject-object dualism that is implied in the natural attitude suggests the world of Martin Heidegger's *Dasein,* where existence is described as always given in a world where the self and world are unified.[32]

---

31. Pearce in "The Last Lesson of the Master," in *The Act of the Mind,* p. 126, claims that in the later poetry "the poems may move toward one of two ends: toward celebrating the power of the subject, the mind which not only wills but makes it knowledge; or toward celebrating the givenness of the object, the reality which is unchanging and unchangeable, perdurably out there." As a description of the poems of *Ideas of Order, The Blue Guitar* and the early poems of *Parts of a World,* Pearce's notion is correct. However, as I will show, the nature of Stevens's poetry of Being will break down this conflict in the poems after this point. Pearce's claim is that the subject-object conflict dominates Stevens's poetry until the final poems of *The Rock,* a claim that I hope to show is wrong.

32. *Dasein* is a normal German word meaning existence or presence and is used by Kant and Hegel in this sense. Heidegger, however, means considerably more, as he indicates in the ontological analysis of the structure of Dasein's Being in *Sein und Zeit* (Halle a.d.s., 1929), translated as *Being and Time* by John Macquarrie and Edward Robinson (New York, 1962). Heidegger describes *Dasein* as an ontological expression for human being which suggests literally *Da-Sein* or "There-Being." He explains that both the "there" and the "Being" of *Dasein* are essential elements of the term, and it always stands for the kind of Being that belongs to persons (*SZ,* pp. 7–8). Hereafter I will use the method of citation of passages from *Sein und Zeit* and *Being and Time* followed by recent commentators: *SZ* for *Sein und Zeit; BT* for *Being and Time.*

5

A Gaiety That Is Being

In many of the poems published in the last half of *Parts of a World,* Stevens presents a stance that differs radically from the dry investigations of consciousness and the acts of the mind (treated as ideas) that dominated the first half. Several aspects of these later poems, such as the tone, the evocations of unusual senses and feelings rather than of clear perceptions, and an insistent reliance on metaphor, mark a turning point in the later poetry. Furthermore, in most of the poems there is a new tone of excitement, including moments of "ecstatic identities" (CP, 258). Yet, the precise nature of Stevens's discovery and of the kind of experience that these poems record is not immediately apparent. Even in "The Latest Freed Man," the identity revealed to the man that makes him "free" stays hidden in the kinds of mental experiences that are described. He is "freed," but of what?

In *Sein und Zeit,* Heidegger's explanation of the goal of his analysis of the ontological structure of human existence begins with an exposition of the way in which *Dasein* finds itself always already "in the world" and related to its world by a sense of Being that unites self and world in a constant process of interaction. Heidegger calls this sense

of Being always, already in the world, *In-der-Welt-sein*
("Being-in-the-world").[1] For Heidegger, the fundamental
and *a priori* unity of the Being of man and the Being of the
world precedes all other considerations. Thus, when he
analyzes the epistemological assumptions of other
philosophers, he declares that the idea of a gap or split
between the mind and the world (usually called the
"Cartesian duality") is a concept of mental experience that
ignores the primordial facts of existence in *In-der-Welt-sein*.
For, as Heidegger explains, *Dasein* exists as *In-der-Welt-sein*
before one can begin (whether for practical, scientific purposes or otherwise) to think in terms of "world as object"
and "self as subject" and thus to pose the problems of
subjectivity and objectivity. For Heidegger, Descartes's
famous method of attaining certainty by asserting the unquestionable priority of thinking (the *cogito, ergo sum*) over
Being is a falsification of ontological priorities.[2] In
Heidegger's system, existence precedes essence. Thus,
Being precedes thinking just as *sum* precedes *cogito*,
though Descartes and later ontologists had it inverted.
The experience of Being-in-the-world (*In-der-Welt-sein*)
that Heidegger describes as the basis of *Dasein*'s existence
is the same experience that is discovered by the protagonist in "The Latest Freed Man," who finds himself
"in-the-world" and immediately related to this world in a
way that precedes thought and abstraction. Thus, one key
to understanding "The Latest Freed Man" is the Heideggerian experience of *Befindlichkeit* or, literally, the way in
which one finds oneself as Being-in-the-world.[3] Heidegger

---

1. See *SZ*, pp. 52–62, 104–10, and 112–80, for Heidegger's full analysis of
In-der-Welt-sein and the full exposition of this structure as it is related to
Heidegger's "fundamental ontology." See also William R. Richardson, *Heidegger:
Through Phenomenology to Thought* (The Hague, 1967), pp. 48–64; Albert
Chapelle, *L'ontologie phénoménologique de Heidegger: Un commentaire de "Sein und
Zeit"* (Paris, 1962), pp. 48–60; and Werner Marx, *Heidegger und die Tradition:
Eine problemgeschichtliche Einführung in die Grundbestimmungen des Seins* (Stuttgart,
1961), pp. 31, 97–101.
2. *SZ*, pp. 24–25, 89–90.
3. *Befindlichkeit* is Heidegger's coinage that suggests literally "the state in which

writes that " . . . ontologically, mood (*die Stimmung*) is a primordial kind of Being for *Dasein,* in which *Dasein* is disclosed to itself prior to all cognition and volition, and beyond their range of disclosure."[4] For Heidegger, the concept of mood and the experience of mood for *Dasein* are the ways in which one becomes aware of the unity of Being that brings self and world together. For the protagonist of "The Latest Freed Man," the disclosure of Being is the result of a state of mind or mood that follows a process of reduction.

The first step of the latest freed man is that of realizing that preconceptions are not adequate to describe his own experience. He proceeds, then, by rejecting all "the old descriptions of the world" and deciding to experience the world by himself:

> Tired of the old descriptions of the world,
> The latest freed man rose at six and sat
> On the edge of his bed. He said,
>   "I suppose there is
> A doctrine to this landscape. Yet, having just
> Escaped from the truth, the morning is color and mist,
> Which is enough: the moment's rain and sea,
> The moment's sun (the strong man vaguely seen),
> Overtaking the doctrine of this landscape. Of him
> And of his works, I am sure. He bathes in the mist
> Like a man without a doctrine. The light he gives—
> It is how he gives his light. It is how he shines,
> Rising upon the doctors in their beds
> And on their beds. . . ."
>
>   And so the freed man said.
>   (CP, 204–5)

---

one may be found" but is translated as "state-of-mind" (*BT*, p. 172). Heidegger stresses that *Befindlichkeit* is the ontological equivalent of *Stimmung* or mood, which is *Dasein's* everyday way of becoming aware of its Being (*BT*, 173).

4. *BT*, p. 175. In the original, this passage is as follows: "Ontologisch die Stimmung als ursprüngliche Seinsart des Daseins zu verleugnen, in der es ihm selbst vor allem Erkennen und Wollen und über deren Erschliessungstragweite hinaus erschlossen ist" (*SZ*, 136).

The poem introduces a man who has just awakened and who gazes upon the world of the early morning. He speaks, describing the morning, in its originality and newness, as something newborn ("having just escaped from the truth" of night). Even in his early morning innocence, the man is aware of the "doctrines" (i.e., the old ideas, presuppositions, the old conceptions, and descriptions) that might be wheeled out to fit the perception that he has. This much of the poem seems familiar enough, since the process of reduction that is implied in the opening rejection of the "old descriptions" is very much like many of the other reductive processes that Stevens uses in the opening poems of *Parts of a World*. "The moment's sun" overwhelms the old ideas and images of this landscape just as the "present moment" in "The Man on the Dump" overcame the old images on the dump. But the similarity stops as the freed man begins to describe what it is about the moment's sun that is stronger and more immediate than the doctrines. He speaks with an almost religious fervor of the sun as he mimics conventional phrases of belief: "Of him / And of his works, I am sure." The sun touches the "doctors" and the freed man both as a physical force and as a metaphysical figure. The doctors represent abstract thinkers (makers of doctrines) who insist on the dominance of structures of ideas, and who as a result are always trapped in the subject-object conflict that has been the central metaphysical problem since Plato. Experiencing the illustration of the sun as a force that dissolves doctrine (that is, abstract thought), the protagonist describes a state of mind that brings him into a new relation with the world. The state of mind that is described is similar to Heidegger's *Stimmung* (mood), which "makes manifest how one is."[5] The mood discloses Being as a process that the latest

---

5. *BT*, 173. In the original, this passage is as follows: "Die Stimmung macht offenbar, 'wie einem ist und wird.' In diesem 'wie einem ist' bringt das Gestimmtsein das Sein in sein 'Da' " (*SZ*, p. 134).

freed man takes part in. He experiences Being with a kind of preconceptual awareness (Heidegger's *Stimmung*) that is explained by the "how" of his experience rather than the "what" or "why." "To be" must remain without a description because it is not an essence or a thing. As Heidegger writes, "Das Sein des Seinenden ist nicht selbst ein Seiendes," thus implying that *Sein* (Being) is a process rather than a thing.[6] One can only describe process in terms of how things change. Thus, for the latest freed man, the sense of freedom is expressed as a series of changes.

> It was how the sun came shining into his room:
> To be without a description of to be,
> For a moment on rising, at the edge of the bed, to be . . .
> (CP, 205)

The disclosure of Being is not, as Heidegger writes, a cognitive process, because "the possibilities of disclosure which belong to cognition reach far too short a way compared with the primordial disclosure belonging to mood, in which *Dasein* is brought before its Being. . . ."[7] The attunement that is described in this section of the poem follows rather closely Heidegger's account of mood. For the freed man is now described by the poet in a series of animal metaphors that attempts to reproduce the feeling or mood that was experienced:

> To have the ant of the self changed to an ox
> With its organic boomings, to be changed
> From a doctor into an ox, before standing up,
> To know that the change and that the ox-like struggle
> Come from the strength that is the strength of the sun,
> Whether it comes directly or from the sun.
> (CP, 205)

---

6. *SZ*, p. 6.
7. *BT*, p. 173. In the original: "Die Erschliessungsmöglochkeiten des Erkennens viel zu kurz tragen gegenüber dem ursprunglichen Erschliessen der Stimmungen, in denen das Dasein vor sein Sein . . . gebracht ist" (SZ, p. 134).

The miniature self of a man whose contact with the world was always mediated through ideas is changed into the animal presence of an ox. The sense of enlargement that accompanies the feeling of attunement is thus dramatized by metamorphosis. Changed from the doctor of abstract doctrines to a physical being (metaphorically, "ox-like"), the man is momentarily free of the ancient philosophical barrier between subject and object (or, at least, he senses the falseness of that barrier) and begins to explore the possibility of a new relation with the things around him. To know the source of the changes that the freed man feels is to know the source of the strength of the sun— "whether it comes directly or from the sun" (CP, 205). The sun is merely an example (as it frequently is in Stevens's late poems) that serves, in this poem, as an illustration of the way in which Being is known through the experience of disclosure. In this case, the man's freedom is an example of the authentic interaction of the man with the ordinary things around him when his mood discloses Being. It is also a sense of freedom:

> It was how he was free. It was how his freedom came.
> It was being without description, being an ox.
>
> (CP, 205)

The speaker describes his access to Being as something that is without description. The phrase "without description" functions in two senses: first, of Being, without the doctrines (specifically the subject-object dualism) that had always provided a false means of describing Being, and second, of gaining, through mood, a sense of Being while remaining unable to describe or express what this sense was. Hence, in the poem, the speaker has difficulty in expressing exactly what it was the latest freed man experienced. Stevens's critics have also had difficulty deciding what this poem is about. For example, Daniel Fuchs quite correctly asserts that "like the modern poet, the free man is in touch with sources of power," but Fuchs does not expand his comment to explain what the power is.[8] I think that without Heidegger's phenomenological description of the way mood discloses Being to *Dasein,* there is a temptation to ascribe the experience (as Fuchs and others imply)[9] to some sort of mystic vision or hallucination. Yet, Stevens is hardly to be accused of mysticism and, in terms of Heidegger's account of mood and attunement in *Sein und Zeit,* the experience of Stevens's protagonist is fully intelligible.

The mood of attunement to Being gives the free man a new sense of the ordinary things of his immediate world, which is expressed in visual terms:

> It was the importance of the trees outdoors,
> The freshness of the oak-leaves, not so much
> That they were oak-leaves, as the way they looked.
> It was everything being more real, himself
> At the center of reality, seeing it.
> It was everything bulging and blazing and big in itself,
> The blue of the rug, the portrait of Vidal,
> *Qui fait fi des joliesses banales,* the chairs.
>
> (CP, 205)

This entire passage functions as a description of the indefinite pronoun *It* that begins every sentence. The indefinite *it* stands for the mood of attunement to Being that the free man experienced. *It* puts the man "at the center of reality" where he is momentarily "free" of the traditional distance between observer and observed. He is described

---

8. Fuchs, p. 150.
9. For example, John J. Enck, *Wallace Stevens: Images and Judgments* (Carbondale, Ill., 1964), p. 135, calls this power a mysterious "animal force," which, "with the sun as an ox, transfers strength to man, who in turn . . . summons similar daring." Ronald Sukenick, *Wallace Stevens: Musing the Obscure* (New York, 1967; paperback ed., 1967), pp. 14–15, writes a Freudian interpretation of the experience of the latest freed man when he notes that "the ego manages to reconcile reality to its own needs and the formerly insipid landscape is infused with the ego's emotion"; he seems to detect symptoms of illness in the hallucination that he thinks is occurring.

as "seeing it" in a moment of vision in which everything
takes on a new value. The man's moment of vision is expressed in images of movement, illumination, and enlargement. "It was everything bulging and blazing and big
in itself" (CP, 205). Each thing is energized by a force that
does nothing other than cause it to stand out as it is. The
things seen are all ordinary: the color of the rug, a portrait
of a French friend (who apparently had made fun of ordinary things), and finally some chairs. Yet each of these
things becomes vital as the free man realizes the similarity
between his "Being without description" and their Being
as they are disclosed to him. The sense of presence unites
man and his world within the field of Being.

For Heidegger, the disclosure of Being through mood is
always a discovery of the finite quality of Being. Each
mood occurs within the limiting instant of temporal existence, and *Dasein* is described as constantly shifting away
from the realization of its potential for Being-in-the-
world.[10] In a similar way, free for a moment, the man in
the poem experiences "everything being more real," but
this experience is instantaneous and cannot be captured,
held, or prolonged. The constant flux of Being adds to the
difficulty of describing or expressing a sense of it in the
poem. The free man, like Heidegger's *Dasein,* must constantly re-create and reexperience the moment of attunement to Being. Nevertheless, the discovery that results
from this attunement marks an important point in the
poet's development. It effectively provides a way of breaking down the subject-object dualism that had led to the
unresolved conflcts between the imagination and reality.
The mood of attunement that is recorded in "The Latest
Freed Man" becomes the poet's way of resolving the ten-

---

10. An essential part of Heidegger's description of the modes of Being
through which Being is disclosed to *Dasein* is dissimulation and the falling of
Dasein away from its potential. It is, in Heidegger's analysis, a natural part of
Dasein's finite quality that it should constantly fall away from the disclosure of
Being. See *BT,* p. 210 and *passim.*

sion between realism and idealism—that is, more clearly, the tension between a poetry of things (which had proved insufficient) and a poetry of ideas (which had proved sterile).

This poem records the beginning of what J. Hillis Miller calls "Stevens' Poetry of Being."[11] But where Miller thinks that only the very last poems in "The Rock" and *Opus Posthumuus* illustrate Stevens's interest in ontology, I suggest that Stevens begins to develop a poetry of Being in *Parts of a World,* and that as he develops his concept of what Being is and how it might be expressed in the poetry, it becomes one of the major themes in the important poems that follow in *Transport to Summer* through *The Rock.* As Stevens writes the major poems of the last part of his career, the various manifestations of his sense of Being are expressed in the poetry, and the concepts that he develops tend to be concepts that fulfill the promise that is projected in "The Latest Freed Man" and developed in "Yellow Afternoon," "The Hand as a Being," and "Extracts from Addresses to the Academy of Fine Ideas."[12] The poem will continue to be the "act of the mind finding," but what the mind begins to seek is the fulfillment of Being. This search takes the form of various visionary experiences in which the poet breaks down the imagination-reality dualism and places the self in the center. The poetry of Being tends to

---

11. "Wallace Stevens' Poetry of Being," in *The Act of the Mind,* pp. 143–62. Miller observes perceptively that "at the heart of Stevens' poetry there is a precise metaphysical experience. Or, rather, this experience is beyond metaphysics, since the tradition of metaphysics is based on a dualism putting ultimate being in some transcendent realm, above and beyond what man can see. Being, for Stevens, is within things as they are, here and now, revealed in the . . . flowing of time, the presentness of things present, in the interior fons of man" (p. 159). As I suggested, though, in the introduction, Miller's insight into Stevens's poetry is suggested, but never analyzed or incorporated into a reading of the later poetry. The notion of finite Being is outside the scope of traditional metaphysics, as Miller suggests, and this is what prevents Miller from a full analysis. My thesis is that Heidegger's investigations of Being (which like Stevens's ideas of Being are beyond metaphysics) will make possible a way of completing the study of "the poetry of Being" that Miller originally suggested.

12. *CP,* 236, 271, 252 respectively.

be a poetry in which vision overwhelms process in much the same way that the sun overtakes the "doctrines" in "The Latest Freed Man." The poems express the vision of Being through mood, discovery, and revelation rather than through discourse, dialectic, and logical argument. In short, Stevens becomes a poet of vision as well as of process, and the process of vision will reappear frequently to supply the satisfactions that the processes of abstract thought and systematic reduction of subject and object had failed to produce.

The difficulty of describing what it is "to be" constitutes a major part of the difficulty of Stevens's later poetry. The poet's problem is that his sense of Being is usually just that—a sense of a vanishing presence that is disclosed through mood almost as if it were discovered out of nothing. There comes to the poet a realization that the source of both the imagination and reality is the same, but this realization occurs with an apparent gratuitousness:

> One's grand flights, one's Sunday baths,
> One's tootings at the weddings of the soul
> Occur as they occur.
>
> (CP, 222)

The poet has a sense of the disclosure that, as the title "The Sense of the Sleight-of-Hand Man" (CP, 222) implies, occurs instantaneously, faster than the eye can see, and that yet, nevertheless, exists. Stevens's intuition of Being displays the same kind of preconceptual status that Heidegger claims for *Dasein's* Being-in-the-world. Being precedes thought just as *sum* precedes *cogito* in Heidegger's system, though Descartes had the order and priority of *cogito* and *sum* inverted. Both Heidegger and Stevens imply that the Being is always "there" before the mind can think. Subsequently, there is no apparent cause of Being or one's sense of it. This thought is expressed in Stevens's poem as the fortuitousness of one's intuition of Being. It resists the intelligence and evades thought. Rather, it is the experi-

ence of an almost physical sensation, much like the mood
that the "Latest Freed Man" describes, which discloses
Being to the poet. He proposes that

> It may be that the ignorant man, alone,
> Has any chance to mate his life with life
> That is the sensual, pearly spouse, the life
> That is fluent in even the wintriest bronze.
>
> (CP, 222)

The word "ignorant" suggests more than a simple defi-
ciency of intelligence. I think Stevens is suggesting a kind
of innocence of conceptual framework that "frees" man
from the preconceptions that conceal his *a priori* relation
to his world. Stevens uses the term *life* in its vague sense
that corresponds to Heidegger's term "Being-in-the-
world." The images of "life" are those images of light and
movement that are associated with Stevens's sense of Being. Hence, the "ignorant man" is similar to the "Latest
Freed Man," both of whom are able to return to a kind of
primordial innocence wherein the disclosure of Being can
occur. For both protagonists, the union of the self with the
world is described in metaphors of physical or sensuous
change. In neither case is there a suggestion of the transcendence that the "flouribund ascetic" mistakenly attempts
in "Landscape with Boat." Instead, the experience is presented as a natural act that would resolve the subject-object
conflict.

To the protagonist of "Yellow Afternoon," the experience of Being is part of a return to earth. The sense of
union with one's world produces a feeling of self-
fulfillment that Stevens suggests is the result of coming in
contact with Being.

> It was in the earth only
> That he was at the bottom of things
> And of himself.
>
> (CP, 236)

Like a man who digs in his garden, the man described in
this poem feels in touch with the source of the union between "things" and "himself" when he is close to the soil.

> There he could say
> Of this I am, this is the patriarch,
> This it is that answers when I ask,
> This is the mute, the final sculpture
> Around which silence lies on silence.
> This reposes alike in springtime
> And, arbored and bronzed, in autumn.
>   (CP, 236)

He is at the center of his existence and, using a spatial
expression, when he is "there" (i.e., "at the bottom," as if at
the source) the man is able to express the fact that he *is*.
The pronoun *This* stands for the indefinite nature of the
poet's sense of his own Being. It is the "patriarch" in the
sense that it precedes and is the source and origin of all
that exists. The sense of Being is then expressed in images
of formlessness, silence, and motionlessness that record
the transient presence of Being that must remain un-
defined. For Heidegger, Being itself grounds all things
that are and is characterized by the same paradoxical attributes that Stevens invokes here. Being stands, the sacred
source (patriarch) which, though mute, answers, and,
though ever-changing, is constant. Taking the form of a
silent work of art, the indefinite subject of this section is
present within the cycle of time that is suggested by the
seasons.

To say more clearly what the "this" of the first stanza
represents, the poet indirectly quotes the protagonist as
he attempts to explain his feelings about the indefinite
quantity that brings about his union:

> He said I had this that I could love,
> As one loves visible and responsive peace,
> As one loves one's own being,
> As one loves that which is the end
> And must be loved, as one loves that

> Of which one is a part as in a unity,
> A unity that is the life one loves,
> So that one lives all the lives that comprise it
> As the life of the fatal unity of war.
>
> (CP, 236)

In a series of similes, the man suggests those attributes which approximate as closely as possible the essence of Being-in-the-world. In each case, the feeling that is compared to all experience is the most intense emotion possible. The separate qualities of "peace," the realization of "one's own being," the finality of death ("the end"), and the satisfaction of being part of a "unity" are all feelings of satisfaction that resemble fulfilling one's potential for Being. But we note that the man uses the past tense of the verb *to have* as he compares his possession to these other, more explicit satisfactions. The poet suggests that what the man "had" is no longer possessed. Like the experience of the "Latest Freed Man," the moment of disclosure that the man experiences is fleeting. It dissolves as soon as it is disclosed. Furthermore, none of the similes suffices individually to describe the full experience, so the poet must describe it again:

> Everything comes to him
> From the middle of his field. The odor
> Of earth penetrates more deeply than any word.
> There he touches his being. There as he is
> He is.
>
> (CP, 237)

Returning to the metaphor of the earth, the poet describes the sense of Being as a field of awareness which, as Frank Doggett perceptively suggests, includes "both inner reality and outer reality, the field of consciousness that in Stevens' brilliant pun is also the field or earth that is both his body and his world."[13] For the man who has momentarily

---

13. Doggett, p. 38.

reached the "middle" of the field, interior and exterior are fused in a sense of the unity of Being that encompasses both self and world. But within this description of the disclosure of Being, there is a suggestion that the experience (like the odor of earth) "penetrates more deeply than any word." The contact with Being is more than either the similes or the direct assertions can communicate.

As a last effort to express the experience, Stevens compares the sensation of unity to physical union of man and woman.[14] The protagonist of the poem is described reflecting on his experience:

> The thought that he had found all this
> Among men, in a woman—she caught his breath—
> But he came back as one comes back from the sun
> To lie on one's bed in the dark, close to a face
> Without eyes or mouth, that looks at one and speaks.
>   (CP, 237)

Here the female figure represents the abstract notion of Being. She personifies the idea and, in this way, the poet makes the vagueness of the preceding stanzas more concrete. No sooner does he suggest this metaphor than it is gone. The experience of disclosure, breathtaking like the contact with a woman, takes no longer than a breath to dissolve. In the final lines, the poet describes the return from experience to reflection, where the formless face ("without eyes or mouth") speaks to the poet its inarticulate language like that of "final sculpture / Around which silence lies on silence" (CP, 236). The man "came back" to the dark of the mind where, like the poet, he is left with only a disembodied memory of the vision, which borders on the inexpressible.

The female figure of Being in "Yellow Afternoon" is also presented in "The Candle a Saint" (CP, 223). She is

---

14. I am overturning the traditional interpretation of the female figure, who is usually seen as "the woman-genius, the queen-consort, the mother of his poems" (Baird, p. 221) or as an earth mother of reality (Nasser, p. 51).

the pervading presence that makes the world come alive for the poet. As the poet discovered in "The Latest Freed Man," the disclosure of Being gives him a new relation to his world and enables him to reject the artificial barriers of the subject-object conflict. The figure of Being can only be conceived as a nameless and somewhat mysterious force. When the poet is in her presence, reality becomes freshened and he is able to know, without explanation, reality as part of the self. The female presence is

> The noble figure, the essential shadow,
>
> Moving and being, the image at its source,
> The abstract, the archaic queen.
> (CP, 223)

We note that the adjectives that are connected with this figure are typical of those descriptive terms which Stevens associated with Being in "The Latest Freed Man," "The Sense of the Sleight-of-Hand Man," and "Yellow Afternoon." The motion of a shadow is something that is not fully visible as a thing, yet is a cause of differing light values. It is "esential" in the sense that it is central to illumination of any kind. "Moving and being," it represents the source of all images, since it is the basis of both the imagination and reality. Being is what causes the things of the world to come to the mind in Heidegger's description and this analysis of the nature of Being seems to fit Stevens's notion of Being as it is expressed in this poem.[15] It is in this sense that Being is "the abstract, the archaic queen." She precedes thought and at the same time exists both in the mind and outside, uniting interior and exterior.

Stevens's sense of Being is expanded in "Contrary Theses (II)" (CP, 270), where the fictive hero is described in a quest for the same abstract figure. In this poem, though, the idea of Being is not represented by a female figure but

---

15. *BT,* p. 95 ff.

rather by a kind of absolute abstraction. The poet presents his quest as a possible solution to his own mortality. He evokes the coldness and finality of nonbeing as he observes the relentless processes of time "one chemical afternoon in mid-autumn, / When the grand mechanics of earth and sky were near" (CP, 270). The cycle of the seasons and the constant movement of his existence toward its end suggest the poet's state of mind as he searches for a confrontation with his own Being. The mood that is evoked is similar to the mood of Heidegger's *Dasein* as he begins to experience a fear that has no evident cause. Heidegger describes this state of mind, *Angst,* as that fear of one's own death which brings *Dasein* into an authentic awareness of his own finiteness.[16] According to Heidegger's ontological analysis of *Dasein,* it is this awareness that concerns *Dasein* with its own Being. *Sein-zum-Tode* or Being-toward-Death "reveals itself in a state-of-mind . . . and belongs primordially and essentially to *Dasein's* Being."[17] In Stevens's poem, the dread of nonbeing causes the poet to seek its opposite, the thesis that is contrary to the thesis of nonbeing. Faced with his finite limitations,

> He wanted and looked for a final refuge,
> From the bombastic intimations of winter
> And the martyrs à la mode. He walked toward
>
> An abstract, of which the sun, the dog, the boy
> Were contours. Cold was chilling the wide-moving swans.
> The leaves were falling like notes from a piano.
> (CP, 270)

The fictive hero faces "intimations" of his mortality. The swans (that were first observed to connote decadence in "Academic Discourse at Havana") and the falling leaves

---

16. *BT,* pp. 228–34.
17. *BT,* pp. 295–96. In the original: "Das Sein-zum-Ende . . . die sich in der Befindlichkeit (der Stimmung) so oder so enthüllt . . . aber das Sein-zum-Tode ursprünglich und wesenhaft dem Sein des Daseins zugehört" (*SZ,* pp. 252–53).

are both Stevens's conventional images for decay, death, and destruction. Filled with the knowledge of his own impending death, the hero, like Heidegger's *Dasein,* is forced to come to terms with Being and his own Being-in-the-world. The metaphor of a walk "toward / An abstract" represents the hero's approach to Being. But, in the same way as the latest freed man and the speaker in "The Sense of the Sleight-of-Hand Man" emphasized, the discovery of Being is always a momentary disclosure. It flickers and flashes before the hero, neither fully idea nor fully object. In the instant of apprehension, the man comes in contact with Being, the abstract that is nameless. Like the man in "Yellow Afternoon" he cannot capture the moment of presence. But he senses that the presence that disclosed itself was what he was looking for.

> The abstract that he saw, like the locust-leaves,
>   plainly:
>
> The premiss from which all things were
>   conclusions,
> The noble, Alexandrine verve.
>
> (CP, 270)

This "abstract" is, as Frank Doggett writes, Stevens's "sense of a world-ground."[18] It is upon this base that existence is posited. For Stevens as for Heidegger, Being is the first premise, the equivalent of Doggett's "world-ground." Stevens suggests here that his sense of Being is that of an energy or a vigor ("verve") that is both noble (in the sense "of the highest order") and poetic (suggested by the adjective "Alexandrine," the traditional line of formal French verse).

Hence it would be a mistake to oversimplify this poem and call the contrary theses of the title merely "life and death," as William Burney does.[19] Rather, I would suggest

---

18. Doggett, p. 139.
19. Burney, p. 116.

that the opposing elements are Nonbeing and Being, since
it is the irrevocable mechanism of time that brings the poet
face to face with the possibility of his own death. The
possibility of Nonbeing (Heidegger's "no-longer-being-
able-to-be")[20] forces the protagonist to accept his own
mortality as part of his Being. It limits and, at the same
time, intensifies his existence. The mood of dread is the
origin, in this poem, of the search for the "abstract," which
includes both life and death.

Stevens's sense of Being includes, then, concepts of
abstractness and impermanence. Both of these aspects of
Being are parts of the poet's developing idea of the
ground or source of both the mind and the world. However, the poet's sense of Being is revealed as the revelation
of a mood or gratuitous circumstance. In fact, the disclosure of Being has resulted from a rejection of ideas and an
attempt to return to innocence, an attempt to return to the
source (abstract though it may be) by way of reduction.
Stevens is not rejecting thought *per se,* but rather is denying the basic assumption of philosophical thought. I think
that each return to "nakedness," "barrenness," "ignorance," and "simplicity" is implicitly a denial of the traditional idea of subjectivity.[21] The poet discovers intuitively
through his moods and experiences the unity of Being
that precedes notions of subject and object (or Husserl's
assumption of consciousness and object of consciousness).
Another illustration of this tendency in Stevens's poetry

---

20. *BT,* p. 294, where "Nicht-mehr-dasein-Können" is translated as "no-
longer-being-able-to-be-there." This is a good example of Heidegger's tendency
to use the German language (which builds words of compounds rather readily)
to make new words.

21. For another interpretation of the images of barrenness, sterility, and emptiness, see C. Roland Wagner, "The Idea of Nothingness in Wallace Stevens,"
Accent 12 (Spring 1952): 111–21. Wagner sees the images of barrenness, coldness, and nakedness as manifestations of nothingness in Stevens. But, as he adds,
nothingness is an absolute, but "it is an upward, rather than a downward or alien
motion" (p. 111). The essence of his argument is that "the nothing that is has
being, but not existence" (p. 115), an idea that is, I think, somewhat contrary to
Stevens's notion that Being exists.

takes place in "The Hand as a Being" (CP, 271). The protagonist of this poem, like the freed man of "The Latest
Freed Man," is at the beginning described as overladen
with ideas, abstractions, and the lucidity of consciousness:

> In the first canto of the final canticle,
> Too conscious of too many things at once,
> Our man beheld the naked, nameless dame.
>   (CP, 271)

I think "our man" in this poem is the "impossible possible
philosopher's man" of "Asides on the Oboe" (CP, 250),
who is Stevens's fictive hero. He "has had the time to think
enough" and hence is a kind of ideal representative of the
contemplative life. But, in this instance, his lucidity seems
to be detrimental to the apprehension of the "naked,
nameless" female figure. He "seizes her" literally, but finds
that she eludes his grasp. His "too conscious" mind com-
mences immediately to "wonder" about the figure that he
beholds. In other words, the contemplative mind asks
questions about the presence that he sees but cannot
name. The images of the hand and the "glittering hair"
(CP, 271) suggest that the hero's "wonder" is also a sense
of awe at her appearance. The hero, who has momentarily
seized Being, loses her in his questions.

> Too conscious of too many things at once,
> In the first canto of the final canticle,
> Her hand composed him and composed the tree.
>
> The wind had seized the tree and ha, and ha,
> It held the shivering, the shaken limbs,
> Then bathed its body in the leaping lake.
>   (CP, 271)

The hand ("as a Being") unites the fictive hero and the
tree, composing them together in the same motion. The
process that the wind effects upon the tree is similar to the
process that the hand effects upon the man. The wind

reduces and cleanses the tree as if it were stripping the symbol of life to an essential simplicity. In a similar way, the consciousness of the hero is "composed" in both senses of the term. The female figure has "ordered" his mind by creating a sense of union (achieved by the reduction of his consciousness) and she has, in the end, composed him in the sense of satisfying and fulfilling him. The symbol of the union achieved is the handclasp, which brings together the figure of imagination and the female figure of Being. "He *was* too conscious of too many things" (CP, 271). This phrase has been repeated three times, but the emphasis is now on the past tense of the verb, which appears in stanza five for the first time and suggests that "consciousness" has been reduced to "Being."

> Her hand took his and drew him near to her.
> Her hair fell on him and the mi-bird flew
>
> To the ruddier bushes at the garden's end.
> (CP, 271)

The female figure here is another version of the "sensual, pearly spouse" of life in "The Sense of the Sleight-of-Hand Man" (CP, 222). However, the image in this poem ("The Hand as a Being") for the union of man and Being is more explicitly sexual and, like the sexual consummation, it releases the philosopher's man from the abstract structures of consciousness and unites him with his Being. The "mi-bird," which James Baird identifies as an image of the poet's lyric self (his capacity to express in language his experience), flies to the garden's end.[22] This is another way of symbolizing the ambivalent quality of the union with Being. The image of the poet's lyric ability "flies"away from the union beneath the tree, unable to express in words the quality of the experience. Yet, the bird flies "to the ruddier bushes," which could mean, if we take the

---

22. Baird, p. 164.

redness to signify reality, that the "life of the imagination" is united with the life of the real during the union of man and Being.[23]

The fictive hero remains, at the end of the poem, in a state of repose where he, alone, "knew / And lay beside her underneath the tree" (CP, 271). In much the same way as the man touching his being in "Yellow Afternoon," the fictive hero in "The Hand as a Being" achieves a state of unification of self and world at the end of thought. This unity is symbolized by the traditional metaphor for the metaphysical experience of union. The image of sexual union declares the satisfaction and pleasure derived from the hero's disclosure of Being which, along with ideas of abstraction and impermanence, constitute an essential part of the poet's sense of the qualities of Being.

This notion of satisfaction and pleasure that is part of the revelation of Being is expanded in "Of Bright and Blue Birds and the Gala Sun" (CP, 248), where the poet explicitly describes the sensations that are associated with the disclosure of Being. The poet speaks in the role of a teacher of a youth as he explains this aspect of the nature of Being.

> Some things, niño, some things are like this,
> That instantly and in themselves they are gay
> And you and I are such things, O most miserable . . .
>
> For a moment they are gay and are a part
> Of an element, the exactest element for us,
> In which we pronounce joy like a word of our own.
> (CP, 248)

The instantaneous "moment" in which the poet is "a part" of the whole brings a sudden sense of satisfaction. The

---

23. For the color symbolism in Stevens, I am indebted to Nasser, p. 26, who writes that "red is the color of reality unfalsifed." I am also indebted to an earlier study of color by George McFadden, "Probing for an Integration: Color Symbolism in Wallace Stevens," *MP* 57 (February 1961): 181–93.

poet's recognition of the unity of Being is expressed as a
sense of joy at sharing existence with the "exactest element."

> It is there, being imperfect, and with these things
> And erudite in happiness, with nothing learned,
> That we are joyously ourselves and we think
>
> Without the labor of thought, in that element,
> And we feel, in a way apart, for a moment, as if
> There was a bright *scienza* outside of ourselves,
>
> A gaiety that is being, not merely knowing,
> The will to be and to be total in belief,
> Provoking a laughter, an agreement, by surprise.
>   (CP, 248)

In the same way that each of the previous poems has expressed the disclosure of Being, this poem emphasizes the
presence of Being as a fleeting sensation ("instantly," "in a
moment"). The poet's sense of Being precludes any notion
of an absolute or ideal. Being is "being imperfect," and
thus is a finite concept (both temporally and intellectually
finite). The disclosure of Being occurs both inside ("we
think / without the labor of thought") and outside ("as
if / There was a bright *scienza* outside ourselves") the self,
interfusing and uniting exterior and interior. Being is
more than thought, "not merely knowing." The disclosure
of Being is an experience that brings all the disparate elements of the self together. More simply, "the will to be" is
"to be total in belief" in a moment of wholeness. The last
stanza, as Daniel Fuchs observes, "expresses well Stevens'
faith   in   the   experience   of   a   paradise   unknown . . . which . . . is not a matter of knowledge but of
power."[24] The source of this power is the same source that
Fuchs leaves unnamed in his discussion of "The Latest
Freed Man." In this poem, though, the source is realized

---

24. Fuchs, p. 190.

and named. It is the "bright *scienza* . . . a gaiety that is be-ing."

Each moment of disclosure is a moment of "ecstatic identity" of the self and the world. Thus, Stevens describes this moment as that which will suffice for the act of the mind. At the end of *Parts of a World,* the poet has estab-lished a rudimentary vision of the goal of poetry: the ex-pressing of the disclosure of Being. He proposes that this experience might suffice in "Extracts From Addresses to the Academy of Fine Ideas," where he writes:

> What
> One believes is what matters. Ecstatic identities
> Between one's self and the weather and the things
> Of the weather are the belief in one's element,
> The casual reunions, the long-pondered
> Surrenders, the repeated sayings that
> There is nothing more and that it is enough
> To believe in the weather and in the things and men
> Of the weather and in one's self, as part of that
> And nothing more.
>
> (CP, 258)

6
An Outline of the Poetry of Being

Stevens's sense of Being, as it is discovered and expressed in the poems of *Parts of a World*, is refined and developed into a full aesthetic of the poetry of Being in *Transport to Summer*.[1] In this volume the characteristics of the disclosure of Being that were described in "The Latest Freed Man," "The Sense of the Sleight-of-Hand Man," "The Hand as a Being," "Yellow Afternoon," and "Contrary Theses (II)" as well as in "Extracts from Addresses to the Academy of Fine Ideas"[2] are consolidated in Stevens's long poem about poetry, *Notes Toward a Supreme Fiction* (1942). Stevens classifies the characteristics of the disclosure of Being into three "notes" which form the three-part structure of "Notes Toward a Supreme Fiction."[3] These three

---

1. *Transport to Summer* (New York, 1947) is reprinted in *The Collected Poems of Wallace Stevens* in the same chronological order as it was originally printed. *Notes Toward a Supreme Fiction* (Cummington, Mass., 1942) was first published by a small private publisher in a limited edition. While most of the poems in *Transport to Summer* are collected in chronological order, Stevens placed *Notes* at the end of this edition for reasons that will be obvious from my discussion of the poem.
2. See my discussion of these poems in chapter 5.
3. Stevens comments succinctly in a letter to Henry Church that, while the notes are not in any sense a dialectic, "in the long run, poetry would be the

"notes"—"It Must Be Abstract," "It Must Change," "It Must Give Pleasure"—are stated as imperatives, each of which Stevens considers essential to the creation of the "supreme fiction" that he projects as a possible goal for poetry.

In my discussion of *Transport to Summer,* the next collective volume of Stevens's verse, I want to begin with a reading of the "Notes Toward a Supreme Fiction" that rehearses many of the themes and ideas of Stevens's poetry of Being. "Notes" is a long and difficult poem (659 lines), divided into three parts of ten cantos each. Each canto is a poem in itself of 21 lines composed of seven tercets. "Notes" is the most widely discussed of Stevens's long poems, though, curiously enough, critics such as Bloom, Kermode, and Sukenick, who claim to read the poem line by line, gloss over many sections in need of explication.[4]

---

supreme fiction; the essence of poetry is change and the essence of change is that it gives pleasure" (*Letters,* 430).

4. "Notes Toward a Supreme Fiction" is without a doubt the most thoroughly discussed poem among Stevens's long poems and, to make reference to the criticism as trouble free and simplified as possible, I will list the most important studies of the poem here before I begin a reading of the poem: James Baird, *The Dome and the Rock: Structure in the Poetry of Wallace Stevens* (Baltimore, 1968), *passim;* R. P. Blackmur, "Wallace Stevens: An Abstraction Blooded," in *Form and Value in Modern Poetry* (New York, 1952; paperback ed., 1957), pp. 213–17; Harold Bloom, "Notes Toward a Supreme Fiction: A Commentary," in *Wallace Stevens: A Collection of Critical Essays,* ed. Marie Borroff (Englewood Cliffs, N.J., 1963; paperback ed., 1963), pp. 76–95; Merle E. Brown, "Concordia Discors in the Poetry of Wallace Stevens," *American Literature* 34 (May 1962): 246–69; Glauco Cambon, "Wallace Stevens: Notes Toward a Supreme Fiction," in *The Inclusive Flame: Studies in Modern American Poetry* (Bloomington, Ind., 1963; paperback ed., 1965), pp. 75–119; L. S. Dembo, "Wallace Stevens: Meta-men and Para-things," in his *Conceptions of Reality in Modern American Poetry* (Berkeley, Calif., 1966), pp. 81–107; Frank Doggett, *Stevens' Poetry of Thought* (Baltimore, Md., 1966; paperback ed., 1966), pp. 98–118 and *passim;* John J. Enck, *Wallace Stevens: Images and Judgments* (Carbondale, Ill., 1964), pp. 161–69; Cudworth F. Flint, "The Poem as It Is," *Dartmouth College Library Bulletin* 14 (December 1961): 51–56; Bernard Heringman, "Wallace Stevens: The Use of Poetry," *ELH* 16 (December 1949): 325–36; Frank Kermode, "Notes Toward a Supreme Fiction: A Commentary," *Annali dell' Istituto Universitario Orientale: Sezione Germanica* 4 (Naples, 1961): 173–201; J. Hillis Miller, *Poets of Reality: Six Twentieth Century Writers* (Cambridge, Mass., 1965), pp. 224, 248, 261, 263; Eugene Paul Nassar, *Wallace Stevens: An Anatomy of Figuration* (Philadelphia, 1965), pp. 179–218; Roy Harvey Pearce, *The Continuity of American Poetry* (Princeton, 1961; paperback ed., 1965), pp. 395–400; Joseph N. Riddel, *The Clairvoyant Eye: The Poetry and Poetics*

While the poem is still in need of a full line-by-line explication, this task is beyond the scope and intent of my essay and would result in much needless repetition.[5] I want to approach this difficult poem in terms of the poetry of Being that Stevens was developing during this period in his career. Each section refines one characteristic of the poet's sense of Being that he developed in *Parts of a World*. R. P. Blackmur was the first critic to suggest the direction and implication of the "Notes Toward a Supreme Fiction":

> [the fiction] must, the poet argues, be abstract, beyond, above, and at the beginning of our experience, and it must be an abstract idea of being, which when fleshed or blooded in nature or in thought, will absorb all the meanings we discover. That is to say it must be archetypal and a source, an initiator of myth and sense . . . it must change in its abstractness, depending on the experience of it. . . . The process of change is the life of being, and like abstraction, requires constant iteration and constant experience. Most of all the fiction must change because change is the condition of perception, vision, imagination. . . . in short, an abstract fiction can change and if the abstraction was soundly conceived, the more it is the same the more it will seem to change, and by the feeling of change in identity, identity in change, give the great pleasure of access of being.[6]

This is as succinct an outline as any critic has made of the major limits within which Stevens defines his "notes," but where Blackmur's outline is suggestive, he fails to corroborate his ideas in a reading of the poem. As I have shown in the preceding chapter, each of the ideas that Blackmur brings up has already been suggested, implied, or described in the poems of *Parts of a World*. But each of the

of Wallace Stevens (Baton Rouge, La., 1965; paperback ed., 1967), pp. 165–85; Ronald Sukenick, *Wallace Stevens: Musing the Obscure* (New York, 1967; paperback ed., 1967), pp. 136–63.

5. This is only one of the tasks that needs to be done by scholars in the later poetry of Wallace Stevens.

6. R. P. Blackmur, "An Abstraction Blooded," *Partisan Review* 10 (May–June 1943): 298–99. Reprinted under the title of "Wallace Stevens: An Abstraction Blooded" in his *Form and Value in Modern Poetry*, p. 214.

ideas summarized in the subtitles is then expanded by repetition and variation, by illustration and parable in the
individual poems that constitute the whole. To understand
the implications of the subtitles is a good beginning, but it
is only a beginning.

Perhaps the first question that any reader of the poem
will ask both before and after reading the poem is "what is
the supreme fiction?" I think it will be clear by the end of
my discussion that the supreme fiction, for Stevens, was
the poetry of Being. My discussion will center on the implications of the three subtitles as suggestions toward a
poetry of Being. All three of the subtitles, "It Must Be
Abstract," "It Must Change," and "It Must Give Pleasure"
are introduced in a succinct prologue addressed to an unnamed "you."[7]

> And for what, except for you, do I feel love?
> Do I press the extremest book of the wisest man
> Close to me, hidden in me day and night?
> In the uncertain light of single, certain truth,
> Equal in living changingness to the light
> In which I meet you, in which we sit at rest,
> For a moment in the central of our being,
> The vivid transparence that you bring is peace.
>
>   (CP, 380)

This inscription is addressed to the same female figure
who, in "Yellow Afternoon" (CP, 236) and "The Sense of
the Sleight-of-Hand Man" (CP, 222), was a personification
of the abstract source of the creative power of the poet.
She was source not only of the creativity of imagination but
also of the creativity of the world and, as such, was able to
bring the two together with her presence. Stevens had
previously identified this figure as the "abstract" (CP, 270)
that unites the mind and the world, thus breaking up the

---

7. While several critics have claimed that the prologue is addressed to Henry
Church, Stevens's good friend to whom the poem is dedicated, Stevens makes
clear in the *Letters* that there is no connection between the prologue and the
dedication. See *Letters,* p. 538.

Cartesian dualism. The image of light that is used in the prologue is "uncertain" because the disclosure that the light brings is constantly changing in time ("It Must Change"). The first "light of single, certain truth," the illumination that the "naked, nameless dame" (CP, 271) brings to the mind and throws on reality, is called "equal in living changingness" to a second "light." The second light, Stevens's image of the imagination, which "like light . . . adds nothing except itself" (NA, 61), is a figure for the process that makes the disclosure of the source possible.

In the moment of disclosure described in the poems of *Parts of a World,* the poet and the female figure come together just as they do in this passage. In the duration of this moment, both the female figure and the poet "sit at rest . . . in the central of our being," just as the man in "Yellow Afternoon" attained a union with the center or source when he "touched his being" (CP, 286). In each of the poems of Being discussed in the previous chapter, the disclosure of Being brought an instant of unity wherein the vision brought peace. At the same moment, the protagonist in each poem achieves self-transparency in the sense that the source of the world is seen as the source of the self. Hence, the idea of transparency becomes an important characteristic of the poetic vision. Stevens's concept of transparency is not like the mystical union with the one wherein, as Rudolf Otto writes, "The unification of things is what we may call their 'transfiguration.' They become transparent, luminous, visionary."[8] The things envisioned in the mystical experience become transparent windows to the beyond, outside of time and space in their transparency.[9] Unlike the mystic's timeless vision, the experience that Stevens describes remains within time, fully

---

8. *Mysticism East and West: A Comparative Analysis of the Nature of Mysticism,* trans. B. L. Bracey and R. C. Payne (New York, 1932; paperback ed., 1962), p. 65.

9. Otto, p. 66.

limited by the finite nature of human existence. Stevens's sense of transparency is similar to Heidegger's ontological description of *Dasein*'s full awareness of self and world within a temporally unified projection of its potential. Heidegger's term for this awareness is also "transparency" (*die Durchsichtigkeit*), and his description of this state of mind explains a great deal of what Stevens suggests in each of the poems where the idea of transparency appears:

> In its projective character, understanding goes to make up existentially what we call *Dasein*'s sight (*Sicht*). With the disclosedness of the "there" [of *Dasein*'s Being] this sight *is* existentially [i.e., it exists ontologically] and *Dasein is* this sight equiprimordially in each of those basic ways of its Being. . . . The sight which is related primarily to existence we call "transparency" [*Durchsichtigkeit*]. We choose this term to designate "knowledge of the self" in a sense that is well understood, so as to indicate that here it is not a matter of perceptually tracking down and inspecting a point called the "self" but rather of seizing upon the full disclosedness of Being-in-the-world throughout all the constitutive items that are essential to it [i.e., through *Befindlichkeit, Understanding,* and *Speech*] and doing so with understanding.[10]

The achievement of a state of "transparency" (in Heidegger's description) is the goal of *Dasein* once it has, through mood, experienced the disclosure of Being. The achievement of "transparency" is the way in which the poet or thinker can see through the self and the world to Being, which is the common source of both. As Heidegger explains the ways in which *Dasein* can achieve an authentic

---

10. *Sein und Zeit* (Halle, 1929), translated as *Being and Time* by John Macquarrie and Edward Robinson (New York, 1962), pp. 186–87. In the original German, this passage is as follows:

Das Verstehen macht in seinem Entwurfcharakter existenzial das aus, was wir die *Sicht* des Daseins nennen. Die mit der Erschlossenheit des Da existenzial seiende Sicht *ist* das Dasein gleichursprünglich. . . . Die Sicht, die sich primär und im ganzen auf die Existenz bezieht, nennen wir die *Durchsichtigkeit*. Wir wählen diesen Terminus zur Bezeichnung der wohlverstandenen <<Selbsterkenntnis>>, um anzuzeigen, dass es bei ihr nicht um das wahrnehmende Aufspüren und Beschauen eines Selbstpunktes handelt, sondern um ein verstehendes Ergreifen der vollen Erschlossenheit des In-der-Welt-seins *durch* seine wesenhaften Verfassungsmomente *hindurch. (Sein und Zeit,* p. 146).

relation of self and world, he posits the understanding
(clear sight of Being) as the primary mode from which the
other modes of Being derive. For Heidegger, the goal of
Dasein is a better understanding of Being, and this goal is
achieved through the state of "transparency." Stevens has
previously declared a similar concept to be the goal of the
"impossible, possible philosopher's man," the fictive hero
of the imagination, who is the "transparence of the place in
which he is" and in whose poems "we find peace" (CP,
251).

For Heidegger, the state of "transparency" that is the
goal of *Dasein*'s understanding is to be understood ontologically. That is, for Heidegger, transparency is the understanding of the experience of disclosure of Being that
gives *Dasein* a "full and sophisticated knowledge of the self
in all its implications and possibilities."[11] This is the meaning that Heidegger attaches to the *Selbsterkenntnis* that is
the result of "transparency" and that is to be distinguished
from the ordinary (every-day) awareness of the self, which
he refers to as *sichkennen*. The implications of transparency
for both Stevens and Heidegger are closely related to
man's possible sense of Being as it is revealed to him in the
moments of vision like Stevens's "ecstatic identities" (CP,
258). Such a moment is that instant of "living changingness" in the prologue in which the light of mind and
radiance of Being come together in a "vivid transparence."
Finally, the pleasure of the peace of this moment is the
subject of Stevens's praise as he prefaces his "Notes" with a
prologue to the female presence, the personification of
Being.[12]

---

11. *Being and Time*, p. 187 (see especially the translator's footnote for a full
explanation of these two terms as they are used by Heidegger. The special
meanings of many of his terms often need explanation; some of these Heidegger
gives in the text, but much is left for translators and commentators to puzzle
out).

12. J. Baird, p. 228, connects the person addressed in the prologue to the
ubiquitous female presence addressed at the end of the poem, both of whom he
thinks are the "interior paramour" of the poem by the same name.

It Must Be Abstract

Abstraction, in Stevens's sense of the term, is not a new process in the poems. In the first canto of "It Must be Abstract," abstraction is described as the process of transforming an intuition into the language of poetry. As the speaker assumes the role of instructor for a young poet, ephebe, he describes the first step of the poetic process, and in doing so introduces the concept of the "first idea," which is the theme of the first six cantos of "It Must be Abstract."[13]

> Begin, ephebe, by perceiving the idea
> Of this invention, this invented world,
> The inconceivable idea of the sun.
>
> You must become an ignorant man again
> And see the sun again with an ignorant eye
> And see it clearly in the idea of it.
>   (CP, 380)

The first command of the speaker to his pupil is a description of the processes of reduction and decreation that Stevens had simulated in the poems of *Ideas of Order, The Man with the Blue Guitar,* and *Parts of a World.* Here he suggests that the poet return to a state of innocence ("become an ignorant man again") so that he can see "clearly." The goal of such a procedure is the same goal that both Husserl and Heidegger claim for the phenomenological method.[14] By

---

13. Harold Bloom writes that the first two cantos of "It Must Be Abstract" are "prologues" that introduce the main section of the poem (p. 78).

14. While both Husserl and Heidegger call their respective methods phenomenology, there is a considerable difference between the original meaning of phenomenology as described by Husserl and the method that Heidegger describes in *Sein und Zeit,* pp. 17–39. Both Husserl and Heidegger, however, agree that phenomenology will be a method by which clear perceptions of the world will be achieved. The difference between the two, most simply stated, is in what each expects to see by appropriating the phenomenological method of description. Husserl expects the original intuition to form the basis for a philosophy without presupposition. Heidegger expects that phenomenology will reveal "the Being of the things that are" (*das Sein des Seienden*). Both have the idea that the phenomenological method will make accessible something not normally

removing all preconceptions, the perceiver can achieve an original intuition of the sun. This intuitive grasp or original perception Stevens calls the "first idea," but the word *idea* is not used in its Platonic sense,[15] for it more closely approximates Heidegger's phenomenological disclosure of Being than a Platonic ideational or eidetic essence. The difference between Plato's ideational essence and Stevens's "first idea" is the difference between conception and perception. The "first idea" is "inconceivable," but it can be seen or perceived. It comes as a result of perception that is essentially phenomenological:

> Never suppose an inventing mind as source
> Of this idea nor for that mind compose
> A voluminous master folded in his fire.
>
> How clean the sun when seen in its idea,
> Washed in the remotest cleanliness of a heaven
> That has expelled us and our images . . .
>
> The death of one god is the death of all.
> Let purple Phoebus lie in umber harvest,
> Let Phoebus slumber and die in autumn umber,
>
> Phoebus is dead, ephebe.
>
> (CP, 381)

The perception of the sun "in its idea" cleanses it of all mythological and religious accretions. Here, the process of

---

perceived and both maintain that the method will, figuratively speaking, brush away the dust and dirt of preconceptions and assumptions so that what is "present" in the act of observing will be "seen." The disagreement between the two philosophers rests most deeply in their opposing views of what philosophers are supposed to do. For Heidegger, philosophy is the investigation of the meaning of Being. For Husserl, philosophy is the science of thought, which will provide a basis of certainty for all other sciences.

15. Here I take issue with the accepted reading of the "first idea" as a Platonic ideational essence. The full implications of Stevens's Platonism are discussed by Daniel Fuchs in his *The Comic Spirit of Wallace Stevens* (Durham, N.C., 1963), pp. 120–54, where he finds that Stevens rejects all notions of a world of ideational essences that is beyond appearances and that thus would form a higher or "true" reality. For other views of Stevens's "first idea," see Cambon, pp. 84–85; Heringman, pp. 330–31; Miller, p. 248; Nassar, p. 186; and Riddel, pp. 168–70.

decreation implied in the method of phenomenological perception functions to clear away all the old constructs of the imagination. The figure of the young poet must learn that the old fictions about the sun as a mythical god (Phoebus) have been set aside. "The death of one god is the death of all" because the premise involved in this process of decreation permits no exceptions. Only by banishing all the gods can the poet have a way to perceive "the first idea" (the original perception of the sun). The effect of the process that Stevens presents is that of letting the sun be as it exists. Only in this way can the Being of the sun be disclosed as an intuition and not an old idea. The difference between the old ideas about the sun and the "first idea" is again played upon in these lines, for the speaker rejects the old ideas about creation, the sun, and the heavens, yet presents the "first idea" as a positive value.

The sun had formerly served as one of Stevens's figures for unquestionable reality as this reality was contending with the imagination. In these lines it serves both as an example of a thing (one part of the real) and as an emblem for the universe of things that could be apprehended through the intuition of the "first idea."

> But Phoebus was
> A name for something that never could be named.
> There was a project for the sun and is.
>
> There is a project for the sun. The sun
> Must bear no name, gold flourisher, but be
> In the difficulty of what it is to be.
>   (CP, 381)

That the sun could not be named is Stevens's way of saying that the attempt to fix the thing with an old name puts the thing itself at one remove of abstraction. The poet's task is first the disclosure of the Being of the thing in its immediacy. The project for the sun that is both of the past and of the present is simply "to be." But the term "project" has another connotation.[16] It is both the sun's project and the poet's project. The poet's project is to uncover the Being of the sun. Perceiving the sun in the first idea of it is defined as the never-ending project of establishing the Being of the sun "in the difficulty of what it is to be." In spite of the statement that the sun must bear no names, each presentation of the sun in the poem involves a renewal of the poetic function, which always moves from the unnamed "first idea" to the expression of that perception in language. Hence we see, even in the denial of the name, the poet calling. the sun "gold flourisher," which illustrates the movement from nameless vision to named existent. The concept that Stevens is suggesting in this rather dense passage is similar to Heidegger's concept of the essence of poetry, which he discusses in the essay "Hölderlin und das Wesen der Dichtung," where he writes:

> Poetry is the act of establishing by the word and in the word. . . . What is established in this manner? The permanent. . . . Being must be opened out so that the existent may appear. But this very permanent is the transitory. The poet names the gods and names all things in that which they are. This naming does not consist merely in something already known being supplied with a name; it is rather that when the poet speaks the essential word, the existent is by this naming nominated as what it is. So it becomes known as existent (i.e., what it is). Poetry is the establishing of being by means of the word. Hence that which remains is never taken from the transitory . . . . Being is never an existent *(Seiende)*. But because Being and the essence of things can never be calculated and derived from what is present, they must be freely created, laid down and given. Such a free act of giving [and creating] is

---

16. Nassar suggests that the word *project* in Stevens's use is "ambiguous . . . it means, in part, that there is a *'raison d'être'* for the 'sun' (implying, one would suppose, some sort of supernatural projector). It also means that there are satisfactory imaginative projections for inexplicable reality that the poet can project ('throw out') though not believe" (P. 187). While Nasser's speculations are interesting, I think that he pushes the noun *project* into a verb without adequate support from Stevens's context.

the way in which poets establish Being. Hence, it is the essence of poetry to establish (make known) Being through language.[17]

Thus, when Stevens writes that "Phoebus was / A name for something that never could be named," he is in accord with Heidegger. The poetic act is integrally related to the first perception of Being. Heidegger's idea of poetic naming no more consists of using the old ideas (like Stevens's "Phoebus") to name a thing than does Stevens's concept of the "first idea." Both the poet and the philosopher are concerned with the act of establishing the Being of the things that exist. Every poem is a process of renewal, a new attempt to "nominate the existent as what it is" in Stevens's "first idea of it." For both Heidegger and Stevens, the task of the poet is to let the sun (i.e., the things of the world) "be in the difficulty of what it is to be." In doing so, the poet can "see the sun in the idea of it." The fresh perception that results from such a poetry is an intuition of the source of both the world and the imagination.[18]

The "first idea" of the sun cannot be named. The poet's task of nominating things as they are is thus doomed to eventual failure. Naming is one of the inevitable tasks of the poet, but it is not his sole function. The phenomenological reduction that permits the poet to perceive the object "in the idea of it" (to envision the Being of the sun as it is) is also a function of the imagination. What is described in this poem is the decreative cycle of the decreating and creating imagination. The original intuition of the "first idea" is the basis for each new creation of the Being of the sun. As Heidegger writes, "Being and the

---

17. "Hölderlin und das Wesen der Dichtung" in *Erläuterungen zu Hölderlins Dichtung* (Frankfurt, 1944), pp. 31–45. Translated as "Hölderlin and the Essence of Poetry" by Douglass Scott in *Existence and Being*, ed. Werner Brock (Chicago, 1949; paperback ed., 1967), pp. 280–81.

18. I want to make it clear that I mean *intuition* in Heidegger's sense of the word: intuition is a preconceptual awareness that is characterized by both sense perception and internal state of mind. When people intuit things, they grasp them unthinkingly, by a kind of leap beyond a purely rational process.

essence of things . . . must be freely created . . ."[19] by the poet, but always in the sense of expressing or representing in language what is intuited. Once again, the difference between perception (the first idea) and conception (the finished poem) is the difference between the beginning and the end of the poetic process. Hence, "the difficulty of what it is to be" is not merely a difficulty for the sun. What is hard is also the task of the poet, who must suggest or evoke the unnamable "first idea" through a language composed of names. Or, as Stevens explains in the first canto of "It Must Give Pleasure":

> . . . the difficultest rigor is forthwith
> On the image of what we see, to catch from that
> Irrational moment its unreasoning.
>
> (CP, 398)

The full sense of the admonition "It Must be Abstract" concerns the necessary and unavoidable task of the poet, who must begin, without preconceptions, to "see the sun again with an ignorant eye." The reductions and decreations make possible the intuitive grasp of the "first idea," but after the original intuition, the movement of the mind is always toward abstraction. The poet's role in creating his own world is certain to end in abstraction because it is the nature of language to be abstract. The "invented world" of the first stanza of the first canto is the "supreme fiction" that Stevens writes of in "The Noble Rider and the Sound of Words":

> There is, in fact, a world of poetry indistinguishable from the world in which we live, or, I ought to say, no doubt, from the world in which we shall come to live, since what makes the poet the potent figure that he is, or was, or ought to be, is that he creates the world to which we turn incessantly and without knowing it and that he gives to life the supreme fictions without which we are unable to conceive it.[20]

---

19. "Holderlin and the Essence of Poetry," p. 281.
20. NA, p. 31.

The world that the poet creates is the "invented world" which, as Stevens suggests in this passage, is the double of the real world. The difference that he is stressing is again the difference between the world that we perceive (however badly) and the world that the poet helps us to imagine (to conceive). The poet conceives this world (and the supreme fictions) by abstracting, from the immediate experience of "the first idea," a version of the world.[21] The "first idea" is thus described in canto II as

>   the quick
> of this invention; and yet so poisonous
>
> Are the ravishments of truth, so fatal to
> The truth itself, the first idea becomes
> The hermit in a poet's metaphors,
>
> Who comes and goes and comes and goes all day.
>   (CP, 381)

Stevens uses the term *quick* to describe the "first idea" as the source and origin of the poet's "invented world." The problem for the poet, as Canto I made clear, lies in the difficulty of expressing the "quick," the transient and evasive quality of Being. Unable to name Being and refusing the attempt to fix or make permanent what is by nature

---

21. Doggett takes a slightly different view when he writes that " . . . to see the world in immediate experience without transforming it into conventional human terms is the difficult vision. This direct experience is an approach to what Stevens calls 'the first idea' and it is irrational because it is close to the non-human, external world. It is later and through conception that we abstract experiences, that we 'reason about them with later reason' and understand them in reflection" (pp. 103–4). While I am indebted to both Doggett and Kermode (see especially the latter's definition of abstraction in his *Wallace Stevens* [Edinburgh, 1960; paperback ed., New York, 1961], pp. 112–13), both of these critics insist, wrongly I think, upon the absolute split between mind and world. Doggett's phrases "close to the non-human, external world" seem to me to miss the meaning of both the "muddy centre" of Canto IV and "The complicate, the amassing harmony" (CP, 403) of the last sections. For a complete discussion of the humanizing elements of Stevens's *Notes*, see the recent article by Riddel, "It Must Be Human," *College English* 56 (April 1967): 525–34, where he emphasizes the unity of mind and world as a fully human idea.

fleeting (another sense of *quick*) and not to be seen in the
things that tell of it, the poet watches the freshness of each
disclosure of Being disappear in his lines. The poet is
caught between the desire to express the first idea and the
knowledge that adequate expression is impossible:

> . . . not to have is the beginning of desire.
> To have what is not is its ancient cycle.
> It is desire at the end of winter, when
>
> It observes the effortless weather turning blue
> And sees the myosotis on its bush.
> Being virile, it hears the calender hymn.
>
> It knows that what it has is what is not
> And throws it away like a thing of another time,
> As morning throws off stale moonlight and shabby sleep.
>   (CP, 382)

These lines suggest the constant cycle of creation and decreation that is both the glory and the distress of the poet.
The nameless "it" that observes the "effortless" changes of
nature refers to the poet's desire. The virility of the poet's
desire is its ability to reproduce through intuition another
experience of the "first idea." Hence, each decreation and
each creation take place within the temporal boundaries of
human existence. The "calendar hymn" suggests the temporal quality of each perception. More clearly, the "desire
at the end of winter" is the desire of the poet who has
reached the psychic equivalent of winter, the barren phase
of the decreation-creation cycle and, in imitation of the
cyclical destruction of the season, begins the imagination's
cycle with nothing ("it knows that what it has is what is
not"). Each creation is subsequently "thrown away" because it is no longer fresh. The "quick" of the invention is
lost in each succeeding moment and becomes literally "a
thing of another time" (i.e., the past). The cycle must begin
again. As Stevens develops the poetry of Being, the natural
cycles of the seasons and the days are often used as psychic

equivalents for the cycle of the creative imagination. After *Ideas of Order,* the idea of place and the relation of place to state of mind are no longer so important to Stevens's imagination as the temporal qualities of creation. "Notes Toward a Supreme Fiction" establishes the images of time as the figures of the creative mind. The archetypal figures of time (the seasons, phases of the moon, and the period of the day) become the central representations of the temporal basis of the imagination. As I will show in my discussion of "It Must Change," Stevens expands his concept of the poetry of Being by including the integral relation of finite Being and human time.

After treating the constant frustration that accompanies the poet's attempt to capture the "first idea" in his poems, Stevens expands his meditation upon the first idea and its relation to poetry in the third canto of "It Must Be Abstract." This passage is the most positive explanation of Stevens's theory of the poetry of Being in "It Must Be Abstract." It also serves as the explanation for the following three sections.

> The poem refreshes life so that we share
> For a moment, the first idea . . . It satisfies
> Belief in an immaculate beginning
>
> And sends us, winged by an unconscious will,
> To an immaculate end. We move between these points:
> From that ever-early candor to its late plural
>
> And the candor of them is the strong exhilaration
> Of what we feel from what we think, of thought
> Beating in the heart, as if blood newly came,
>
> An elixir, an excitation, a pure power.
> The poem, through candor, brings back a power again
> That gives a candid kind to everything.
>
> (CP, 382)

In principle, as the speaker announces, the poem makes possible the sharing of the original intuition of Being and, for a moment, satisfies the poet's faith in the phenomenological process that was implied in Canto I. An "immaculate beginning" is the barrenness and emptiness that is evoked in order to arrive at the first perception of the Being of the thing. Each "beginning" comes as a result of a process of decreation. The religious overtones that Stevens uses ironically parody the old myths that are removed by the reductive process described in the first canto.

But the establishing of the Being of the world is a never-ending process. The poet moves between the first perception ("the ever-early candor") and the necessity to reject what was perceived as soon as it has been abstracted (expressed in language). This movement is temporal and explains more fully the "calendar hymn" that frustrates the poet's desires for permanence in Canto II. After the instant of perception, the "first idea" is no longer valid and must be re-created. The nature of the Being disclosed in the "first idea" of it cannot be fixed. The poem, then, is a process that moves between the act of intuition wherein the "first idea" (the Being of the thing) is disclosed and the final necessity to decreate the abstraction that takes form as soon as the experience is expressed in language. The experience is, nonetheless, ecstatic for the poet. The sense of joy that was first associated with the disclosure of Being in "Of Bright & Blue Birds & The Gala Sun" (CP, 248) and the "ecstatic" quality of the experience of the unity of Being that was evoked in "Extracts From Addresses to the Academy of Fine Ideas" (CP, 258) are both suggested in the last two stanzas of this passage. An "elixir, an excitation, a pure power" are all expressions of the poet's sense of an invisible power that discloses itself within the constant cycle of decreation and creation. This presence is described as a power or force that is similar to the source of energy that made the chair, the portrait, and the rug shine out in "The Latest Freed Man" (CP, 205). The function of the poem is to "bring back a power again / That gives a candid kind to everything." The unnamed force brings the abstraction to life like "thought / beating in the heart, as if blood newly came." This is the "abstraction" that is "blooded" in Canto VI (CP, 385) as it is given life by the poet's words. Being is disclosed as the "candor" of the things themselves (using the original, Latin root-meaning of candor: "a purity or radiance") and the poem is, as Joseph N. Riddel aptly writes, "a way of knowing what it is 'to be.' "[22]

From Heidegger's descriptions of the poetic act, a more precise description of this poem would be that it demonstrates a way of establishing the poet's sense of Being itself. And where Heidegger insists that the function of the poet is to "establish Being through language," he illustrates the close affinity that his concept of poetry has to Stevens's elevated concept of poetry. Stevens's notion about the role of the poet as creator of the human sense of Being who reestablishes the existence of things is considerably clearer when compared to Heidegger's discussion of the essence of poetry. And, when Stevens writes that "a poet's words are of things that do not exist without the words" and continues this line of thought by concluding that "poetry is a revelation in words by means of the words,"[23] he is expressing an idea of the function of poetic language and its relation to Being that is very similar to Heidegger's concept of the essence of poetry. Furthermore, where Stevens's ideas about the relation between Being and poetry are rehearsed implicitly in the first sections of "It Must Be Abstract," in the later poem, "Description Without Place," the function of the poetry of Being is explicitly proposed.

In "Description Without Place," Stevens defines a theory of description as the way in which poetry makes manifest

---

22. Riddel, *The Clairvoyant Eye*, p. 170.
23. NA, pp. 32–33.

the Being of the things that exist.[24] He first defines "description" as "composed of a sight indifferent to the eye" (CP, 343), where what is seen is not dependent upon or imagined by the perceiver, yet the vision fulfills the perceiver's projections.

> It is an expectation, a desire,
> A palm that rises up beyond the sea,
>
> A little different from reality:
> The difference that we make in what we see
>
> And our memorials of that difference,
> Sprinklings of bright particulars from the sky.
>
> (CP, 344)

As Stevens contemplates the relation between vision and perception, he describes the process of description as an essential part of the poetry of Being. Description, then, is not simply the measuring of appearances, the summary of spatial perspectives, the listing of qualities of color, size, and texture, or the attempts to reproduce or imitate in words the things seen. Stevens's sense of the word *description* includes the "difference" that the perceiver makes in what he sees. The "difference" is the process of vision by which the poet achieves an intuition of Being. More succinctly, the poetry of Being makes poetic description a process similar to Heidegger's phenomenological method of description. Like Heidegger's definition of phenomenology, Stevens's "description" is a method that seeks to uncover the Being of the things that exist. Thus, where Heidegger declares that phenomenological description "is the science of the Being of entities—ontology,"[25]

---

24. None of the critics who comment on this poem have attempted to explain completely the kind of theory of description that Stevens is proposing. For other readings of this poem, see especially Fuchs, pp. 124–25; Doggett, pp. 167, 201–2; Riddel, pp. 197–99; and Enck, pp. 172–74.

25. *Sein und Zeit*, p. 37.

Stevens writes that poetic "description" makes possible "a change immenser than / A poet's metaphors in which being would / Come true" (CP, 341). For both philosopher and poet, "description" makes manifest the Being of the things that appear. Hence:

> Description is revelation. It is not
> The thing described, nor false facsimile.
>
> It is an artificial thing that exists,
> In its own seeming, plainly visible,
>
> Yet not too closely the double of our lives,
> Intenser than any actual life could be,
>
> A text we should be born that we might read,
> More explicit than the experience of sun
>
> And moon, the book of reconciliation,
> Book of a concept only possible
>
> In description, canon central in itself,
> The thesis of the plentifullest John.
> (CP, 344–45)

If description in poetry is revelation, what is revealed? The poet's method brings something to life that is neither "the thing described, nor false facsimile." In other words, the poet's description reveals something that is otherwise not possible to see. Yet, this "something" is not a thing like other things. One cannot feel or touch what is revealed. To repeat Heidegger's statement, "Das Sein des Seienden ist nicht selbst ein Seiendes"—[26] "The Being of the things that exist is not itself a thing." Yet, neither is it a nonexistent quality ("a false facsimile"). Stevens's "description" does not deal with fact but rather with ontology, creating a text, in theory, that reveals the Being of the world of things and the Being of the poet. Being is the artificial

---

26. *Ibid.*, p. 6.

thing that exists (artificial because not a thing in itself—not a *Ding an sich* in Kant's terms). When disclosed by the process of vision (the intuition that is described in the first section of "It Must Be Abstract"), Being is "plainly visible / Yet not too closely the double of our lives." There is no identity of Being and appearance except where the intuitive process discloses that "to seem, it is to be" (CP, 341). But such an equation wherein "to seem" (appearance) is identified with "to be" (Being) is only possible within the theory of description Stevens defines.

Stevens proposes the possibility of uncovering the source of the real through a poetry of description, but, as Helen Hennessey Vendler points out, "the untoward modulations of tense [from "might" to "would" to "is"] are simply not available to the critic who tries to paraphrase Stevens in prose, and so an apprehension becomes a statement, an intuition becomes a dogma."[27] In other words, the theory of description that Stevens offers in "Description Without Place" is too frequently taken as doctrine that supports practice rather than an intuition of the poetry of Being that projects a possible poetic method.[28] In this matter of distinguishing between what critics sometimes take to be Stevens's evasiveness and what others take to be his hermetic way of explaining his poetry in his poems, I want to be very clear about the nature of both Stevens's and Heidegger's statements, for both philosopher and poet are dealing with possibilities (potential states of mind and potential functions of language) rather than actual, concrete, and provable theorems. The interest of both in ontology is largely a speculative interest,

---

27. "The Qualified Assertions of Wallace Stevens," in *The Act of the Mind: Essays on the Poetry of Wallace Stevens,* ed. J. Hillis Miller and Roy Harvey Pearce (Baltimore, Md., 1965), p. 165.

28. Cambon thinks that the theory stated here is proved by the poem of "Nanzia Nunzio" in Canto VIII of Part II, "It Must Change," and thus seems to see an actual realization of the theory. I think that he illustrates Vendler's statement, since he seems to accept the poet's intuitive projection of a possible kind of "description" as a dogma. See Cambon, pp. 107–8.

which is what Heidegger means when he explains of his phenomenological method that "Höher als die wirklichkeit steht die Möglichkeit. Der Verständnis der Phänomenologie liegt einzig im Ergreifen ihrer als Möglichkeit."[29] The importance of phenomenology is in its possibility rather than its reality (actuality). As Mrs. Vendler implies, "intuition" and "apprehension" are not to be confused with doctrine and dogma. In "Description Without Place" Stevens's theories, his "possibles" and "potentials," are speculations on the poetry of Being, the "supreme fiction" of the "Notes Toward a Supreme Fiction." Only in the heightened perception of poetry can this possibility be realized.

Stevens proposes the possibility of a poetry that would contain:

> The outlines of being and its expressings, the
>   syllables of its law
> *Poesis, poesis,* the literal characters, the vatic
>   lines.
>
> (CP, 424)

In this late expression of the goal of poetry (it is from "Large Red Man Reading"), the poet figure reads from his book the poetry that is, in summary, a precise definition of the poetry of Being. As Canto III of "It Must Be Abstract" asserted, this possibility is part of the theory of the poetry of Being, the "supreme fiction" in which the intuition of

---

29. *Sein und Zeit,* p. 38. In *Being and Time,* this passage is translated to read: "Higher than actuality stands possibility. We can understand phenomenology only by seizing upon it as a possibility" (p. 63). Heidegger's concept of the importance of something as a "possibility" is a vital part of the structure that he describes of *Dasein's* modes of Being. To Heidegger, *Dasein* exists authentically as a possibility rather than as an actuality. The actual is related to the essence and, for Heidegger, existence precedes essence. Where Goethe could say "Beome what you are," implying that there was an undiscovered essential self, Heidegger would say "you are what you become," with an understanding that your essence is always a possibility, never an actuality. This is why Heidegger will say later that *Dasein* exists primarily in the future, a concept that I will compare to Stevens's aesthetic at the end of this chapter.

the "first idea" will lead to a new poetry. If appearance (seeming) is the disclosure of Being through vision, this kind of appearance is made possible by the source itself. In "Description Without Place" the unnamed female figure is once more a personification of the source.

> It was a queen that made it seem
> By the illustrious nothing of her name.
>
> Her green mind made the world around her green.
> The queen is an example . . . The green queen
>
> In the seeming of the summer of her sun
> By her own seeming made the summer change.
>
> In the golden vacancy she came, and comes,
> And seems to be on the saying of her name.
>
> Her time becomes again, as it became,
> The crown and week-day coronal of her fame.
>
> (CP, 339)

In a compressed and highly figurative statement filled with internal rhyme and alliteration, the speaker again represents the disclosure of Being by the appearance of a mysterious female figure. Each appearance of the "green queen" as she "came, and comes" (as she is disclosed and vanishes in time) makes possible the revelation of the Being of the world of things.[30] She stands for the force of presence (a transcendence in immanence — the only possible transcendence in a demythologized world[31]) that brings the world into the mind. She is an "illustrious noth-

---

30. See my discussions of the female figure as she appears in the poems of *Parts of a World* (above in chapter 4).

31. I am indebted for this phrase, "transcendence in immanence," to Mircea Eliade, whose discussions of the mythic patterns of existence in primitive religions end with a suggestive chapter on the presence of mythic patterns in modern, profane, "demythologized" life. See particularly his *Myth and Reality*, trans. Willard R. Trask (New York, 1963), pp. 162–94, and *The Sacred and the Profane: The Nature of Religion,* trans. Willard R. Trask (New York, 1959; paperback ed., 1959), pp. 162–98.

ing" who cannot be named except as an abstraction. Yet, "on the saying of her name," the act of poetic description that involves the naming process of poetic language, her existence is established. That act establishes her Being but, at the same time, covers it up in the evasions of metaphor. As Stevens attempts to describe the evasive nature of Being, he again suggests the double movement of poetry (which moves in time "between these points, / From that ever-early candor to its late plural" [CP, 382]) that he describes in "It Must Be Abstract," Canto III.

In such a poetry of constant movement, the necessity for change that is demanded in the note "It Must Change," is here explicitly associated with the nature of Being. The cyclic decreation and creation are formal ways of paralleling the transitory nature of Being. By simulating the fluctuations that are observed, the poet can project that

> There might be, too, a change immenser than
> A poet's metaphors in which being would
>
> Come true, a point in the fire of music where
> Dazzle yields to a clarity and we observe,
>
> And observing is completing and we are content,
> In a world that shrinks to an immediate whole,
>
> That we do not need to understand, complete
> Without secret arrangements of it in the mind.
>   (CP, 341)

This change, where, in poetry, "Being would come true," defines the goal of the poetry of Being. But this change must remain a "possibility." Stevens's use of the conditional "would" qualifies the entire statement of the goal as a possibility rather than a doctrine, something latent rather than actual.

The "dazzle" of the world of appearances "yields to a clarity" where mind and world become transparent to each other as they are brought together in the presence of Be-

ing. This moment of vision, "where observing is completing," shrinks the world "to an immediate whole" as the
poet envisions the unity of Being "without secret ar-
rangements of it in the mind." More clearly, the vision
occurs without imposing or forcing the unity through
metaphor or metamorphosis. Not that the process of
metaphor is denied, for it is a minor example of the kind
of change that is projected in the poet's version of the new
poetic. Rather, the poet's metaphor-making is treated as a
paradigm of the larger process of change. Hence, where
the metaphor brings together the associations of two disparate things or concepts to form a third or metaphorical
meaning, the intuitive apprehension of Being brings a
change of meaning that is a similar transformation, but
"immenser." The universe of things is brought together in
a larger metaphor.[32] The nature of the revelation is qualified in these lines. Description will not be the concrete
description of things (their material or physical properties), but rather a description of the interaction of the mind
and world that reveals the nature of Being itself. This
theory is a refinement of the "poem of the act of the mind"
(CP, 240) that the poet had described in "Of Modern
Poetry." In this case, description is no longer comparable
to Husserl's common-sense meaning of the term, wherein
the Being of the things described was never in question.
Stevens's theory of description parallels Heidegger's concept of phenomenology as explained in *Sein und Zeit*.[33]
Both methods are calculated to let the Being of the things

---

32. The most suggestive discussion of the nature of metaphor in Stevens's
poetry is Northrop Frye's essay, "The Realistic Oriole: A Study of Wallace Stevens," *Hudson Review* 10 (Autumn 1957): 353–70. See also Donald Sheehan, "Stevens' Theory of Metaphor," *Papers on Language and Literature* 2 (Winter 1966):
57–66, for a recent analysis of Stevens's use of metaphor. Unlike Frye, Sheehan
discusses only the theory and not the practice in the poems.

33. In *Sein und Zeit,* pp. 17–39, Heidegger explains what he means when he
claims that phenomenology is the only fitting method for the study of ontology.
Briefly, his argument is that the phenomenological method (and he makes clear
that he is discussing a method and not a subject matter) is the proper method for
letting the Being of the things that exist (*das Sein des Seienden*) appear or make

that exist (*das Sein des Seienden*) show itself. This explains the allusion to "the thesis of the plentifullest John" (CP, 345). The logos that begins the gospel of John functions as the first revelation of Being. The new logos, for both Stevens and Heidegger, is the word of the poet, whose function, like that of the creators of the Gospel, is to create the essential word ("the supreme fictions") that will reveal the nature of Being. The difference is that the New Testament logos revealed a source that was divine, sacred. Both Heidegger and Stevens want to disengage the nature of Being from all religious or divine connotations.[34] Stevens continues the refinement of a concept of poetic logos that approximates Heidegger's theory of the ontological function of poetic language in the concluding lines of "Description Without Place."

> Thus the theory of description matters most.
> It is the theory of the word for those
>
> For whom the word is the making of the world,
> The buzzing world and the lisping firmament.
>
> (CP, 345)

Heidegger's statement that "poetry is the establishing of Being by means of the word"[35] provides a way of explain-

---

itself manifest. For Heidegger, the nature of description is redefined so that description (like Stevens's theory of description) will reveal Being and, since the question of the meaning of Being is the central question of Heidegger's philosophy, phenomenology is the appropriate method. While Heidegger ignores the "reductions" and the concept of "intentionality" that are the keys of Husserl's method, he nevertheless acknowledges his debt to Husserl by insisting on the priority of "intuition" and "moments of vision" over scientific methods of controlled observation.

34. Both philosopher and poet are in accord in their rejection of the religious implications of their theories of the philosophy and poetry of Being, respectively. In Heidegger's "Humanismusbrief," an open letter written to Jean Beaufret and later published in Heidegger's *Platons Lehre von der Wahrheit* (Bern, 1947), pp. 53–119, he explicitly denies any theological implications in his ontology. He refuses to consider as relevant to his concern (i.e., the question of Being) any inference about the existence or nonexistence of God. Stevens is considerably more explicit in his atheism, both in the poetry and in his prose.

35. "Hölderlin and the Essence of Poetry," p. 281.

ing Stevens's compressed theory. The poet's language (the word) establishes what otherwise would remain unintelligible and thus unknown, for the world without the poet's words is a "buzzing" and "lisping," inarticulate mass. The Being of the world is then:

> . . . a world of words to the end of it,
> In which nothing solid is its solid self.
> (CP, 345)

As the poet had suggested in "It Must Be Abstract," Canto III, only the words of the poem can "give a candid kind to everything" (CP, 382), thus expressing the insolidity of the Being of the things perceived.

In "Description Without Place," the poet proposes the function of description in the poetry of Being. At the same time, he evolves a rather complex theory of the temporal nature of spatial description. The expression of the title, "without place," has a temporal rather than a spatial meaning. For Stevens's "place" is conceived in the present time, the "now" of existence. Neither past nor future is actual. Hence any fictive effort to combine past and future into present time is called "description without place." This is why "the future is description without place / The categorical predicate, the arc" (CP, 344). Since the future toward which the poet projects his possible mode of poetry is not yet actual, such a poetry is called "description without place." A similar concept is proposed to express Stevens's use of the past. Each act of recalling past experience reflects a temporal consideration: ". . . everything we say / Of the past is description without place, a cast / Of the imagination, made in sound" (CP, 345–46). Thus the new mode of "description" proposed in this poem brings both past and future to the present, unifying the three primary temporal modes in much the same way that Heidegger's description of *Dasein*'s modes of Being-in-the-world and Being-toward-death unify the temporality of existence, making use of each tense to project possible ways of Being toward the future.[36]

From the incessant projective activity of *Dasein*, Heidegger derives a concept of unified time. *Dasein*, through its projections (into the future) of possible ways of Being, brings from past experience those possibilities that can be profitably repeated. The movement of *Dasein*, as it assures the possibility of projections into the future by recalling the possibilities of past experience, forms the temporal basis of Heidegger's explanation of how *Dasein* is constantly creating and recreating itself. For Stevens, poetry itself becomes a way of Being and the projections of possibilities in poetry are the ways in which the poet creates and re-creates himself in poetry. As the poet imagines the tasks of poetry, he can begin to fulfill them. Just as Heidegger's *Dasein* projects its own possibilities for Being into the future and then lives in the possibilities that it has imagined, so Stevens writes that poetry matters

---

36. While one is forced to distort Heidegger's complex and carefully constructed concepts of temporality and historicity in any summary, the profound unity of the three modes of time (Heidegger's *ekstases* of time) is maintained throughout his analysis of the temporal basis of Being that is described in *Sein und Zeit*, (pp. 231–436) in the *Zweiter Abschnitt*, which is entitled simply 'Dasein und Zeitlichkeit' (*Dasein* and Temporality). While I have attempted to abstract those ideas which are helpful for understanding Stevens's use of time in the later poems, needless to say, Stevens does not develop a theory of temporality that is as complete and systematically consistent as Heidegger's. Nor, for that matter, did Stevens ever claim that he did. Since a complete explanation of Heidegger's analysis of the ontological structure of time is beyond the scope of this study, I can only refer the reader who seeks a full comprehension of Heidegger's study of time and temporality to the sections of *Sein und Zeit* (see above); *Kant und das Problem der Metaphysik* (Bonn, 1929), pp. 92–95, 146–59, 170–78; and to several commentators on Heidegger's concept of *Zeitlichkeit* whose analysis and explanations are both clear and faithful to the philosopher's basic assumptions. See Alphonse De Waelhens, *La Philosophie de Martin Heidegger* (Louvain, 1942), pp. 181–240; Albert Chapelle, *L'Ontologie Phénoménologique de Heidegger* (Paris, 1962), pp. 135–96; Werner Marx, *Heidegger und die Tradition* (Stuttgart, 1961), pp. 74–80, 108–21, and *passim;* Thomas Langan, *The Meaning of Heidegger: A Critical Study of an Existentialist Phenomenology* (New York, 1959; paperback ed., 1961), pp. 41–55, 72–76, and *passim;* Karl Löwith, *Heidegger: Denker in dürftiger Zeit* (Frankfurt, 1953), *passim;* and William J. Richardson, *Heidegger: Through Phenomenology to Thought* (The Hague, 1967), pp. 85–90, 145–50, 173–74, 243–50.

Because what we say of the future must portend,

Be alive with its own seemings, seeming to be
Like rubies reddened by rubies reddening.
(CP, 346)

The metaphor is precise. The future is possessed only by
the man who has, as Stevens insists, "imagined well" (CP,
383). Like the "rubies reddening" (becoming red) in time,
the poetry of Being is brought to life by the imaginative
projection of its possibilities. The insistence that "it is possible" (CP, 339, 342), (a phrase that is frequently reiterated
in Stevens's later verse) is fulfilled for the poet by the
poems of the possible. The ontological possibilities of *Dasein* are more important than the actual present reality.
"*Dasein*'s primary [temporal] meaning is the future."[37] For
Stevens, the poetry of Being is ultimately the poetry of
possibility, always "Prologues to What Is Possible," as the
title of one of the late poems phrases it (CP, 515), rather
than a verification of what is self-evident. The poetry of
Being, like Heidegger's authentic Being-in-the-world, is of
the future, dependent on the concept of possibility.

Following these descriptions of the positive aspects of
the proposed poetry of Being, I want to return now to the
final three tercets of Canto III of "It Must Be Abstract," a
passage that has caused a great deal of consternation
among Stevens's commentators.

We say: At night an Arabian in my room,
With his damned hoobla-hoobla-hoobla-how,
Inscribes a primitive astronomy

Across the unscrawled fores the future casts
And throws his stars around the floor. By day
The wood-dove used to chant his hoobla-hoo

---

37. *Sein und Zeit*, p. 327. In the original, the statement is "Ihr [Daseins] pri-
märer Sinn ist die Zukunft."

> And still the grossest iridescence of ocean
> Howls hoo and rises and howls hoo and falls.
> Life's nonsense pierces us with strange relation.
>
> (CP, 383)

In this passage the narrator observes the multiple relations
that exist between apparently unrelated things. The observation is carefully qualified by the conditional introduction: "We say." The first thing to note about the passage is
that the relation between the three figures—the Arabian,
the wood-dove, and the ocean—is the repeated sound and
not the sense or symbolism of the figures.[38] The imagination can bring together things that are apparently without
any inherent order or relation because it has the power to
make sense (arbitrarily) of "life's nonsense." If the Arabian
is a figure for the imagination, projecting with his strange
chant possible versions of the future ("the future casts")
and the wood-dove is a figure of memory recalled from
the past (who "used to" sing a similar song), then the
ocean, acting in the present tense, is a figure for the immediate chaos of reality.[39] Each of the three figures acts in
a different time and a different place. The relation that
the imagination (poem) creates in this illustration brings
the three figures together, thus bringing three separate
modes of time into one, and three figures into a single
relation, all because of an analogy of sound ("nonsense").
While such arbitrary relations can be demonstrated, they
are nevertheless "strange." They can scarcely be said to

---

38. Stevens adds to the confusion by commenting that "The Arabian is the
moon; the undecipherable vagueness of the moonlight is the unscrawled fores:
the unformed handwriting. . . . the fact that the Arabian is the moon is something that the reader could not possibly know. However, I did not think it was
necessary for him to know" (*Letters*, 433–44).

39. For other readings of this passage, see particularly Bloom, p. 79, who
concludes that the Arabian is connected with Wordsworth's Arabian in *The Pre-
lude;* Sukenick, p. 139, who thinks that the Arabian is portentous, even if only the
moon; and Cambon, p. 89, who considers all three figures as "images that sym-
bolize the utter naturalness of poetry." None of these writers seems to have paid
much attention to Stevens's own explanation, and while as a rule that is a safe
thing to do, in the case of this passage, Stevens's "gorgeous nonsense" is exactly
that.

illustrate the kind of poem that was proposed in the first part of the canto. I do not think that we "share for a moment the first idea" in this passage. In fact, if anything, I think that this passage illustrates the false imagination, which Stevens calls at one point "the false conception of the imagination as some incalculable vates within us . . ." (NA, 61).

After this strange example of the minimal imagination, Stevens moves to the central statement of "It Must Be Abstract" in Canto IV, where he restates the nature of the "first idea" and its role in the making of poetry.[40] The "first idea," Stevens repeats, is not of men or gods (neither an "inventing mind" nor "a voluminous master folded in his fire" [CP, 381]). Rather, it comes from the "inconceivable" generative core or center, the origin of both the creativity of the mind and the incessant creations observed in nature.

> The first idea was not our own. Adam
> In Eden was the father of Descartes
> And Eve made air the mirrors of herself,
>
> Of her sons and of her daughters. They found themselves
> In heaven as in a glass; a second earth;
> And in the earth itself they found a green—
>
> The inhabitants of a very varnished green.
> But the first idea was not to shape the clouds
> In imitation. The clouds preceded us.
>
> There was a muddy centre before we breathed.
> There was a myth before the myth began,
> Venerable and articulate and complete.
>
> From this the poem springs: that we live in a place
> That is not our own and, much more, not ourselves
> And hard it is in spite of blazoned days.
>
> (CP, 383)

---

40. Riddel sees this section of Canto IV as a parable of the "fortunate fall," and thus connects it to the theme of *Paradise Lost*.

To get to the center of this passage, "the first idea" must be understood as the intuitive apprehension of Being. If that is clear, then the poem is straightforward. The allusions to Adam and Descartes concern the celebrated relation between thinking and Being that Descartes's method of systematic doubt elucidated. For Adam, the mythical first man, every perception would have been the "first idea," for he had no preconceptions. Any statement that Adam made would have been the poetry of the "first idea" because it would have, in the sense of both Heidegger and Stevens, established the Being of whatever the statement concerned. However, each statement that Adam made would also have falsified the "first idea," because his act of naming would place the "intuition" at one remove of abstraction. Hence, the original function of language both reveals and covers up the Being of the things spoken of. It is in this sense that Adam is the father of Descartes, for Descartes merely formalized the process of reason in his experiments in epistemology. For both Adam and Descartes, the *cogito* led away from the intuitive disclosure of Being. Descartes is no doubt chosen because he stands, in Stevens's mind, as the archetypal rationalist who attempted to establish the authority of the science of reason over ontology.

The efforts of both Adam and Descartes resulted in their seeing the world as a reflection of their own mind. Hence "Eve made air the mirror of herself" instead of attempting to see it in the "first idea" of it. The initial impulse of the mythical first humans was the same as that of Descartes. Both constructed a dual world, one of the mind and one of reality (the earth and "the second earth"). The point of the parable of Adam and Eve and Descartes is that the implied difference between mind and world is a false difference that is erroneously imposed upon a world whose origin and source are the same as those of the mind. Hence, the "first idea" was "not to shape the clouds" in the fancy. Nor was it the shaping or forming of natural things by some anthropomorphic deity (an assumption of both Adam and Descartes). The "muddy centre" preceded both mind and world and was the source of both.[41] The intuition of this "muddy centre" is called the "first idea" and both Adam and Descartes stand accused of falsifying both the generative center and the "first idea" of it. The narrator of the poem wants to uncover the source of creativity by revealing its origins. By presenting a parable about Adam and Descartes, he can suggest both the mythic and philosophical implications of his insight without sounding too much like a philosopher expounding "first causes" or a historian investigating the historical facts.[42]

The project of "It Must Be Abstract" is to disclose the nature of the muddy center of the mind and the world, where both the creative forces of man and the re-creative powers of nature are brought together. The poverty of the human condition is supported by the fictions that are created to make sense of a world that seems alien. Yet, while each fiction is destined to be false in its "late plural," in a world without meaning, man must nevertheless create meaning, for neither the pathetic fallacy nor anthropomorphic views are possible:

> The air is not a mirror but bare board,
> Coulisse bright-dark, tragic chiaroscuro

---

41. Frank Doggett, p. 180, sees the "muddy centre" as an archetype of the mind. "Mud," Doggett writes, "like clay, is an archetype of the idea of prime substance; for example, clay or better, mud conceived thus recurs in . . . Stevens' muddy centre. With this conception of mind as mind (as functional, not as mere physical brain) the idea of mind as the creative source of whatever experience impends [is a recurrent theme]." It is difficult to see how Doggett would interpret the muddy center, in this case, without having to talk about an original mind, like a deity or an absolute.

42. Nassar, p. 189, sees this passage as a rejection of God and an acceptance of Descartes's dualism. I think he has it half right. For a clearer reading of this passage see Sukenick, p. 139, who writes that "the garden of Eden was the primary example of conceiving reality in man's image. Thus Adam is the father of Descartes—'a symbol of reason' according to Stevens [Letters, 433]—since through Adam reality was first conceived on the basis of the reality of the reasoning ego."

And comic color of the rose, in which
Abysmal instruments make sounds like pips
Of the sweeping meanings that we add to them.
(CP, 384)

The background behind the stage upon which the human drama is played ("Coulisse bright-dark") has neither tragic nor comic qualities, for it is the neuter ("bare board") element into which men are thrown. Only the intuition of a "muddy centre" can provide a new beginning from which men can begin again to make sense of a world that "is not our own and, much more not ourselves" (CP, 383). This description of the human condition parallels Heidegger's description of *Dasein*'s "thrownness," the way in which *Dasein* finds itself already in the world with no choice but to make of this condition what it can.[43] For both Stevens and Heidegger, the realization of this *a priori* condition of existence necessitates the creation of projections. Stevens writes that "From this the poem springs" (CP, 383), implying that the condition in which man finds himself, as already in the world and related to the things around him, is part of the reason that he must create the fictive "sweeping meanings that we add" (CP, 384) to the meaningless world that he finds.

The particular trials of the young poet who realizes both the grandeur and the poverty of the human condition are dramatized in Canto V. The ephebe is described as attempting to create meaning where there is no meaning inherent. His "bitter utterance from his writhing, dumb,/ Yet voluble dumb violence" (CP, 384) characterizes the anguish of creation in the face of a world that will not sustain the human explanations of it. The speaker in this canto relates the parable of the roaring lion, the blaring elephant, and the snarling bear to demonstrate the difference between the purely physical relation of these animals

---

43. *Sein und Zeit,* pp. 175–80.

to their surroundings and the partly physical and partly
spiritual relation of the ephebe to his world. Each of these
animals seems the master of his situation, but each is more
helpless than any man before the powers of nature (symbolized by the "enraging desert," its emptiness, the darkness of the jungle, the summer thunder, and winter snow).
Compared to the torments of the ephebe's partial ignorance, the animals may seem to be better off in their total
ignorance. In the end, man is the victor who learns "to lash
the lion, / Caparison elephants, teach bears to juggle" (CP,
385). But like the victories of Adam and Descartes of the
previous canto, the victory over the dumb animals is hollow. It perverts their nature just as Descartes had per-
verted the nature of human existence by insisting (along
with a rather impressive group of predecessors) that man
is merely "the rational animal." This explains why "these
are the children time breeds against the first idea" (CP,
385), for they are the children of rationality. Stevens's concept of the first idea is an attempt to return to the source of
the relation of the mind and the world, an attempt that he
characterizes at the end of "Notes" as "the more than rational distortion" that fulfills man's desires. As both Stevens and Heidegger contend, the disclosure of Being (the
muddy center that is the source of both mind and world) is
beyond the limitations of reason.[44]

In Canto VI the narrator continues this theme as he
begins another variation upon the intuition of the "first
idea." Here Being (the inaccessible abstract) is

> Not to be realized because not to
> Be seen, not to be loved nor hated because
> Not to be realized. Weather by Franz Hals,
>
> Brushed up by brushy winds in brushy clouds,
> Wetted by blue, colder for white. Not to
> Be spoken to, without a roof, without

---

44. For Heidegger the nature of disclosure is "prior to all cognition and
volition, and beyond their range of disclosure" (*Being and Time*, p. 175).

First fruits, without the virginal of birds,
The dark-blown ceinture loosened, not relinquished.
(CP, 385)

The artist's attempt to capture the presence of the "first idea" in art is destined to become "false flick, false form, but falseness close to kin" (CP, 385). The example used by Stevens is a landscape by Franz Hals ("whose forte," Ronald Sukenick observes, "was not landscape"[45]). Art (poetry included) can only intimate the vision of the first idea, since the evasiveness of Being precludes its complete or lasting disclosure in man's fictive representations. Stevens comments on this passage that

> The abstract does not exist, but it is certainly as imma-nent . . . in the mind of the poet, as the idea of God is imma-nent in the mind of the theologian. The poem is a struggle with the inaccessibility of the abstract. First I make the effort; then I turn to the weather because that is not inaccessible and is not abstract. The weather described is the weather that was about when I wrote this. There is a constant reference from the abstract to the real, to and fro.[46]
>
> (*Letters*, 434)

While Stevens is seldom his own best critic and frequently contradicts himself in his comments on his own poems, this comment does provide a notion of what he might have intended. The poet must try to contain the abstract and inaccessible qualities of the "muddy centre" by references to concrete, accessible phenomena. His task is to suggest the "centre" by its concrete manifestations even though the "centre" itself is "not to be seen."

---

45. Sukenick, p. 141. He also considers this whole passage about major man and, in doing so, ignores the cantos that both precede and follow this passage.

46. Again, in spite of what Stevens writes, in January 1943 to Hi Simons, the interpretations of this passage vary to the extent that it is thought to be about everything from "Major man" (Sukenick, p. 141) to a painting (Baird, p. 142). And these two examples are from critics who are aware of what Stevens writes of the passage in *Letters*, p. 434.

It must be visible or invisible
Invisible or visible or both:
A seeing and unseeing in the eye.

The weather and the giant of the weather,
Say the weather, the mere weather, the mere air:
An abstraction blooded, as a man by thought.
                                        (CP, 385)

The poem should suggest both the concrete thing that is
accessible (the weather) and the abstract, "first idea" of the
weather (the giant of the weather). In these lines, the process of moving back and forth from perception to conception, from representation to intimation, is meant to
suggest the difficulty of the poet's task (certainly only
another variation of the theme of the first six cantos of "It
Must Be Abstract"). The fluctuating movement from perception to conception illustrates the theory that was proposed in Canto III. Moving from the "ever-early candor to
its late plural," the poem is an attempt to suggest how the
abstraction is blooded by the poet's "revelations" of the
"muddy centre."[47]

The process illustrated in the last six lines of Canto VI
reduces the opposing elements to "mere air," which (like
Kant's "mere appearance"), when given form in poetry,
becomes "blooded" by human feelings. No longer can the
personified idea (the abstract presence of the weather) be
thought of as a neutral abstraction, for it is transformed by
the poetic process into something that can take on life in
the poem, even though the life is fictive and known to be
such. Hence the meditation of the "first idea" brings the

---

47. Doggett, p. 113, finds the paradox of "a seeing and unseeing in the eye"
difficult to understand. In rational terms Doggett has a point, but if he is insisting on reason from a poet who praises the "irrational" moment's "unreasoning,"
he will not go far with visionary poets. There are paradoxes in Stevens's verse,
but they should not bewilder the critic as much as they do in the readings of
Doggett and Fuchs, to name two, who refuse to consider the possibility of the
coexistence of contradictions, a phenomenon that I will discuss later in terms of
the "principle of complimentarity."

original intuition of Being to the poem even though the act of representing it in language makes it "a false flick, false form" that must immediately be rejected. The poet then performs the transformation that "refreshes life so that we share, / For a moment the first idea" (CP, 383).

Stevens then expands the temporal quality of the "first idea" (the intuition of Being) in the ten cantos of "It Must Change," but before returning to the nature of the "first idea" and its relation to time, he concludes "It Must Be Abstract" with a series of poems that treats the theme of "major man." Rather than trace the variations upon the theme, I will go straight to the passage that culminates the final distinctions and functions of "major man." This passage is the beginning of Canto X and a close reading of it will make clear what the variations upon the theme of "major man" in Cantos VII, VIII, and IX have been leading toward. I am not claiming that Stevens follows a logical argument in these cantos, but the movement of the poetic discourse in the previous cantos leads directly to the statement that I quote in full:

> The major abstraction is the idea of man
> And major man is its exponent, abler
> In the abstract than in his singular,
>
> More fecund as principle than particle,
> Happy fecundity, flor-abundant force,
> In being more than an exception, part,
>
> Though an heroic part, of the commonal.
> The major abstraction is the commonal,
> The inanimate, difficult visage.
>   (CP, 388)

To make the distinctions clear so that I do not, as Harold Bloom does, confuse "major man" with "the idea of man," I would like to stress the difference between an idea and its exponent.[48] Major man, most simply defined, is a person-

48. Bloom, p. 82.

ification of the process of the imagination. He is thus, logically, an exponent (someone who expounds or explains) of
the idea of man. Since *The Man with the Blue Guitar*, Stevens
has proposed that the major task of poetry is to evolve a
man. Thus it is not surprising that he still maintains that
"the major abstraction is the idea of man," since it is the
most general and most difficult of all concepts. The processes of the imagination are called upon to take up this
difficult task (i.e., to evolve an adequate idea of man that
would be the sum of his existence). When Martin Heidegger set out to evolve an idea or structure of the existence of
man (the ontological structure of *Dasein*) the result was a
450-page treatise that accomplished only one-third of
what he had announced in his preface.[49] Perhaps this
example of the impossibility of such a task suggests why
the process of the imagination is more "fecund as principle
than particle." Another reason for this statement is Stevens's preference for the possible rather than the
actual—that is, for the idea of creative potential in place of
a single, and thus, limited example.

The major man is called "the happy fecundity, flor-
abundant force" because he is a personification of the potential, human, creative force that is contained in the imagination. He is not, as some critics have suggested, a hero
or a giant who epitomizes a kind of Nietzschean *Übermensch*, the apocryphal new man.[50] As a personification of
a force rather than a person or a thing, major man is
similar to Stevens's other personifications. The poet's tendency is to personify ideas and abstractions to give them a
kind of human stance in his poems. Personification is a
feature of Stevens's later poetry that mitigates and makes

---

49. *Sein und Zeit*, pp. 39–40.
50. Riddel, p. 152, writes that "clearly enough, Stevens' hero owes his image
to Nietzsche (the philosopher of the moment for Stevens in the later thirties)"
and suggests the *Übermensch* as the source of Stevens's major man. Stevens, in
fact, denies any such idea. See *Letters*, p. 409, where he writes "About Nietzsche;
I haven't read him since I was a young man. My interest in the hero, major man,
the giant, has nothing to do with the *Biermensch* [*sic*]."

human poems that would otherwise be unbearably abstract and lifeless.[51]

The power, represented by "major man," to conceive the fictions that explain man to himself is praised as "an heroic part, of the commonal" (CP, 388). Major man is a symbol of the heroic part of everyman—the power of imagination to create and re-create the fictions without which life would no longer be bearable.[52] The "inanimate, difficult visage" is the idea of man—the commonal, "the man in that old coat, those sagging pantaloons" (CP, 389) who symbolizes the poverty and nakedness of every man.[53] The narrator, having instructed the ephebe on the difference between major man and the idea of man, then exhorts the young poet to take on the power symbolized by "major man" in order to expound the "idea of man." To become an exponent of the major abstraction is to become fully human by fulfilling the possibilities of creative activity:

> It is of him, ephebe, to make, to confect
> The final elegance, not to console
> Nor sanctify, but plainly to propound.
> (CP, 389)

At the conclusion of "It Must Be Abstract," the narrator has addressed a rather long lesson to his student on the source of creativity ("the first idea") and how this source

---

51. In my discussion of the personifications of Being, the abstract idea or sense of presence that was presented in human forms in *Parts of a World,* I began to develop a theory that I will expand in the next chapter in my discussions of "Chocorua To Its Neighbor" (CP, 296–302), "The Auroras of Autumn" (CP, 411–20), and several other poems in which Stevens again personifies ideas. I will refrain from adding to that theory until I begin to discuss those poems. However, for the best discussions of Stevens's practice of personifying abstractions, see Baird, pp. 217–30, and Doggett, pp. 90–93.

52. Nassar, p. 183, insists that "major man" is both the power of the imagination and an idealized hero who is "an example" of what men ought to be like. That is, Nassar seems to want the personification to stand for a force and an ideal person at the same time. He refuses to see, and this is his error, the distinction that the poet makes between the "major abstraction" and "major man."

53. Cambon suggests that the vision of the man "in that old coat, those sagging pantaloons" (CP, 389) represents a view of a Charlie Chaplin character (p. 97).

unites both the imagination and the world. Having completed this lecture, he then personifies the process of the
imagination as major man and proceeds to demonstrate
how this process is essential to the fiction-making function
of the poet. It should be clear by now that the first section
of "Notes Toward a Supreme Fiction" is not directly a
definition of the supreme fiction. Rather, the lessons are
meditations of the qualities of a new poetry of Being.
While the new poetry, which is described and refined as a
possibility for the young poet, might become a supreme
fiction, it is never stated explicitly that this is what the
narrator has in mind.

I have followed the argument and implications of "It
Must Be Abstract" rather closely, because Stevens's progress in these early sections is elliptical and often dense to
the point of obscurity. Furthermore, each of the ideas that
Stevens develops in these cantos is essential to the poetry
of Being.

It Must Change

The following two parts of "Notes Toward a Supreme
Fiction," "It Must Change" and "It Must Give Pleasure,"
are considerably less didactic and, as a result, less sequen-
tial in argument than "It Must Be Abstract." The dramatic
device of a narrator lecturing to a student on the theory of
poetry is dropped and the narrator proceeds to meditate
the possibilities of a poetry of Being without the implied
presence of the ephebe. In the second part, "It Must
Change," the fourth canto is the central section toward
which the others move. In Canto IV, Stevens bases the
necessity of change upon a theory of complementarity.[54]

---

54. I am indebted to Kermode for the idea of a principle of complementarity
which he discusses in his *The Sense of An Ending: Studies in the Theory of Fiction*
(New York and Oxford, 1966; paperback edition, 1968), pp. 59–64. Kermode
explains the principle of complementarity in the following way: "This principle
arose from a precise scientific need. Light behaves in such a way that you think of
it in terms of waves, and it behaves also so that you can think of it in terms of

As I pointed out in the preceding chapter, the impermanence of the experience of disclosure was a crucial part of Stevens's sense of Being and the relation of poetry and temporality is clearly implied in the subtitle of this part of "Notes." Just as the temporal qualities of the perception of the "first idea" were the source of both the decreative and creative functions of the imagination, so the concept of change in its various manifestations becomes an essential part of Stevens's theory of a poetry of Being. The relation of the poetry of Being and time is demonstrated both in terms of the "change" that is imperative for any poetry that is written to express a sense of a constantly changing subject and in terms of the empirical observation of "change" in the world. Whether the change involved is the fluctuation and repetition observed in the natural world or the kind of change that is the essential condition of consciousness and creativity, the base of all of Stevens's explanations and illustrations of change is his sense of the complex structure of time and its relation to both mind and world. He discovers that the changes he observes, which at

---

particles; it proved possible, mathematically, to develop a single set of equations to cover both wave and particle effects, but outside mathematics you could only speak of them as being 'complementary' " (p. 59). Kermode goes on to explain that the acceptance in theory of both wave theory and particle theory for the same thing is logically contradicatory. Rationally, a thing can not both be and not be at the same time. However, the idea of complementarity has become a respectable explanation in the sciences for what visionary poets have been insisting upon for quite some time: that two mutually exclusive things can coexist at the same time in the same place. As Kermode suggests, "one can imagine the Principle [of complementarity] being used to establish a consonance between what is so and what is not so; propositions may even yet be true and false at the same time" (p. 62). "[The principle of complementarity] . . . is an interesting example of the way in which an operationalist fiction outgrows its immediate purpose . . . . Its object can be generalized as being the establishment of concord between the world of normal thought and the world of nuclear physics, between observations originally hard to categorize and somewhat disquieting, and an order acceptable to our mental set. Now it is extended to cover other disquieting gaps, intervals in thought and experience; it is doing a job analogous to that of literary fictions. It is, in short, what I call a concord-fiction" (p. 62). Thus, by uniting contradictory or opposing things without abandoning the essential qualities of either and at the same time providing an interaction that generates a new fiction, the principle of complementarity is used to explain the fiction of concord. My discussion of the following sections of "Notes" will use this principle several times to explain facets of Stevens's aesthetic.

first seem separate and discrete, are actually the same for the mind and the world.

Much of the final part of "Notes Toward a Supreme Fiction" is concerned with the similarity of the exterior and interior manifestations of time. The poet discovers that whenever the unity of Being is disclosed, both the world and the mind are integrally united by the temporal nature of the disclosure. The passing of days, the changing months, and the four seasons serve as both the literal and the symbolic, physical manifestations of temporality. But, in the poems of *Transport to Summer, Auroras of Autumn,* and "The Rock," these time measurements become more and more importantly the psychic equivalents for human time as it is experienced and imagined. As mind and world are brought together, empirical time and human time become interchangeable metaphors and Stevens uses specific references to solar, lunar, and seasonal temporal variations to suggest the internal realization of time as a fictive duration that makes possible not only the unique existential birth and death, but also numerous repetitions of the story of life. These variations, with their concomitant beginnings, middles, and ends, both fulfill the poet's projection of Being and provide pleasure. He can partake fully in the changes that occur because he can end them. The "supreme fiction" may in fact never appear, but the fictions generated during the poet's search for it suffice as paradigms of the poetry of Being. These fictions demonstrate both the means (the genesis through revelations) and the end (usually a new genesis) without invoking a final fiction.[55]

Perhaps the clearest way to explain the similarity between Stevens's view of exterior and interior time and thus

---

55. I want to cite two sources here that I have used in the discussions of Heidegger's temporality and Stevens's use of time in the poetry. Although neither of these writers talks specifically about either Heidegger or Stevens in the books I have found helpful, both writers were extremely stimulating. They are Georges Poulet in his *Studies in Human Time,* trans. Elliott Coleman (Baltimore, Md., 1956) and Paul Fraisse, *The Psychology of Time* (London, 1964).

clarify his sense of the complexity of time and its relation to the poetry of Being will be to show how several of the cantos of "It Must Change" illustrate the poet's sense of time as the origin of change. However, first I want to make it clear why Heidegger's concept of time as the ground of Being helps explain the temporal basis of Stevens's supreme fictions.

Heidegger organizes his entire phenomenological description of *Dasein*'s modes of Being on a temporal structure, which is carefully constructed to include the complexity of temporality (*Zeitlichkeit*). The notion that time is simply a linear progression of now-points is never denied by Heidegger. He calls this the "everyday" idea of time, which is correct as far as it goes. However, this notion of empirical time does not explain the temporal nature of human existence (*Dasein*), which is constantly aware of both past and future, bringing both modes of time into present existence. The received idea that the future is simply a "now" that is not yet and that the past is composed of those present moments that are no longer present does little to explain the human ability to make use of both past and future time in the projection of its own ontological possibilities for Being.[56]

Heidegger formulates a complex explanation of how each of the three modes of time is primary for one of the three modes of existence(an explanation that need not be described in detail here). The purpose of his careful explanation of the temporal qualities of each mode of *Dasein's* Being-in-the-world is to show how each human brings all three kinds of time into play. Heidegger's theory is based on the human ability to unify past, present, and future. For the ontologist, the way in which *Dasein* makes use of time shows the profound unity of time that forms the finite horizon (i.e., limitation) of every human possibility for Being.[57]

---

56. *Sein und Zeit*, pp. 334–49, 367–72 (*Being and Time*, pp. 383–430).
57. *Sein und Zeit*, pp. 338–40.

Dasein exists ontologically in the future since it is toward the future that it projects its own possibilities for Being. More clearly, when Heidegger wants to describe the way in which humans can fulfill their potential for Being-in-the-world, he refers to that mode of Being which he calls *Sein-zum-Tode* (Being-toward-death), which *Dasein* becomes when aware through *Angst* (the state-of-mind characterized by anxiety about one's own impending death) of the finite duration of existence.[58] Time, then, for *Dasein,* is first understood as the duration of existence. However, this kind of time-consciousness only intensifies *Dasein*'s concern for its own Being. *Dasein* cannot remain in a state of vague fear of its own death (the final possibility of Being, which is nonbeing). Instead, man must begin to make sense of existence by creating it. The self-creation that Heidegger describes occurs through a process of projection wherein *Dasein* makes use of both its past experience and its present existence to project toward the future its possibilities for Being (and it would seem that the source of projection in Heidegger's analysis is similar to Stevens's imagination, which creates the fictions that make the human condition of *Sein-zum-Tode* bearable).

The past is an important measure of both the present existence of *Dasein* and its future possibilities. *Dasein* recalls from its past experience a knowledge of both its limitations and its potential for Being. Heidegger names two kinds of activities that *Dasein* performs in its use of the past. The first activity is the process of repetition (*Wiederholung*), which is the act of making present the possibilities of the past.[59] The second activity is the destruction of those things from the past that are no longer feasible. Heidegger's *Destruktion* of the past is illustrated by his treatment of the history of philosophy. Each of the famous philosophers of the Western tradition is made present

---

58. *Ibid.,* pp. 235–67.
59. For a full discussion of *Wiederholung* and *Destruktion,* see William J. Richardson, pp. 89–93, 374–91.

(repeated) insofar as his thought is useful to Heidegger's projected "fundamental ontology." Whatever is not deemed useful is destroyed. Each destruction is, in effect, a decreation of an old idea that is no longer useful. The decreation clears the way for repeating the possibilities of the past. This repetition gives *Dasein* a valid paradigm from which it can project original possibilities into the future. Heidegger insists upon a balance between repetition and destruction so that *Dasein* can retain the ability to make use of its past while rejecting those elements of past experience that are no longer helpful. Each projection (like each of Stevens's fictions) is created in the present, based on paradigms of the past, and projected toward the future as a possible mode of Being.

Using this brief analysis of Heidegger's ontological structure of time, I want to show how Stevens's sense of time functions as the central idea of "It Must Change" and provides an explanation of the pleasure that is derived from the poetry of Being as it is illustrated in "It Must Give Pleasure." For Stevens, the first origin of change is the fluctuation between opposing orders that "seem to depend on one another" for their Being. The theory is not simply that contrasting things tend to illuminate one another, but that the coexistence of contraries brings a constant alteration. The central idea in this theory is the concept of complementarity wherein "two things of opposite natures seem to depend / On one another" (CP, 392). Where opposites find a common source and are united, the reality of change is most directly demonstrated. The nature of change is understood as the passage of time that makes the disclosure of "the muddy centre" possible.

The first three cantos of "It Must Change" describe the phenomenology of change through variations upon the theme of time. The first canto presents examples of change and permanence wherein the contradictory ideas coexist in the cyclical repetition of the seasons and birth. Stevens approaches a mythic point-of-view through the persona of the "Gilded Seraph," who observes change as if he were eternal.[60] From the point of view of one who exists outside of time, the changes observed in nature are only examples of the tedious repetition of an eternal cycle that repeats itself *ad infinitum*. The same boring thing is observed in the regenerative cycle of existence, where birth and death are simply recurrent patterns. From this point of view, the cyclical nature of change is constant, and thus change itself is evidence of the eternal.

However, the speaker contrasts this mythic time-consciousness to his own existential time-consciousness. The "Gilded Seraph" presents one fiction of time, the fiction of eternity. The speaker balances this view:

> We say
> This changes and that changes. Thus the constant
>
> Violets, doves, girls, bees, and hyacinths
> Are inconstant objects of inconstant cause
> In a universe of inconstancy.
>
> (CP, 389)

He is aware of both the fiction that claims these appearances as proof of a constant universe and the fiction that sees these changes as proof of the inconstancy of the universe. The first view is based on mythic, cyclical time, while the second view is based on a view of simple linear time. Neither is satisfactory.

> It means that the distaste we feel for this withered scene
> Is that it has not changed enough. It remains,
> It is repetition.
>
> (CP, 390)

---

60. Mircea Eliade in his *Cosmos and History: The Myth of the Eternal Return*, trans. Willard R. Trask (New York, 1954; paperback ed., 1954), p. 20, writes of the nature of mythic temporality when he explains that "through repetition of the cosmogonic act [Eliade's term for the act of the creation or birth of the world] concrete time, in which the construction takes place, is projected into mythical time, *in illo tempore* when the foundation of the world occurred." Stevens's "Gilded Seraph" is a good example of a character who lives in mythic time where all acts of creation are repetitions of the original act of creation and hence seem to take place in mythical rather than empirical time.

Neither the cyclical explanation of the myth of the eternal return nor the linear explanation of the fiction of serial time[61] suffices to explain the human experience of the moment:

> An erotic perfume, half of the body, half
> Of an obvious acid is sure what it intends
> And the booming is blunt, not broken in subtleties.
>
> (CP, 390)

This is description without explanation, for the narrator does not evaluate either of the temporal explanations of change that he has suggested, except to say that neither is adequate to his experience of spring.

In Canto II, the narrator points out the futility of attempting to impose permanence on a changing world. "The president ordains the bee to be / Immortal" (CP, 390), but the bee dies and is survived only by the form of the species. This is not the answer either. The "booming and booming of the new-come bee" (CP, 391) defies the attempts of men to establish the immortality of nature. Only the pattern of repetition seems permanent. As Harold Bloom suggests, "against an imaginative denial of the reality of change, the booming of the bees asserts a beginning, not a resuming."[62] For while each spring brings intimations of mythic immortality, the narrator questions the adequacy of all mythic concepts of time:

> Why, then, when in golden fury
>
> Spring vanishes the scraps of winter, why
> Should there be a question of returning or
> Of death in memory's dream? Is spring a sleep?

---

61. Kermode, *The Sense of an Ending*, pp. 44–58, suggests that the cyclical time of myth, the "crisis" time of apocalyptic theory, and the notion of serial time are fictions that men use to explain their experience of time. In fact, one might add, all concepts of time are fictions since, like Being, time is both a most evident and most difficult concept to understand with any degree of intelligibility.

62. Bloom, p. 84.

> This warmth is for lovers at last accomplishing
> Their love, this beginning, not resuming, this
> Booming and booming of the new-come bee.
>
> (CP, 391)

Like Heidegger's secularized *Dasein,* the narrator lives within the finite duration of existence. He thus sees the new season not as one more example of the eternal return of the similar, but as an entirely new beginning for him. The originality of each moment is best achieved by those who are most fully aware of the mutability theme ("the lovers"). "Death is the mother of beauty" (CP, 68, 69), since without change both nature and art would be dead. Without change, the quality of human existence would also be impoverished, since, for Stevens

> The greatest poverty is not to live
> In a physical world, to feel that one's desire
> Is too difficult to tell from despair.
>
> (CP, 325)

To live in "a physical world" where "lovers at last" can accomplish their love is to live in a finite world. To accept the limits of time that are implied by the constant changes of physical existence is to know the difference between one's "desire" for fictions of change and the "despair" that results in creations of the myths of eternal return. This difference, most simply stated, is the difference between *fictions* that incorporate change and celebrate human existence and *myths* that deny change and thus deny the reality of physical existence. The third canto of "It Must Change" illustrates the necessity of change by the example of the "great statue of General Du Puy," which attempts to achieve a permanence of sorts. Yet, the rigidity of the form is satirized as "a bit absurd" and "was rubbish in the end" because "nothing had changed" (CP, 393).

Each of these cantos has described methods of accounting for the origin of change through the theories of time

that are implied in myth, science, and art. None of these
theories was adequate, for none could account for the contradictions that each theory of time implied. Thus, in
Canto IV, the narrator proposes a theory that will account
for the complexities of change as they are to be incorporated in poetry. The theory, as Riddel points out, "is quite
simply an aesthetic which finds the origin of change not in
the creation myth but in the instant of human consciousness."[63]

> Two things of opposite natures seem to depend
> On one another, as a man depends
> On a woman, day on night, the imagined
>
> On the real. This is the origin of change.
> Winter and spring, cold copulars, embrace
> And forth the particulars of rapture come.
> (CP,392)

The opposing things depend on one another for their
Being. From the interaction of opposites comes change
and from change come the "particulars of rapture" (the
fictions that account for both interior and exterior time).
The rapture comes from taking part in the change that is
an essential characteristic of "living in a physical world":

> The partaker partakes of that which changes him.
> The child that touches takes character from the thing,
> The body, it touches.
> (CP, 392)

Just as the poetry of Being helps us share for a moment
the "first idea," so the active participation in change is a
sharing wherein the opposites share a center. The center is
literally the mind of the observer, but as he partakes in
Being, he also partakes in change. To the observer whose
duration (whether in a fiction or in a Bergsonian *durée*)

---

63. Riddel, p. 176.

brings opposing things together, music and silence, morning and afternoon, and North and South "are an intrinsic couple" (CP, 392). Each act of bringing opposites together emphasizes the dependence of opposing forces on each other. This dependence is another variation on the marriage motif that Stevens repeats several times (particularly Canto VIII of "It Must Change" and Canto IV of "It Must Give Pleasure"). Marriage for Stevens is the symbol of a union of opposing forces that does not impair the self-identity of either of the individual partners. The opposites are not reconciled or synthesized in a higher form.[64] Rather, they are brought together by a common bond so that they can change through interaction and yet retain their individual identity within the process of change. These marriages that transform without changing are concrete examples of the theory of complementarity upon which Stevens bases his aesthetic of change.

The parable in Canto V is an example of the complementarity of change. The planter made his island a place dependent on himself. By partaking in the changes of nature and self, he became wedded to his plantation. After his death, the evidence of his love for the place disappears as passing time erodes his work. The same inevitable change that he took part in and celebrated during his life destroys him and his work. Yet, he is a positive figure. The narrator summarizes his existence with negations that add up to an affirmation.[65]

> An unaffected man in a negative light
> Could not have borne his labor nor have died
> Sighing that he should leave the banjo's twang.
>
> (CP, 393)

---

64. Bernard Heringman, on the other hand, sees all these marriages as part of a Hegelian synthesis. See "Wallace Stevens: The Use of Poetry," *ELH* 16 (December 1949): 325–36; Reprinted in *The Act of the Mind,* ed. R. H. Pearce and J. Hillis Miller (Baltimore, Md., 1965), pp. 1–12, esp. p. 6.

65. Roy Harvey Pearce, p. 398, was the first to observe that "the use of negatives here [in this passage, which summarizes the planter's existence] literally forces the positiveness of the statement on us."

The opposite of Stevens's theory of the complementarity of identity and difference is demonstrated in the onomatopoetic birdsongs of Canto VI. William Van O'Conner writes that the parody of the bird's incessant "Be thou me" is a direct allusion to Shelley's impassioned plea in the "Ode to the West Wind."[66] Both Shelley's cry and the bird's song are calls for identity with a force that is more powerful than they. For the narrator, this kind of identity is wrong. Each "Be thou me" asks for a universal identity that will take away the individuality of the caller and immerse him in the larger power invoked. For Shelley this power is the West wind. For the birds this power is all of nature. Both call for an identity that implies a loss of self within the force of some greater power that will preserve their efforts from change. This desire, like the desire of the myth-maker and the mystic, implies a denial of the temporality of the human condition. Each of the birds calls for a mindless union, implicitly rejecting the uniqueness of the self in the quest for fusion with the wholly other. All these "Be thous" are heard by the narrator as

> One voice repeating, one tireless chorister,
> The phrases of a single phrase, ké-ké,
> A single text, granite monotony,
>
> One sole face, like a photograph of fate,
> Glass-blower's destiny, bloodless episcopus,
> Eye without lid, mind without any dream—
>
> These are of minstrels lacking minstrelsy,
> of an earth in which the first leaf is the tale
> Of leaves, in which the sparrow is a bird
>
> Of stone, that never changes.
>   (CP, 394)

While certain critics have thought this passage a praise of

---

66. William Van O'Conner, *The Shaping Spirit* (Chicago, 1952), p. 72.

the bird's "heroic" song,[67] the tone and direct statement both make fun of the bird's monotonous song. These singers with their redundant songs are representatives of a changeless world where "the first leaf is the tale / Of leaves" (CP, 394). They are falsifiers of nature as well as of their own individuality. Proof of this is scarcely needed, but the kind of world they sing of implies a similarity of all leaves that certainly contradicts the observations of anyone who has looked carefully at leaves. Hence, the "granite monotony" of their chant "is a song like any other. It will end" (CP, 394).

The birds and their song are the last of a series of examples, all of which falsify the nature of change. Each of these examples is finally rejected because none penetrates the complexity of time that is the basis of change. Any theory of change must take into account the "easy passion and ever-ready love" that "are of our earthy birth and here and now / And where we live and everywhere we live" (CP, 395). This is the state of mind that is described in Canto VII, where Stevens praises the possible satisfactions that are to be found in *Sein-zum-Tode* (Being-toward-death). The visionary experiences possible for a fully human existence preclude the "need of any paradise," for with the full acceptance of the human condition "We have not the need of any seducing hymn" (CP, 394). The entire canto is a song in praise of the human passions that fill the life of the man of imagination, who partakes in change because he realizes that each "accessible bliss" is possible only in "the fluctuations of certainty, the change / Of degrees of perception in the scholar's dark" (CP, 395).

Through a full realization of the finite duration of existence, man exists as *Sein-zum-Tode*. The decision to participate in such an existence makes each instant a cause for joy

---

67. Ronald Sukenick, for example, p. 149, calls the sparrow a kind of hero, because his "song, which here seems the dominant one," is thought by the critic to be heard "in contrast . . . to the repetitions of the other birds" (p. 148).

as well as for sorrow, each love a cause for celebration in the knowledge (which is like the planter's knowledge in the parable of Canto V) that there is a definite end and "Death is absolute and without memorial" (CP, 97). Part of the complex human sense of time, the narrator implies, is the appreciation of the irretrievable quality of each instant. The present then becomes a possible moment of vision in which one projects toward the future the authentic possibilities of Being ("another accessible bliss"). Each possible satisfaction must be projected within the finite horizon (limit) of human time. Each fiction must be projected within "the fluctuations of certainty" that are an undeniable part of human existence.

Man can never know the ultimate or absolute and, as the parable of Canto VIII demonstrates, each attempt to transcend the finite quality of existence must be rejected. "Nanzia Nunzio," whose last name suggests, as Glauco Cambon indicates, "Good messenger or accredited ambassador,"[68] presents herself as the potential spouse of Ozymandias, the mythical representative of an eternal order. She claims to be stripped "more nakedly / Than nakedness" (CP, 396) so that she can be clothed "in the final filament" (CP, 396). The reference to Shelley's King of Kings, whose Sphinx-like figure stood for an inflexible order that was destroyed by time, adds a curious ambiguity to this passage.[69]

Here the statue is a figure for a timeless order, and Nanzia Nunzio's attempt to achieve union with this order is denied because "a fictive covering / Weaves always glistening from the heart and mind" (CP, 396). Her attempt to reach the absolute (like that of the floribund ascetic in "Landscape With Boat") is an attempt to transcend human temporal boundaries by achieving a kind of absolute purity outside the changes of time. Stevens's denial of this attempt is, at the same time, an affirmation of the constant

---

68. Cambon, p. 105.
69. I am following the accepted reading here of the figure of Ozymandias. See, for example, Bloom, p. 87; Cambon, p. 106; Riddel, p. 177.

changes that emanate from the imagination and the emotions. The poem is another illustration of the necessity of change that is both interior (for Nanzia Nunzio) and exterior (for Ozymandias).

As Stevens approaches the end of "It Must Change," he confronts the relations between language and change in Canto IX. The problem is similar to the problem of the relation between language and Being ("the first idea") that was suggested in the first cantos of "It Must Be Abstract" and treated extensively in the later poem, "Description Without Place." Since I have already discussed the implications of the possibilities that were proposed in both of these poems, I will limit my commentary on Canto IX to a few remarks on how the questions that the narrator asks here are the same kinds of questions that have haunted several other major modern poets. T. S. Eliot in *The Four Quartets,* Hart Crane in *The Bridge,* Paul Valéry in his essays, and William Carlos Williams in the concluding sections of *Paterson* all question the potential of language to sustain the poet's meanings. While all of these questions are essential to the narrator (and, one might add, implicitly to Stevens as implied author), he avoids any theory of the permanence or constancy of language. Thus, the question "Does the poet evade us, as in a senseless element?" (CP, 396) goes unanswered. Do the words "strain / Crack and sometimes break, under the burden / Under the tension, slip, slide, perish" as Eliot writes in "Burnt Norton"?[70] Such questions are the proper study of poetry, particularly a poetry whose subject is poetry, but, as the narrator admits,

> There's a meditation there, in which there seems
>
> To be an evasion, a thing not apprehended or
> Not apprehended well.
> (CP, 396)

---

70. *The Collected Poems and Plays of T. S. Eliot: 1909–1950* (New York, 1952), p. 121.

Instead of continuing the series of questions, the narrator evades the issue by suggesting the poet's function, which is

> To compound the imagination's Latin with
> The lingua franca et jocundissima.
>
> (CP, 397)

He seeks the peculiar combination of ordinary language ("the vulgate") and strange language ("the poet's gibberish"—"the imagination's Latin") that will, hopefully, express his vision. This description is not particularly startling compared to the theory of language, Being, and time that is implied in the propositions in "Description Without Place." The meditation is evaded in this poem, but it is taken up again in the later poems of *Auroras of Autumn* and "The Rock," which I will discuss in the next chapter.

At the end of the second part of "Notes Toward a Supreme Fiction," Stevens has presented variations upon the idea of impermanence (his initial intuition of the nature of Being) and has expanded it into a full concept of change. The basis of this change is time as it is humanized by the fictions that both take part in and cause change. Like its symbol, the West Wind in Canto X, time is both the creator and destroyer of Being. Through time, life is refreshed in the changes that occur both in the exterior, empirical world and in the interior, psychic world. This fusion of exterior and interior time is illustrated by the scene described in Canto X. As Doggett points out, "the water of the lake becomes a metaphor for the consciousness"[71] as it evolves the "artificial things," the images of the imagination. The image of the West Wind operates on both a literal level (a force that changes the scene described) and a symbolic level ("a will to change / A will to make iris frettings on the blank" [CP, 397]). The wind then is, in

---

71. Doggett, p. 114.

Shelley's sense (as Harold Bloom suggests), a figure for the deep structure of time.

The effect of time requires "a will to change, a necessitous / And present way, a presentation, a kind / Of volatile world, too constant to be denied" (CP, 397). The full understanding of Stevens's concept of change includes both "the casual" transformation of the "volatile" world (which "is not enough" [CP, 397]) and the purposeful transformation of creative activity. Each transformation is a new beginning that takes the participant back to the start of a new duration, as he begins a new fiction with the original intuition of the "first idea." The interrelation of Being of man and Being of the world within time is fully suggested by the similarity wherein

> The freshness of transformation is

> The freshness of the world. It is our own,
> It is ourselves, the freshness of ourselves. . . .
>   (CP, 397–98)

The basis of change or rather the basis of Stevens's aesthetic of change is not only that time transforms (self-evident and inevitable) but that Being in time is partaking in the transformations by actively projecting possibilities (creating fictions) that explain the relation of Being to time. More clearly, each act of projection tends to make human (and thus understandable) the poet's sense of time as the basis of change. What might have seemed on the surface a simplistic platitude turns out to be a fully articulated aesthetic of time that is incorporated into the poetry of Being.

It Must Give Pleasure

The final part of "Notes Toward a Supreme Fiction" brings together the processes and concepts that have been described in "It Must Be Abstract" and "It Must Change."

The value of any fiction is neither its truth content (though Stevens would not deny a kind of truth to his fictions) nor the reality principle, although both of these criteria are used to measure philosophical speculation. In a way that is similar to Freud's theory of the unconscious, Stevens's theory of the poetry of Being is measured by the pleasure it makes possible. The pleasure comes, as Blackmur suggests, "from access to being,"[72] which begins a kind of aesthetic of pleasure in much the same way that Stevens's "Esthétique du Mal" describes a peculiarly existential "aperçu" of pain.[73] Both pleasure and pain are fully human in Stevens's theory, and together they expand the poetry of Being to include a more comprehensive view of human existence. But, as I have insisted before, Stevens's view is not a philosophy of existence.[74] More properly speaking, I think Stevens attempts to project an aesthetic of existence, since he believed that "the aesthetic order includes all other orders but is not limited to them" (OP, 166). But, like Heidegger's philosophy of Being, Stevens's "poetry of Being" never denies the essential finite quality of existence.

"It Must Give Pleasure" opens with a rejection of the "facile exercise" (CP, 398) of worship of dead myths, which is contrasted with the new poetic process in a suc-

---

72. Blackmur, "Wallace Stevens: An Abstraction Blooded," p. 214.
73. Stevens defines his own sense of the title "Esthétique du Mal" when he writes "I am thinking of aesthetics as the equivalent of *aperçus*, which seems to have been the original meaning. I don't know what would happen if anybody tried to systematize the subject, but I haven't tried" (*Letters*, 469).
74. Here, I am following the distinction between philosophy and poetry that Stevens made numerous times. I am also followwng the suggestion of James Baird that the word *existentialist* really doesn't apply to Stevens just as it doesn't apply to Heidegger. (*The Dome and the Rock*, p. 268). I do not agree, though, with everything that Baird has to say about ontology, and I will discuss our differences more fully below. Baird's notions about Being, existence, time, and phenomenology all show a familiarity with European philosophy which, no doubt, comes from his reading of Jean Wahl's *Les Philosophes de l'existence*. While Wahl is interesting as a philosopher, he has his own peculiar ideas, some of which distort Heidegger as well as Jaspers and Husserl. Baird mentions Stevens's friendship with Wahl as a way of justifying using some of Wahl's distinctions and terms (see pp. 269–70).

cinct juxtaposition of the theory of myth and the theory of
fiction. After this introduction to the idea of pleasure as it
is to be conceived in fictions, the narrator presents three
mythic parables, each of which suggests a new way of seeing opposing female and male principles of the myth of
creation.[75] In Cantos II, III and IV, the mythic elements
are either decreated or else explicitly denied.[76] They may,
as a number of critics insist, suggest paradigms for the
process of creation, but in each of the examples it is precisely at those points where the paradigm suggests a
mythic origin that it is attacked by the narrator. Following
Cantos II and III, which effectively deflate the mythic
elements of female and male principles, the narrator relates the "mystic marriage" of a new couple who are fully
human and whose union provides a definitive way of explaining Stevens's marriage motif as it is developed in
"Notes." The central portion of "It Must Give Pleasure" is
the poet's explanation of the failure of Canon Aspirin.
The parable of the Canon Aspirin is described in Cantos
V–VII. He is Stevens's final personification of the hero of
the imagination in "Notes Toward a Supreme Fiction."
His attempts to transcend human spatial and temporal
limits fail, not because as a human character he must fail,[77]
but rather because his assumptions about the nature of the
mind and the nature of the world remain unchanged even
though he has perceived the unity of mind and world. He is
certainly more admirable than many of Stevens's fictive
men of imagination, even though he is "surpassed by the

---

75. For a complete account of the structures of the myth of creation, see
Mircea Eliade's *Myth and Reality,* trans. Willard R. Trask (New York, 1963), pp.
21–53.
76. While few of the commentaries on these passages have suggested certain
mythic elements, only Ronald Sukenick, pp. 151–54, and Roy Harvey Pearce,
p. 398, recognize the decreation that is being performed.
77. Harold Bloom, p. 91, writes that the Canon is fully admirable and is like
"that brave man, our abstraction of the sun" without explaining what that means.
He then concludes that "the Canon is the cure for our current headache of
unreality" (p. 91), thus playing upon the word aspirin, but distorting the meaning of the fable.

narrator,"[78] who corrects the errors of imposition that result
from the Canon's refusal to accept the vision of "the
whole, / The complicate, the amassing harmony" (CP,
403). I take Cantos VIII and IX to be the central statements of "It Must Give Pleasure," for in these cantos the
poet brings together all the elements of the poetry of
Being into a unified aesthetic of existence.

I want to look briefly at the three mythic parables (Cantos II, III, and IV), then explicate the Canon Aspirin
group to show how Stevens, through a description of
Canon Aspirin's adventures in speculation, reaches the
fullest statement of the poetry of Being, an aesthetic of
existence. In Canto VIII the narrator affirms the possibility of vision that is beyond the limits of rational thought.
This vision is expressed in fictive projections, but each
vision forms the core of the poet's affirmation of the
poetry of Being, a poetry made possible by the intuition of
the "first idea" that was brought up in "It Must Be
Abstract."

In Canto I, the ritual repetitions of joy in the worship of
outworn beliefs (whether these are mythic or religious) are
contrasted to the joys of individual experience, which are
both more valuable and more difficult. As Stevens has insisted since "Sunday Morning," the pleasures of belief in
myths are no longer valid possibilities since "the death of
one god is the death of all" (CP, 381) and "Phoebus is
dead."

Thus, for Stevens,

> . . . The difficultest rigor is forthwith,
> On the image of what we see, to catch from that
>
> Irrational moment its unreasoning,
> As when the sun comes rising, when the sea
> Clears deeply, when the moon hangs on the wall

---

78. Bloom, p. 91.

Of heaven-haven. These are not things transformed.
Yet we are shaken by them as if they were.
We reason about them with a later reason.
                                                  (CP, 398–99)

The narrator returns to the "first idea" of "It Must Be
Abstract" as he describes the irrational moment of vision
that discloses the "inconceivable idea" of the sun (i.e., the
Being of the sun). What is perceived is what is there ("not
transformed") and yet the ecstasy of the vision moves the
poet as if a metamorphosis had taken place. The last line
introduces Stevens's idea of memory ("later reason")
which he adds to his theory of a poetry of Being. His
concept of "memory" is scarcely a Wordsworthian "emotion recollected in tranquillity." Rather, it is the imaginative recognition of the possibilities of past experience.[79]
Like Heidegger's *Dasein,* Stevens's poet is not a man without a past. He actively recalls and repeats the possibilities
of past experience and, by this process of active (rather
than tranquil) repetition, brings to mind, through the decreative power of the imagination, aspects of his past that
he can project toward the future in a new fiction.

After suggesting the function of the past in the creative
act, the poet moves, in Canto II, to a parable of the "Blue
Woman." She rejects the imaginative "late plurals" by
which myth and religion attempt to make permanent the
temporal quality of experience. "It was enough for her
that she remembered" (CP, 399) that the things she saw
were intuited in their Being, without the distortion of the
mythic imagination. There was no need to explain the
clouds, the waves, the blossoms, and the summer season in
terms of some larger cosmic purpose. Neither space nor

---

79. Stevens writes that this passage "validated the memory. In the memory,
(the past, the routine, the mechanism) there had always been a place for
everything . . . (*Letters,* 444). Stevens implies that the process of decreation is the
act that "validated" the memory and made possible an "intensity expressible in
terms of coldness and clearness" (*Letters,* 444).

time for the "blue woman" was purposive as each is in myth. Thus, while she does represent the female creative force, she is not a "mythical Venus" or the moon, as some critics have claimed.[80] Rather, she is the naked power of the imagination, which will have none of mythic transformations that previous fictions have constructed. Her function is primarily decreative. She sees clearly and names what she sees. She thus fulfills the admonition of the first cantos of "It Must Be Abstract" to "see again with an ignorant eye" (CP, 380) and, from this seeing, to establish the Being of what she sees by naming it. Thus she

> . . . looked and from her window named
>
> The corals of the dogwood, cold and clear,
> Cold, coldly delineating, being real,
> Clear and, except for the eye, without intrusion.
>   (CP, 399–400)

The whole theory of the phenomenological intuition suggested in "It Must Be Abstract" is based on the ability of the "ignorant eye" to add nothing to what is seen. This method of seeing permits the Being of the thing to show itself. The processes of "seeing" and "naming" that were implied in the first canto of "It Must Be Abstract" are projected in this passage as possibilities for memory as well as for immediate vision.

With this process of seeing, the narrator looks, in Canto III, at "the lasting visage in the lasting bush" (CP, 400) and sees the face of a dead god. The first five tercets present a rather decimating portrait, since the new way of seeing illustrated by the "blue woman" detects the flaws that mar the grandeur of the face of God.[81] The portrait starts with

---

80. For a reading of the "blue woman" as a Venus figure, see Bertholf, pp. 241–43. For a reading of the "blue woman" as the moon, see Harold Bloom, p. 89.

81. Thus, while critics like Joseph N. Riddel end up crying for help, it is clear that the processes demonstrated make this poem considerably less difficult than Riddel would like to make it. See Riddel, p. 180.

"A face of stone in an unending red" (CP, 400) and from
that point the narrator proceeds to decreate the visage to
"red-in-red repetitions never going / Away, a little rusty, a
little rouged . . . An effulgence faded, dull cornelian / Too
venerably used" (CP, 400). The vision of the "blue woman"
is put to use in this image from the racial or mythic memory that has served as a paradigm for the countless representations of the face of God in paintings, sculpture, and
literature. Like the statue of General Du Puy in Canto III
of "It Must Change," this face has grown stale in its
stonelike refusal of change. The decreation of the god-
head is completed by the allusion to an Orphic-Christ
figure ("A dead shepherd brought tremendous chords
from hell / And bade the sheep carouse" (CP, 400). In
myth ("Or so they said"), the figure of the shepherd
brought the old deity to a ritual end by celebrating the
rebirth of a new order. The ritual resurrection is recognized by the "children in love with them" (apparently in
love with both the old god and the new), who thus
"brought / Early flowers and scattered them about, no two
alike" (CP, 400). Both the sheep and the children are traditional Christian and mythic symbols for the disciples, who
by scattering "early flowers" (testaments or poems), attest
to their belief in the permanence of both the deity and the
cyclical process of death and rebirth.[82] However, like the
"Blue Woman," in Canto II, the narrator in Canto IV
reflects with an "ignorant eye" upon these mythic patterns:

> We reason of these things with later reason
> And we make of what we see, what we see clearly
> And have seen, a place dependent on ourselves.
> (CP, 401)

More clearly, the phenomenological method of percep-

---

82. My reading of the "dead shepherd" as a suggestion of the Christ-Orphic
figure in myth and religion is the standard reading; see Cambon, p. 111; Riddel,
p. 180; Sukenick, p. 154; Bloom, p. 90; Brown, p. 259.

tion creates our present world, not through reconstruc-
tions of mythologies, but through the clear sight of present
vision and the selective process of an actively decreating
memory. Both the past and the present are repeated only
to the extent that they will be useful for the projections
toward the future created in our fictions.

Having related the two parables of Cantos II and III,
the narrator then illustrates the statement that place, like
time, is dependent on the self. In this parable, the male
and female figures are brought together in a marriage.
But neither the male nor the female is directly associated
with the male and female myths that were rejected in Cantos II and III. Their marriage is not accomplished
through mutual physical attraction ("Anon / We loved but
would no marriage make" [CP, 401]) nor by the repetition
of the ritual ceremony of marriage ("Anon / The one refused the other one to take, / Foreswore the sipping of the
marriage wine" [CP, 401]), which was denied in Canto I.
Rather, the union was "a mystic marriage in Catawba" (CP,
401), in which love of place brings the male and female
creative forces together. This is a union that does not ask
for identity in fusion or a total submission of individuality.
Rather, it is a union that affirms a love of earth, a love of
the physical condition of human existence.

> Each must the other take as sign, short sign
> To stop the whirlwind, balk the elements
> (CP, 401)

because, as Harold Bloom suggests, "this is a marriage
between sun and moon, the natural meeting that shatters
the context of nature. But it remains a confrontation in
this world, the human making choice of a human self."[83]

> They married well because the marriage-place
> Was what they loved. It was neither heaven nor hell.
> They were love's characters come face to face.
> (CP, 401)

---

83. Bloom, p. 90.

The love and complete acceptance of earth ("neither heaven nor hell") sanctifies the natural love of man and woman. From this union, as Bloom continues, "proceeds the supreme fiction" which, like the fruitful union of opposites (as in "It Must Change," Canto IV), initiates as well as takes part in change.[84] Time in such a union is recorded at the midpoint of duration for, in Stevens's concept of time, the middle is the point of fulfillment. The rejection of myth implies the creation of a fiction that will serve the same kind of purpose for poetry: that is, a fiction that will suggest the full meanings of mythic paradigms without implying their temporal and religious explanations. Thus, in Stevens's fiction, the union of opposites occurs between the beginning and end of his fictional structure of time: the midpoint of the day in the midpoint of summer, which is the middle of Stevens's year. Each of these points in the temporal cycle suggests the middle of the duration of existence, the time in which any pleasurable fulfillment must take place. The difference between this kind of temporal structure and that of mythology is clearly stated by Mircea Eliade:

> It is the divine hierogamy, which took place *in illo tempore,* that made human sexual union possible. The union between the god and goddess occurs in an atemporal instant, in an eternal present whereas sexual unions between human beings—when they are not ritual union—take place in duration, in profane time.[85]

At the midpoint, both space (the earth) and time (change) are present and the "mystic marriage" is consummated in the present. A fully mystic marriage would take place outside of time, but for Stevens, time ends at the end of the duration, only to begin again. The mythical *in illo tempore* is not suggested or stated, for this fictive marriage is fully human: "They were love's characters come face to face" (CP, 401).

---

84. *Ibid.*
85. *The Sacred and the Profane,* p. 89.

Following the marriage, the way is cleared for an understanding of the adventures of the Canon Aspirin in Cantos V, VI, and VII. Much has been made of the fable of the Canon Aspirin who has been called "like Milton's Satan,"[86] and a figure "who comes as close to a true self-portrait of Stevens as we will find in the poetry."[87] Both interpretations have missed the point of the entire fable. For the most part, the commentaries on these cantos tend to make entirely too much of the figure of the Canon Aspirin.[88] I take the fable of this attractive character to be an illustration of one of the limits of creative imagination.

In Canto V, the Canon Aspirin is contrasted to his sister. He represents Stevens's man of capable imagination, a sophisticated, speculative thinker. His ability to appreciate the utter realism of his sister who, he declares, lives in "a sensible ecstacy" (CP, 401), marks him as a connoisseur of opposites. For the Canon, the connotations of "sensible" tell us much about both his sophistication and his sister's lack of it. She is very nearly like a peasant in her mundane existence.[89] Where her creations are the purely physical products of the body (her daughters) and are dressed plainly as a reflection of their mother's poverty of the imagination, Canon Aspirin's creations are fully metaphysical (angel's "wings") and are decorated rather than dressed. Where the Canon's sister thinks of night as a fitting period for dreamless sleep ("by rejecting dreams"), he conceives night as the appropriate time for metaphysical speculations.

---

86. See, for example, Nassar, p. 212.
87. Nassar, p. 211.
88. I am indebted to Riddel whose sensibleness in reading the Canon Aspirin poems is a refreshing breath of air. Riddel writes that the Canon is "a dreamer of Angels [who] has the capacity to live beyond his canonical law, to grasp the first idea. But when he has it he awakens to the world and makes his canonical choice—he submits his experience to the formal ordering of dogma. His order violates his experience" (p. 182).
89. Nassar, p. 212, claims that the sister "is the interior paramour" while Bloom claims that the sister "is the moon" (pp. 90–91).

> When at long midnight the Canon came to sleep
> And normal things had yawned themselves away,
> The nothingness was a nakedness, a point,
>
> Beyond which fact could not progress as fact.
>   (CP, 402)

As the Canon begins his speculations, he has reached
the point in time between the end of one day and the
beginning of the next. Rather than the midpoint of duration, between beginning and end (between birth and
death), the Canon is between end and beginning, a period
when, in Stevens's theory of time, change stops in the same
way that a pendulum must stop before it can go the other
way. During that moment, fact can go no further because
it is at its temporal limit. The Canon's speculations are
then forced inward toward the limit of thought. He travels
toward "the very material of his mind" (CP, 403).

Within his own mind, he conceived "night's pale illumination" (the imagination's beginnings),

> So that he was the ascending wings he saw
> And moved on them in orbits' outer stars
> Descending to the children's bed, on which
>
> They lay. Forth then with huge pathetic force
> Straight to the utmost crown of night he flew.
> The nothingness was a nakedness, a point
>
> Beyond which thought could not progress as thought.
>   (CP, 403)

Having reached the end of fact, he then imagines the end
of thought to be "a point" of nothingness like Heidegger's
nonbeing (*das Nicht*). But as the parallel sentences and
identical diction have already suggested, the end point of
fact and the end point of thought are the same. For, as
Stevens writes in his notebook, "to be at the end of fact is
not to be at the beginning of the imagination, it is to be at

the end of both" (OP, 175). Thus, the attempt to imagine a different limit requires "huge pathetic force," for the Canon Aspirin has pathetically conceived a difference between mind and world, between imagination and reality.

At the barrier of thought, he finds himself faced with a choice:

> He had to choose. But it was not a choice
> Between excluding things. It was not a choice
> Between, but of. He chose to include the things
> That in each other are included, the whole,
> The complicate, the amassing harmony.
>
> (CP, 403)

His choice then was to include both the world and the mind, both "fact" and "thought." But, as the narrator implies, where the Canon thought himself forced to choose, there was no choice possible, since reality and imagination are united in the "muddy centre" of Being. The Canon's choice then is false, because it presumes an inherent division between opposing forces. The point of the fable is that while the Canon's decision to include "the whole, /
The complicate, the amassing harmony" is correct, it is made for the wrong reasons and from the wrong assumptions. The old idea of a division between mind and world is still maintained by the Canon, in spite of his decision to include each within a larger whole.

Thus in Canto VII, having made the right choice, the Canon does not realize the full meaning of what he has chosen. He immediately attempts to assert his reason as if the world were still an object or utensil and not part of himself.[90]

> He imposes orders as he thinks of them.
> As the fox and snake do. It is a brave affair.
>
> (CP, 403)

---

90. Sukenick, p. 209, writes that the "he" of Canto VII "is not demonstrably Canon Aspirin, the problems concerning whom have, on the contrary, been

Even though the Canon has experienced the vision of
"the amassing harmony" of the "muddy centre" of Being,
he is unable to make the leap of apprehension necessary to
throw aside the habitual Cartesian dualism. He fails to
realize that "to impose is not / To discover" (CP, 403). At
this point the narrator provides the corrective to the fable
of the Canon Aspirin. The essential lesson of the corrective is the difference between the actual and the possible.
For the Canon, the possibility revealed in the vision of
unity is confused with the actuality of his everyday experience. For the poet of the supreme fiction, the projection of
possible modes of Being is still more important than descriptions of fact. Thus the possibility of discovery is the
lesson of vision.

> To discover an order as of
> A season, to discover summer and know it,
>
> To discover winter and know it well, to find,
> Not to impose, not to have reasoned at all,
> Out of nothing to have come on major weather,
>
> It is possible, possible, possible. It must
> Be possible. It must be that in time
> The real will from its crude compoundings come,
>
> Seeming, at first, like a beast disgorged, unlike,
> Warmed by a desperate milk. To find the real,
> To be stripped of every fiction except one,
>
> The fiction of an absolute—Angel,
> Be silent in your luminous cloud and hear
> The luminous melody of proper sound.
> (CP, 403–4)

The lesson of this passage is directed at the angel that
the Canon Aspirin imagined himself to be in Canto VI.

---

resolved in VI." This is an interesting claim, but it ignores the sequence of the
poems and the reference to the angel in VII, which ties VI and VII together.

Here the narrator reaffirms the fortuitous nature of the disclosure of Being that Stevens first described in *Parts of a World*. The disclosure of Being is the essential beginning of the poetry of Being and it is consistently described as a purely intuitive apprehension, one that is neither imposed nor reasoned ("not to have reasoned at all"). The moods that lead to this disclosure are preconceptual and, like Heidegger's concept of *Befindlichkeit* (the "state of mind" in which one finds oneself through mood), these moods make possible a kind of knowledge that is beyond the limits of cognition. Like the freed man of the poem "The Latest Freed Man," the narrator of this passage insists that the disclosure comes "out of nothing" to reveal "major weather."

The "real" that will be discovered "in time" is not a thing, but the presence of the thing.[91] The beginning of the poetry of Being is projected here as the possibility of discovering the "amassing harmony" that is envisioned through the disclosure of Being. By stripping the mind of every fiction but the one that is sought, "the fiction of an absolute," the poet will partake of the vision of the center, the source of both the imagination and reality. This source, though not recognizable as a thing ("like a beast disgorged, unlike"), will nevertheless be made accessible. The difference between *an* absolute and *the* absolute is, as Stevens emphasized in "Extracts from Addresses to the Academy of Fine Ideas," "that difference between *the* and *an*" (CP, 255), the difference, then, between *the* absolute of the idealists, transcendentalists, and mystics (the unchanging, timeless essence) and the fiction of *an* absolute (a possible source that is present, changing, and finite).

Having corrected the errors of the Canon Aspirin, the narrator then begins a meditation of the function of poetry of Being when he asks in Canto IX if he is not part

---

91. Of all Stevens's critics, only Nassar claims, pp. 213–14, that man cannot ever experience these moments of discovery. They are not actual, and for Nassar they are not even possible because they are incorrigibly romantic, which is a problem for his thesis.

of his fictions. Referring to the angel of Canto VI, the narrator asks "Is it he or is it I that experience this?" (CP, 404). If the angel that he creates is satisfied with the joy of free flight in "deep space," is the poet less satisfied, having created the angel? The point of these questions is not whether creator and created are identical, but whether the pleasures of the fiction are experienced by the creator. The answer to this interrogation points to another source of pleasure.

Throughout the cantos of "It Must Give Pleasure," the narrator has told the parables of pleasure. When he appears to ask, at this point, if these are not affirmations of the joy of creative power, he is beginning, through a rhetoric of questions that act as assertions, to formulate a profoundly humanistic statement of the goal of the poetry of Being.

> Is it I then that keep saying there is an hour
> Filled with expressible bliss, in which I have
>
> No need, am happy, forget need's golden hand,
> Am satisfied without solacing majesty. . . .
>   (CP, 404–5)

In posing this question, the narrator refers to the "times of inherent excellence" (CP, 386) and to the "accessible bliss" (CP, 395) where he has expressed the joy of the visionary experience. In each case the ecstatic experience was a discovery rather than an imposition, a fortuitous event rather than the result of rational planning, and most important, a fully temporal and finite experience rather than the "solacing majesty" of mystical or religious experience. Thus he continues:

> And if there is an hour there is a day,
> There is a month, a year, a time
> In which majesty is a mirror of the self:
> I have not but I am and as I am, I am.
>   (CP, 405)

The actual moment of disclosure expands temporally to the fullest possible duration—the finite duration of existence—one interpretation of the word *time*. The projected expansion in time, then, is again from actual time to possible time, wherein the imagined joy is but a mirror of the actual joy of the self. The source of joy in creation is fulfillment of Being, a fulfillment that is projected into the future as a necessary part of an aesthetic of existence. The final line summarizes Heidegger's distinction between the actual existence of Being-in-the-world, which is like having a world, and the potential existence that is projected in each of *Dasein*'s possible modes of Being. Stevens realizes that the conditional "as" of the fictive mode ("as I am") can become identical to Being itself, the "I am" that is asserted. The full pleasure of creation is the fulfillment of Being in the fiction. Heidegger's *Dasein* has nothing but its own projections of possible ways of Being. In each of these projections, it does not establish anything like self-definition. Rather, it establishes its Being as a process of projection. Being for Heidegger is always Being-possible (*Sein-können*) in the future. There seems to be little chance of present pleasure. Stevens's statement explicitly announces that the creation of self that takes place in the creative act is an assertion of fulfilled Being.

> These external regions, what do we fill them with
> Except reflections, the escapades of death,
> Cinderella fulfilling herself beneath the roof?
>   (CP, 405)

While the fictive "mundos" are simply reflections (both in the sense of speculations and in the sense of double images) of *Sein-zum-Tode* ("the escapades of death"), they fulfill the potential of Being in the same way that Cinderella might become what she has projected for herself without the help of a fairy godmother.

The narrator continues his speculations on the nature of aesthetic pleasure in Canto IX. Having proposed one way in which fictions make fulfillment possible, thereby mitigating the poverty of existence, he then realizes, in a kind of sudden leap, the full power of the poetry of Being, and in so doing, provides another distinction between aesthetics and philosophy. Like the bird's singing, which was rejected in Canto VIII of "It Must Change," the poet's endless processes of creation and decreation are seen as repetitious. Yet they are good, for they form an occupation. If this were all that was implied in this passage, it would hardly be worth commenting on, and several of Stevens's critics have skipped this entire canto.[92] But there is more involved in his richly repetitious meditation on repetition than simply the assertion that it keeps the mind occupied. Each process of creation becomes

> A thing final in itself and, therefore, good:
> One of the vast repetitions final in
> Themselves and, therefore, good, the going round
>
> And round and round, the merely going round
> Until merely going round is a final good,
> The way wine comes at a table in a wood.
>
> And we enjoy like men, the way a leaf
> Above the table spins its constant spin,
> So that we look at it with pleasure, look
>
> At it spinning its eccentric measure. Perhaps,
> The man-hero is not the exceptional monster,
> But he that of repetition is most master.
>
>   (CP, 405–6)

The basis of the pleasure in repetition is the human comprehension of time, wherein, as Kermode writes, the idea of endless time, the conception of time without beginning or end, "just one damn thing after another," is an unbearable concept.[93] This is the beginning of the expla-

----

92. For example, Bloom, p. 95, writes that "the rest is epilogue," and dismisses the final two cantos with a few sentences.
93. *The Sense of an Ending*, p. 47.

nation of the time concepts that archaic man invented when he invented myths which, as Eliade explains, were his way of controlling the terror of history and the certainty of annihilation. The paradigmatic myths that man created were all concerned with inventing a concept of time wherein the beginning and the end of time could be ritually reenacted in order to give man a way to experience time as a meaningful duration.[94]

As Stevens has maintained since "Sunday Morning," the modern equivalent of the mythic experience of time is not the creation of new myths of eternal return, *in illo tempore* and eternity. In place of myth, the modern mind creates fictions wherein time is again made meaningful with a beginning, middle, and end. The fiction makes sense of the experience of time, whether this fiction takes the shape of the entire human life-span (which is essentially the way *Dasein* must conceive of its existence as *Sein-zum-Tode*) or the shape of Stevens's seasons of the imagination, wherein the temporal changes of the creative process are visualized as a recurrent cycle with beginning, middle, and end. Each of Stevens's fictions illustrates a theory of human time where the repetition of the process of creation is always possible. Furthermore, the poet can take pleasure in each completed period of creative activity, for each creation both takes part in and is an example of time as a duration. Each creation makes time meaningful. Since the poet can conceive of the difference between temporal existence and temporal duration, he can create fictive durations that will be self-fulfilling and hence pleasurable. The crucial difference between Heidegger's concepts of Being and time and Stevens's aesthetic of Being and time is that Stevens can project and then fulfill his projection. The conscious use of fictions permits Stevens to project pleasure from his activity whereas the satisfactions of Heidegger's *Dasein* seem rather limited. When the fundamental duration is

---

94. *Cosmos and History*, pp. 18–19.

that of human existence, the possible fulfillment promised by the end of the duration is scarcely something to be anticipated with pleasure. For Heidegger, the only pleasure, or rather the source of pleasure, is access to Being, but this access is always a potential, placed in the future. The possibility of fulfilled Being for *Dasein* is death. The difference, then, between the philosophy of Being and the poetry of Being is best defined by Stevens's fiction of fulfilled Being, which is neither available nor important to philosophy. A fiction that has numerous endings and hence numerous fulfillments can achieve ends that Heidegger's *Dasein* (for which there is only one end) cannot. The idea of projecting all one's possibilities toward an end that is, as Stevens writes, "absolute and without memorial" may be a realistic way of explaining human existence. But it leaves out the possibility of attaining satisfaction and fulfillment within the duration of existence.

At the end of "Notes Toward a Supreme Fiction," Stevens proposes the fitting end to his meditation of an aesthetic of existence: the pleasure that comes from fulfilling the theory in the actual poetic experiences of the poems. After this point in Stevens's development, in the late poems of *Transport to Summer, The Auroras of Autumn,* and "The Rock," the poetry of Being will rarely develop issues that are not already suggested, proposed, or implied in "Notes Toward a Supreme Fiction." In this sense, the aesthetic proposed in "Notes" is the central statement of Stevens's poetic, and each of the later poems can be seen as a development of the "aesthetic of existence" that Stevens projects in this poem.

7

After the Outlines of Being: Its Expressions

In "Notes Toward a Supreme Fiction" Stevens rehearsed the possible criteria of a new aesthetic that proposed the possibility of a "poetry of Being." In doing so, he refined and expanded the characteristics of the disclosure of Being that he had expressed in *Parts of a World*. But it is one thing to propose a poetry of Being and quite another to express in the poems the modes of the poet's vision of Being. The major concerns of the later poems are the ways of fulfilling these proposals in the poetry. These later poems, collected in *Transport to Summer, The Auroras of Autumn,* and *The Rock,*[1] have been the subject of a great deal of critical disagreement. For both the early reviewers of the separate volumes and the later critics, who were able to look at the complete development of the poetry from beginning to the end, the later poetry remained something

---

1. While both *Transport to Summer* and *The Auroras of Autumn* were published as separate editions by Alfred Knopf in 1947 and 1950 respectively, *The Rock* constituted the final section of *The Collected Poems of Wallace Stevens* and was not published separately as a volume, though many of the poems in the last section were published individually in journals and little magazines.

of an enigma. The range of opinion about it varies from Randall Jarrell's early review, which found that the later Stevens resembled "G. E. Moore at the spinet,"[2] to Louis Martz's contention that the later poetry develops a meditational mode that is very similar to the meditative poems of the seventeenth-century religious poets.[3] While both Jarrell and Martz build adequate cases for their conflicting arguments, neither has managed to account for the difficult and sometimes obscure qualities of the later verse. Nor does either Jarrell or Martz attempt to explain why Stevens's later poetry is different from the earlier verse. For while it is the consensus of Stevens's recent critics that the late poetry decidedly did change, in spite of the claims of Yvor Winters, Ronald Sukenick, and Robert Pack,[4] neither the early critics nor the more recent commentators provide an adequate explanation of the difficult later

---

2. Randall Jarrell, "Reflections on Wallace Stevens," *Partisan Review* 17 (May–June 1951): 341–42. Reprinted in Jarrell's *Poetry and the Age* (New York, 1953), pp. 121–34.

3. Martz, "Wallace Stevens: The World as Meditation," in *Literature and Belief: The English Institute Essays for 1957*, ed. M. H. Abrams (New York, 1958), pp. 139–65. Reprinted in *Wallace Stevens: A Collection of Critical Essays*, ed. Marie Borroff (Englewood Cliffs, N.J., 1963), pp. 133–50.

4. All three of these critics argue that Stevens is more or less the same poet who writes the same kind of poetry from 1930 on. In fact, each of these critics sees the poetry of Stevens growing progressively worse, more abstract, and more "hedonistic," to use Winters's term. See Yvor Winters, "Wallace Stevens, or the Hedonist's Progress," *In Defense of Reason* (Denver, 1943), pp. 431–59; Ronald Sukenick, *Wallace Stevens: Musing the Obscure* (New York, 1967; paperback ed., 1967), pp. 2–10; and Robert Pack, *Wallace Stevens: An Approach to his Poetry and Thought* (New Brunswick, N. J., 1958), pp. 3–18. For other views of the later poetry that are more in line with the consensus, see particularly Roy Harvey Pearce, *The Continuity of American Poetry* (Princeton, N. J., 1961; paperback ed., 1965), pp. 389–419; Roy Harvey Pearce "The Last Lesson of the Master," in *The Act of the Mind: Essays on the Poetry of Wallace Stevens*, ed. R. H. Pearce and J. Hillis Miller (Baltimore, Md., 1965), pp. 121–42; Joseph N. Riddel, *The Clairvoyant Eye: The Poetry and Poetics of Wallace Stevens* (Baton Rouge, La., 1965; paperback ed., 1967), pp. 187–89, 224–26; J. Hillis Miller, *Poets of Reality: Six Twentieth Century Writers* (Cambridge, Mass., 1966), pp. 217–84; Howard Nemerov, "The Poetry of Wallace Stevens," *Sewanee Review* 65 (Winter 1957): 1–14; and Mildred Hartsock, "Wallace Stevens and the Rock," *Personalist* 42 (Winter 1961): 71–73. While none of the critics cited above is in complete agreement about the nature, value, causes, or extent of the change or development in Stevens's later poetry, they do agree that there are differences between the Stevens of *Harmonium* and the Stevens of *The Auroras of Autumn* and "The Rock."

period of his verse.[5] I want to use the proposals of "Notes Toward a Supreme Fiction" as a guide in tracing the development of three related aspects of Stevens's poetry of Being in the later poetry. Each of the elements that I discuss has numerous antecedents in Martin Heidegger's studies of the relation between language and Being.[6] As I develop my discussion and compare Stevens's treatment of the problem of expressing his sense of Being, his notion of the nothingness, and the late aesthetic that defines poetry as a projected mode of Being with similar ideas from Heidegger, I want to pay close attention to Stevens's concept of time as it was expressed in "Notes Toward a Supreme Fiction." I hope to make clear how Stevens incorporates his own sense of temporality into his poetry. Time, in Stevens, is the essential form in which Being is revealed. A clear account of the relation of time and Being in Stevens's poetry provides an explanation that clarifies the obscurities of his later poetry. As in the previous chapter, I will use the theories and concepts of Heidegger's meditations on Being and poetry to explain the development of Stevens's later verse and to provide a way of understanding the typical modes of the poetry of Being.

The last poems of Wallace Stevens move in the seasonal sequence that was proposed in "Notes Toward a Supreme Fiction." The seasonal and diurnal cycles serve as a paradigm of the cycle of creative activity (or, more clearly,

---

5. The most complete and persuasive accounts of Stevens's later poetry are those of Pearce, Miller, Riddel, and Jarrell cited above. Two other studies that are especially perceptive, although neither intends more than a limited explanation of one or two points of development, are Ralph J. Mills, "Wallace Stevens: The Image of the Rock," *Accent* 17 (Spring 1958): 75–89. Reprinted in *Wallace Stevens: A Collection of Critical Essays*, ed. Marie Borroff (Englewood Cliffs, N.J., 1963), pp. 96–110; and Marjorie Perloff, "Irony in Wallace Stevens' *The Rock*," *American Literature* 36 (November 1964): 327–42.

6. While Heidegger begins his study of the relation of language and Being in *Sein und Zeit*, pp. 160–67, 269–73, 406–8, the specific relations between Being and poetry are analyzed in the Hölderlin studies collected in *Erläuterungen zu Hölderlins Dichtung* (Frankfurt, 1944) and later in *Holzwege* (Frankfurt, 1950), where other studies of poetry appear.

these natural temporal revolutions are metaphors for the cycles of the imagination). The final proposal of "Notes" was a positive affirmation of the pleasure of an aesthetic of Being wherein the poet could project possibilities of Being that could be fulfilled in fictions.

I begin with "Credences of Summer." It is a fairly long poem written in 1947, five years after the completion of "Notes Toward a Supreme Fiction," and is the high point of *Transport to Summer*. It fulfills two of the propositions of "Notes Toward a Supreme Fiction." First, it is an example that substantiates the theory of fulfillment in the fictions that Stevens had proposed in the last three sections of "It Must Give Pleasure." In "Credences of Summer" the poet expresses the experience of fulfilled Being that was presented but not realized in "Notes." Second, "Credences of Summer" introduces one of the crucial images of the later poetry, the image of the rock, which is expanded through the final stages of Stevens's development.[7] In the last poem I will discuss, "The Rock," which is the title poem of the final section of the *Collected Poems,* the image of the rock is fully formed as one of the final images of Being itself. "Credences of Summer" names the result of fulfilled Being (the "Credences") and establishes summer as the season of the imagination's fulfillment. The opening section presents the central motif of the poem: the nature of fulfilled Being at the apogee of the imagination's cycle:

> Now in midsummer come and all fools slaughtered
> And spring's infuriations over and a long way

---

7. For other readings of "Credences of Summer" see especially Frank Doggett, *Stevens' Poetry of Thought* (Baltimore, Md., 1966; paperback ed., 1966), pp. 176–78, 196–97; John J. Enck, *Wallace Stevens: Images and Judgments* (Carbondale, Ill., 1964), pp. 175–77; Frank Kermode, *Wallace Stevens* (Edinburgh, 1960; paperback ed., New York, 1961), pp. 106–7; Ralph J. Mills, Jr., pp. 98–102; Eugene Paul Nassar, *Wallace Stevens: An Anatomy of Figuration* (Philadelphia, 1965), pp. 174–78; James Baird, *The Dome and the Rock: Structure in the Poetry of Wallace Stevens* (Baltimore, Md., 1968), pp. 66, 98–100, 103, 108, 164–65, 240; Henry W. Wells, *Introduction to Wallace Stevens* (Bloomington, Ind., 1964), pp. 81–84; Riddel, pp. 218–23.

To the first autumnal inhalations, young broods
Are in the grass, the roses are heavy with a weight
Of fragrance and the mind lays by its trouble.

Now the mind lays by its trouble and considers.
The fidgets of remembrance come to this.
This is the last day of a certain year
Beyond which there is nothing left of time.
It comes to this and the imagination's life.

There is nothing more inscribed nor thought nor felt
And this must comfort the heart's core against
Its false disasters—these fathers standing round,
These mothers touching, speaking, being near,
These lovers waiting in the soft dry grass.

(CP, 372)

Each season of the year represents part of the cycle of creative activity. If one were to visualize the cycle of decreation and creation in terms of a sine curve or a graph of an alternating current, the place of summer within the cycle of the seasons would become apparent. The period described in this section is a point in time that represents both the fictive time of the creative act and the existential time of the poet's life. For both kinds of time, midsummer is the highest point on the graph, for it is the time of maximum production both in the imaginative cycle and in the cycle of nature. The fertility of this period is suggested by the presence of various human and natural figures of sexual activity (the young broods, fathers, mothers, and "lovers waiting in the soft dry grass" for fulfillment). During this period of the cycle, time is fulfilled by ripeness. Shakespeare's "ripeness is all" has seldom been so beautifully illustrated as in the opening sections of "Credences of Summer." Within the casual cadences of the first stanza, Stevens compresses an entire complex of cyclical allusions by naming not just summer, but also the preceding and following seasons. He suggests that even though progress stops at this point (which is the endpoint of the upward surge of this phase of the cycle) there is nevertheless a continuity and each endpoint is also a new beginning. In this particular time (and the whole poem, I want to stress again, is about one moment in the imagination's life, one part of the creative cycle that is presented as one day in the concrete calendar year), the troubles of the mind are forgotten in the vision that accompanies the account of ripeness and fulfillment. All the conflicts that had characterized the spring and autumn phases are dissolved. All divisions between mind and world that had dominated the poetry of the thirties are forgotten.

At this point in the fictive duration, time does not end. That is, the point, "beyond which there is nothing left of time" is a point in the continuous movement of the fictive duration where time ends and a new year (not a calendar year) begins. After this point, both the imagination and nature begin the downward movement toward the nothingness of winter, a phase that I discuss at the end of this chapter. Stevens's concept of time as a cycle (that is, his fiction of time that encompasses both empirical and fictive time), makes this endpoint the "end of a certain year," which is not the year 1946, but the fictive year of the creative cycle. This time period represents the fulfillment of projected Being, wherein the imagination can go no further. It is functioning in phase with reality, and at this point, the exact point of ripeness, growth has ended, but decay has not yet begun. The explicit comparison between the natural scene (described in the first two stanzas) and the cycles of the imagination is made at the end of the second stanza: "It comes to this and the imagination's life."

The exact point imagined here is the point of fulfillment for which the rest of the year and the entire cycle of decreation and creation have been preparing. Hence there need be "nothing more inscribed nor thought nor felt / And this must comfort the heart's core against / Its false disasters—" (CP, 372). The subsequent images of fathers, mothers, and lovers are not the heart's false disasters.

Rather, the disasters are the doubts and uncertainties of the human condition, mortality, limited knowledge (in general, the "troubles" that are put aside at this moment). The human figures are symbols of the natural sexual fertility that is fulfilled at this moment. They present the creative possibilities that are brought to fruition in the moment of ripeness that is described. Moreover, this moment must be remembered after the cycle has turned to autumn, where the dominant modes of thought (uncertainty, dread, and the movement in time toward nothingness) haunt the human speaker and his audience.

In contrast to autumn and spring, this moment in summer is the moment of unity. The speaker's command is to

> Postpone the anatomy of summer, as
> The physical pine, the metaphysical pine.
> Let's see the very thing and nothing else.
> Let's see it with the hottest fire of sight.
> Burn everything not part of it to ash.
>
> Trace the gold sun about the whitened sky
> Without evasion by a single metaphor.
> Look at it in its essential barrenness
> And say this, this is the centre that I seek.
> Fix it in an eternal foliage
>
> And fill the foliage with arrested peace,
> Joy of such permanence, right ignorance
> Of change still possible. Exile desire
> For what is not. This is the barrenness
> Of the fertile thing that can attain no more.
>   (CP, 373)

This section (II) explains the full meaning of the summer cycle. With fulfillment comes a vision of unity. The unity of Being is beyond the powers of rational analysis to pull apart and explicate.[8] Any explication (any "anatomy of

---

8. Nassar, p. 175, writes that "there is a great deal of pathos in these lines which call for a realization that nature is barren, but that imaginative desire in man endures anyway." Nasser seems to see the entire moment in midsummer as

summer") is put off, since both the physical and the
metaphysical (both existence and Being, the concrete and
the abstract) are brought together without special effort.
In this period, the full disclosure of the unity of Being as
the source of subject and object, mind and world is not just
possible, it is actual. For the speaker, all the tensions of
"becoming" ("spring's infuriations") and "passing away"
("autumn's inhalations") are dissolved in a vision of the
whole. This section reenacts, in a less compressed way, the
initial directions to the ephebe in the first canto of "Notes
Toward a Supreme Fiction." Just as the "muddy centre"
was the source of both mind and world, so in this case a
center is sought (and again the image of the sun is used as
a metaphor to suggest a source that is both radiant and
life-giving). It accounts for both the visible effects (light)
and the invisible sense of presence (heat). Just as the
speaker in "Notes" (Canto I of "It Must Be Abstract") insisted that the "sun must bear no name," so the "very thing"
cannot be named by "the evasions of metaphor." In this
section, the center that is sought evades direct identification (only the metaphorical sun is suggested). But Being,
the center that is sought, must be named by the poet in
order that it may be established. Thus the speaker continues his command by directing the poet to "fix" the indefinite "it" in "eternal foliage / And fill the foliage with
arrested peace . . ." (CP, 373). The poet's desire to reveal,
once and for all, the source or center of his vision is expressed in these lines, where he is directed to put his vision
into a work of art, to make it a lasting expression of the
peace, the joy, and the serenity of the fulfilled vision of
Being. For a moment, the poet's hope is to evade temporality through art as though "right ignorance / Of change"

---

a pathetic experience for the frustrated romantic poet who cannot fulfill his
desire to break through the subject-object barrier. Such a reading would seem to
ignore the later visions as well as the full meaning of this "moment" in the
imagination's cycle. Nassar thinks it "ominous" (p. 174) that midsummer is called
the last day of the year because, apparently, he can conceive of no way for this to
be so.

were "still possible." Each of these commands defines the
desire of the poet of Being. That goal is, in Heidegger's
terms, "to establish Being and the essence of things
through the word."[9] Though neither the speaker's command nor Heidegger's goal can be fully achieved, the
poet's sense of his vision is completed as he exclaims "This
is the barrenness / Of the fertile thing that can attain no
more" (CP, 373). At the ultimate point of the fictive duration, the mind fulfills itself by fulfilling its projections of
Being. Here, at this point, the unreal fiction coincides with
the real moment in experience as imaginative vision and
actual perception coincide.

The vision is fully expressed in the metaphors of section
III, which serve as examples to show that the desire to
evict metaphor is combined with the full awareness that
metaphor is, in effect, poetic language and must be present if any poetic expression of the experience of Being is
to take place.

It is the natural tower of all the world,
The point of survey, green's green apogee,
But a tower more precious than the view beyond,
A point of survey squatting like a throne,
Axis of everything, green's apogee

And happiest folk-land, mostly marriage hymns.
It is the mountain on which the tower stands,
It is the final mountain. Here the sun,
Sleepless, inhales his proper air, and rests.
This is the refuge that the end creates.

It is the old man standing on the tower,
Who reads no book. His ruddy ancientness
Absorbs the ruddy summer and is appeased,
By an understanding that fulfills his age,
By a feeling capable of nothing more.
                                         (CP, 373–74)

---

9. Heidegger, "Hölderlin and the Essence of Poetry," trans. Douglas Scott in
Existence and Being, ed. Werner Brock (Chicago, 1949; paperback ed., 1967), p.
281.

Thus the metaphors of this section expand and change
with each stanza. Initially the time of ripeness is explained
in terms of a vision of a tower. The concrete spatial images
are attempts to telescope the meanings of the moment into
a unified spatial picture. The recurrent images of high
points serve to illustrate the top (apogee) of the cycle of the
imagination as it is expressed in first temporal, then spatial
terms. From this top point, the view is not so important as
the suspended moment in the imagination's life, where the
limit of both the mind and the world is reached in the full
disclosure of the center. This point is the "axis of everything," "green's green apogee" and "happiest folk-land,
mostly marriage hymns." These three short phrases are
Stevens's shorthand symbols for the characteristics of the
moment of fulfillment. Toward this point, the summit, so
to speak, of the metaphorical mountain of the cycle, everything moves (hence it is like the axis of a planet or the
point toward which the revolutions of the cycles move in
time). The ultimate point of time (represented by the
highest point in space) is where opposites come together in
their common source. It is a period of "mostly marriage
hymns," which suggests the kinds of unions of opposite
natures that take place within the revelation of Being.[10]

In my discussion of the final cantos of "Notes Toward A
Supreme Fiction," I explained the projected pleasures of
beginnings and endings of fictive durations in terms of
Stevens's idea of the value of repetition, which was not an
identical reiteration of the same words or acts but rather a
repetition of the same patterns of creativity. The fulfillment of a form in each individual example of the form
gave the poet a sense of pleasure and fulfillment from
having completed his projections of possible modes of Being. These were the fictive equivalents of *Dasein*'s projec-

---

10. Compare, for example, the vision of the Canon Aspirin in "Notes Toward
a Supreme Fiction" (CP, 401–3) where the opposites of fact and thought are
united in a vision of the "amassing harmony," at the opposite limit, the extreme
of midnight.

tions of possibilities into the indefinite, but finite future. These passages of "Credences of Summer" describe most fully the result of Stevens's theory. "This is the refuge that the end creates," for without ends there are no new beginnings and hence no possible moments of fulfillment until the last moment of factual existence (i.e., death).

In the third stanza, a figure appears at the top of the mountain. He is that which is revealed at the moment of fulfillment. He represents the abstract source of fulfillment. He is not human ("reads no books"), but rather is a figure for Being who, like the figure for "collective being" in the poem "Chocorua to Its Neighbor," is a "metaphysical metaphor" (CP, 301) that provides "a clearing, a detecting, a completing / A largeness lived and not conceived, a space in an instant . . ." (CP, 301). Fully envisioned at the completed duration, the figure for Being is fulfilled by being understood ("is appeased, by an understanding that fulfills his age" (CP, 374). The poet, though, does not understand him rationally. He is not a product of calculation or of reason. He is disclosed through a feeling and thus is disclosed in accord with Heidegger's description of the way in which Being is disclosed to *Dasein* through mood and state of mind rather than by cognition.[11]

The "feeling capable of nothing more" is then illustrated in concrete, accessible terms in the landscape evoked in section IV:

> One of the limits of reality
> Presents itself in Oley when the hay
> Baked through long days, is piled in mows. It is
> A land too ripe for enigmas, too serene.
> There the distant fails the clairvoyant eye
>
> And the secondary senses of the ear
> Swarm, not with secondary sounds, but choirs,

---

11. Heidegger writes that "ontologically mood is a primordial kind of Being for *Dasein*, in which *Dasein* is disclosed to itself prior to all cognition and volition, and beyond their range of disclosure" in *Being and Time,* trans. John Macquarrie and Edward Robinson (New York, 1962), p. 175.

> Not evocations but last choirs, last sounds
> With nothing else compounded, carried full,
> Pure rhetoric of a language without words.
>
> Things stop in that direction and since they stop
> The direction stops and we accept what is
> As good. The utmost must be good and is
> And is our fortune and honey hived in the trees
> And mingling of colors at a festival.
>
> (CP, 374)

Here, the speaker presents a concrete illustration of the temporal point in the experience of time and Being that he is attempting to render. He describes one summer day in a valley in Pennsylvania when the natural season is complete and the associations of the hay baking in the sun, its rich aromas, and the suggestions of a finality of ripeness all are brought together in a composite image. As a concrete metaphor for the mind's fulfillment, this landscape is described as "a land too ripe for enigmas," for there is no suggestion of mysteriousness or unsolved riddles. The fulfillment of the season is present in time and in space and hence is fully realized without special vision or a "clairvoyant eye." The "distant" fails because the source of vision is nearby, represented as a concrete limit of reality, beyond which the land presented cannot go. At this stage in both the real world that is presented and in the fictive world that is suggested, "Things stop in that direction and since they stop / The direction stops and we accept what is / As good" (CP, 374). There is no need to proceed further. "The utmost must be good and is" (CP, 374). These sections have all traced the experience of summer in purely descriptive terms.

The next sections attempt to explain the temporal basis of the endpoint of both the fictive duration and existential duration.

> One day enriches the year. One woman makes
> The rest look down. One man becomes a race,

Lofty like him, like him perpetual.
Or do the other days enrich the one?
And is the queen humble as she seems to be,

The charitable majesty of her whole kin?
The bristling soldier, weather-foxed, who looms
In the sunshine is a filial form and one
Of the land's children, easily born, its flesh,
Not fustian.

(CP, 374–75)

Each of the human figures is an example of the ways in which a paradigm can provide an example for the rest. They are all metaphors for a particular instant in time. Both the "one woman" and the "one man" could be any heroine or hero of legend or myth (one critic has suggested Mary and Christ.)[12] The point of the parable is that a single example or occurrence can affect the whole. Thus, the passage begins with the theory that one day ("the last day of a certain year") can suffice to "enrich" the entire cycle of the year. But then there is a pause, and a question that implies a mutual exchange: "Or do the other days enrich the one?" The answer is that both enrich each other. The moment of fulfillment requires the continuity of the cyclic process to bring it to a point of fulfillment. Without the continuous change there would be neither final instant nor first moment, neither beginnings nor ends. Hence, "the other days" do enrich the "one." Each example—the queen, the man, and the soldier—is a part of a larger whole. Each performs his role in making the whole meaningful. In the same way, the unique moment makes all the others worthwhile, since this moment fulfills the cycle of time. The underlying structure, time itself, is fulfilled on the last day.

---

12. Robert J. Bertholf asserts that the Christ figure is definitely intended in this passage and interprets the "one man" and the "soldier" as well as all the other male figures in this passage as figures for Christ. See his Ph.D. diss., University of Oregon, 1968, "The Vast Ventriloquism: Wordsworth and Wallace Stevens," pp. 265–67.

As a result of the mutual interdependence of the part and the whole, "the more than casual blue" of the unity of the imagination and the real world

> Contains the year and other years and hymns
> And people, without souvenir. The day
> Enriches the year, not as embellishment.
> Stripped of remembrance, it displays its strength—
> The youth, the vital son, the heroic power.
>
> (CP, 375)

The moment of completion comes from access to Being. It is not only an end (in the sense of fulfillment of the previous seasons and previous days), but also a new beginning from which the fresh creations of future days will come. This is the "strength" of this period. It makes possible a sense of renewal figured by "the youth, the vital son," and "the heroic power" of the rebirth of the imagination.

The full power of this moment is then presented metaphorically in the image of the rock, a figure for the all-inclusive and yet difficult realization of the source or center.

> The rock cannot be broken. It is the truth.
> It rises from land and sea and covers them.
> It is a mountain half way green and then,
> The other immeasurable half, such rock
> As placid air becomes. But it is not
>
> A hermit's truth nor symbol in hermitage.
> It is the visible rock, the audible,
> The brilliant mercy of a sure repose,
> On this present ground, the vividest repose.
> Things certain sustaining us in certainty.
>
> It is the rock of summer, the extreme,
> A mountain luminous half way in bloom
> And then half way in the extremest light
> Of sapphires flashing from the central sky,
> As if twelve princes sat before a king.
>
> (CP, 375)

The rock has been taken by Stevens's critics as a symbol of "bare reality"[13] and, on the other hand, a symbol of "objective certainty,"[14] but each reading of "the rock" that attempts to associate it with a solid thing called "reality" fails to account for the description of the rock as the figure expands in the following stanzas. It is a metaphor (rather than a symbol) for the ground of both reality (the world) and the imagination (the mind). The rock is the metaphor for Being that is "half way green" (part reality) and half "immeasureable" transparency ("such rock as placid air becomes"), thus bringing both parts of the divided world together in one unified vision. As Riddel points out, the rock "is the physical transmuted in imagination and raised to vital form (metaphysical) of poetry."[15]

The poem presents the metaphor in such a way as to make it as clear as possible that the truth that is expressed is present and visible at the moment of vision. It is neither mystic sign ("a hermit's truth") nor secluded symbol ("symbol in hermitage"), because it expresses the vital, changing qualities of "this present ground," the source of both world and mind. The rock of summer is the ultimate form that the imagination can conceive for the presence of Being. Heidegger's metaphors for Being, which include light, movement, and a flashing presence, are paralleled by Stevens's expanding metaphor.[16] The rock changes to "a mountain luminous half-way in bloom" (half earth) and then "half-way in extremest light . . ." (half mind). The brilliance of the vision described in the final stanza of this passage makes it difficult to understand how Nassar could refer to the rock as "barrenness of reality" or how Mills could write that the rock is a static symbol of "objective certainty."[17] What the rock represents "is the truth," in

---

13. Sukenick, p. 195.
14. Mills, p. 98.
15. Riddel, p. 220.
16. See Heidegger, *Erläuterungen zu Hölderlins Dichtung*, pp. 57–58, 69–73.
17. Nassar, p. 176; Mills, p. 98.

Heidegger's sense of the ontological truth that reveals Being and makes it present for the poet.[18] The poet is positive of his vision, but it is hardly what one could call an "objective" certainty unless the normal connotations of "objective" are stretched considerably. Rather, the poet's vision of the presence of Being is described in terms that merit comparison with John's apocalyptic vision in Revelation:[19]

> in the extremest light
> Of sapphires flashing from the central sky,
> As if twelve princes sat before a king.
>
> (CP, 375)

Here, the poet attempts to render the extremes that accompany the fulfilled vision of Being. The majesty and brilliance of the "sure repose" necessitate allusions to visionary heights that are unequaled in any of Stevens's earlier poems. However, the critic must still measure the full sense of Stevens's all-important qualification in the last line. The "as if" makes sure that the description is taken metaphorically. For this is not prophecy or mystic transcendence. The experience of the fulfillment of time is still a fulfillment of fictive ends, not the absolute apocalypse of the Joachite prophecy.[20]

After the full vision of the rock of Being, the speaker then contrasts the two possible ways of grasping the experience in language. The wrong way is the way of the singers, who avoid the "common fields" of revelation by refusing to face the source of self and world.

---

18. Heidegger, *Vom Wesen der Wahrheit* (Frankfurt, 1943; rev. ed., 1949), p. 18–19.

19. For a full analysis of this passage, see Bertholf, pp. 267–69.

20. Joseph Pieper, *The End of Time* (London, 1954), pp. 15–22, writes of the typical example of a sect of apocalyptic fanatics (i.e., mystics) and cites Joachism as the most influential sect of doomsday prophets who have used the book of Revelation and other prophecies to continue their vision of the end of the world. Frank Kermode, in his *The Sense of An Ending: Studies in the Theory of Fiction* (Oxford, 1966; paperback ed., 1968), pp. 3–31, explains, in a succinct and lucid survey, the basis of apocalyptic thought, particularly as it is related to theories of time and temporality.

> Far in the woods they sang their unreal songs,
> Secure. It was difficult to sing in face
> Of the object. The singers had to avert themselves
> Or else avert the object. Deep in the woods
> They sang of summer in the common fields.
>
> They sang desiring an object that was near,
> In face of which desire no longer moved,
> Nor made of itself that which it could not find . . .
>
> (CP, 376)

Such singers avoid the center, where the truth of Being is available. The speaker admits the difficulty of expressing the direct experience of the Being of the things (the "object" of vision). Nevertheless, the narrator shows that avoiding the direct exposure leads to "unreal songs" in a pejorative sense. The singers hide in the shadow of the woods, away from the radiance that was described in the previous section. Such singers may "sing desiring an object that was near" (CP, 376), but their desire can only be fulfilled in the direct experience of the thing itself, the exposure to the "rock of summer."

The opposite way to express the truth of the experience is then contrasted to the way of singers of "unreal songs":

> Three times the concentred self takes hold, three times
> The thrice concentred self, having possessed
>
> The object, grips it in savage scrutiny,
> Once to make captive, once to subjugate
> Or yield to subjugation, once to proclaim
> The meaning of the capture, this hard prize,
> Fully made, fully apparent, fully found.
>
> (CP, 376)

The "thrice concentred self" has brought together (within the circle or sphere of experience) imagination, reality, and the source of both. Hence, the three circles of possible experience are fused within the single circle of the poet's vision. He stands, as the narrator had directed in section III, directly in the face of the object of his meditation and attempts to make sense of what he sees. He has already possessed this peculiar object through the disclosure of the ground of all objects. But this kind of momentary possession, within a visionary or preconceptual experience, is not enough. The poet, as Heidegger writes, can only reveal Being and the truth of Being by capturing it in language which, in a later essay, the philosopher calls "the house of Being."[21] The poet's goal is the expression of the truth of Being. His process first includes an attentive observation of that which appears at the moment of vision (gripping whatever appears in "savage scrutiny"). He then captures it in his vision. Here, Stevens's sense of the word *capture* is like the act of "catching" proposed in "It Must Give Pleasure," Canto I:

> ... the difficultest rigor is forthwith,
> On the image of what we see, to catch from that
>
> Irrational moment its unreasoning. ...
>   (CP, 398)

The phrase *to catch* or *capture* is used in both cases as a term for verbally catching something. Thus, for a moment, the poet captures in language a sense of his experience. The capture is verbal rather than physical. The object that is captured is metaphysical rather than physical. Each attempt to express Being in poetry results in a give and take or interchange between poet and Being, wherein both are revealed and concealed in the same act.[22] The process then is not concerned with victory or defeat, but with both. The poet must, in Heidegger's terms, "freely give" in order to

---

21. In "Brief über den 'Humanismus,'" included in *Platons Lehre von der Wahrheit* (Bern, 1947), p. 53, Heidegger writes that "die Sprache ist das Haus des Seins...," which he repeats in several places in the later essays on poetry. See also "Wozu Dichter," in *Holzwege* (Frankfurt, 1950), pp. 248–95.

22. The ambivalence of language, which Heidegger claims is unavoidable for *Dasein*, is based first on the finite nature of *Dasein*. Later, in the essays on "Hölderlin and the Essence of Poetry," Heidegger restates this theory in terms of the poet's revelation of Being through the word (language) when he proposes the double function of the language of poetry that both reveals and conceals the truth of Being.

create a sense of Being. Hence he will both "subjugate" and "yield to subjugation" as he attempts to "proclaim the meaning of the capture" by expressing it in his poems. The result of this process of active meditation is the goal of the poetry of Being that "proclaims" the "hard prize, / Fully made, fully apparent, fully found" (CP, 376). The sequence of the final line is an account again of the three-part process. It reverses the steps described in the lines preceding it and thus stresses the interchangeability and simultaneity of the process of expressing the truth of Being. The presence is discovered (fully found), brought into the open (fully apparent), and then created, or rather, "established," in words (fully made) in the same moment of the poetic act. While Martz finds this three-part division similar to the meditative techniques of seventeenth-century religious writers, I suspect that this has little to do with influence.[23] Rather, while Martz's parallel does provide an interesting analogue for explaining this rather compressed passage, it fails to take into account just what is revealed by the process described. The comparison of the description of this technique to Heidegger's comments on the act of poetry and its relation to the revelation of Being gives the reader not only a sense of what kind of process is described, but also what the goal of this process might be. Furthermore, since the rest of the poem supports this reading, Heidegger's description of the poetic act would seem to explain more fully than Martz's meditation theory this difficult and highly compressed passage.

The following section describes this moment in time, the "now in midsummer come," when the imagination and the natural world are in phase and reach their ultimate concord simultaneously.

> The trumpet of morning blows in the clouds and through
> The sky. It is the visible announced,
> It is the more than visible, the more

---

23. Martz, "Wallace Stevens: The World as Meditation," pp. 145–46.

Than sharp, illustrious scene. The trumpet cries
This is the successor of the invisible.

This is its substitute in stratagems
Of the spirit. This, in sight and memory,
Must take its place, as what is possible
Replaces what is not. The resounding cry
Is like ten thousand tumblers tumbling down

To share the day. The trumpet supposes that
A mind exists, aware of division, aware
Of its cry as clarion, its diction's way
As that of a personage in a multitude:
Man's mind grown venerable in the unreal.
                                        (CP, 376–77)

In the moment of revelation, what had before been invisible and mysterious becomes fully visible, announced, as it were, by trumpets. Again this is an allusion to the trumpets of Heaven in John's revelation, the most appropriate Christian analogue to the fulfillment of time at the cycle's end. But, again, as in "Description Without Place" and "Notes Toward a Supreme Fiction," the use of religious analogues and allusions does not imply that the "credences" are religious. In fact, the reverse is the case, for Stevens's concept of Being is fully secular. The projected possibilities of the other seasons of the imagination are fulfilled as a new vision of the source of reality is substituted for the unknown spirits, gods, and transcendental ideas (the "stratagems of the spirit"). The trumpet and the "resounding cry" dramatize, like the "twelve princes" in section VI, the moment's revelation. Each allusion to the fully apocalyptic vision of John functions to suggest the power of the experience of the individual poet. The difference between the two visions is crucial. Stevens describes a purely private vision that affects only the life of the creative imagination. It is his experience, but it foretells neither the fall of kings nor the end of worlds. The similarity to apocalyptic literature is in the form and mode of expression rather than in the meaning.

The "trumpet supposes," as a condition of its having any meaning at all, the presence of the poet, who is aware of the traditional divisions between mind and world and hence fully cognizant of the significance of the last day, which dissolves the divisions in a revelation of the whole of Being. The imaginative vision and the real perception are fused, and thus the real and the unreal (imagination's products) come true together. The result is that "man's mind" grows to impressive dignity (venerable) in his imagination's power to transmit the vision in language.

The "cock bright" that is addressed in the ninth section represents the cold eye of another kind of mind, which looks upon the same landscape without the "unreal" of man's mind and sees a completely different scene. What he sees is what would be there without the poet's vision. The cock sees the scene without vision and hence looks at what human existence would be like without the fictions of the poet. Without the poet's moments of fulfilled Being, the "complex of emotions falls apart, / In an abandoned spot" (CP, 377) because there is no revelation to support the grim realities of death, decay, and the inevitable passage of time that destroys all things. The cock sees with only one eye and thus can perceive only the meaningless passing of time wherein death, absence, and degeneration ruin the works of man and nature,

> The gardener's cat is dead, the gardener gone
> And last years garden grows salacious weeds.
>   (CP, 377)

In this nonhuman view, only "*douceurs, / Tristesses,* the fund of life and death" are seen. The cock's cry of revulsion is "a sound that is not part of the listener's sense" (CP, 377).

After the vision and the moment of fulfillment, ripeness turns to decay, growth to *Sein-zum-Tode,* and unity to division ("another complex of emotions, not / So soft, not so

civil" (CP, 377). This passage contrasts the vision of serenity of the moment of fulfilled Being to the next moment.
But all is not lost. Though the inhuman cock sees with
"one eye" the discouraging facts of mortality, he is
nonetheless limited to the single eye of perception. The
second eye of the imagination's vision creates its own moments of completion. The cock sees only half the truth,
which, without the other half, jaundices his view.

To the poet who has double vision, both the unreal and
the real are present and true. Hence he sees both the cycle
of imaginative or creative activity that leads to fulfilled
Being and the relentless seasonal cycle that leads unerr-
ingly toward the disintegrations of afternoon, autumn,
and an end without memorial. In the poet's eye, the same
scene is seen in section X, where the vision of the unity of
the real and unreal, of the world and the mind, brings a
view of the rebirth that is implied in each death, the beginning that is present in each ending:

> The personae of summer play the characters
> Of an inhuman author, who meditates
> With the gold bugs, in blue meadows, late at night.
> He does not hear his characters talk. He sees
> Them mottled, in the moodiest costumes,
>
> Of blue and yellow, sky and sun, belted
> And knotted, sashed and seamed, half pales of red,
> Half pales of green, appropriate habit for
> The huge decorum, the manner of the time,
> Part of the mottled mood of summer's whole,
>
> In which the characters speak because they want
> To speak, the fat, the roseate characters,
> Free, for a moment, from malice and sudden cry,
> Complete in a completed scene, speaking
> Their parts as in a youthful happiness.
>
> (CP, 377–78)

He sees the joining of opposites in the natural cycle, where blue (the normal color of the imagination) and yellow (one of the colors of reality) are brought together along with "sky and sun" in a union "belted and knotted, sashed and seamed" so that they blend within the light of the common source.[24] Their colors are shared in such a way that the spectrum of color is brought into one circle. The composite unity of the "completed scene" is not a unity of death or decay as the "cock bright" would have it.[25] Rather, there is a new freedom and a new beginning of the cycles of creativity. The "personae" of the first stanza are the "characters" of the "inhuman author" (another way of signifying the abstract source of the unity that is perceived). The unity described is the natural unity of Being that is envisioned at the point in midsummer when the whole of the seasonal cycle is brought to a point in time. Rather than the traditional decline into autumn, there is a new freedom in which the young replace the old and productivity, though only potential, begins again in the natural characters of the summer. In much the same way as the new seeds wait in the ripe fruit for the decay that initiates their growth, these "personae" of both mind and world are envisioned as "speaking their parts as in a youthful happiness" (CP, 378).

Few poems in modern literature so thoroughly meditate the meaning of fulfillment, ripeness, and completed desire. As I suggested earlier, Stevens's vision of the summer phase provides a full expression of Shakespeare's aphorism, but Stevens does not leave this as the final statement. Rather, he shows the full value of the continuity of the creative process and how the projected fulfillment comes true in the completed vision of summer. However,

---

24. I am using the color symbolism established by George McFadden, "Probing for an Integration: Color Symbolism in Wallace Stevens," *Modern Philology,* 57 (February 1961): 186–93.

25. Nassar, p. 177–78, identifies this cock as "the cock of reality," which should lead to some problem in his reading of the poem since he also calls the rock of summer the "rock of reality."

never again would Stevens reach the full expression of ripeness, and "Credences of Summer" stands as the only full expression of the certainty of Being within a completely temporal context.

The following phase, autumn, is fully described in several poems of *Transport to Summer* and reaches its most complete treatment in *The Auroras of Autumn*. Unlike Keats's "season of mellow fruitfulness," autumn, for Stevens, is a season of uncertainty. The third phase of the creative cycle, like the spring phase, is characterized by an absence of vision. The truth of Being cannot be experienced in autumn, and this fact leads to the extended meditations on the adequacy of poetic language to express the truth of Being that is no longer "fully apparent" nor "fully found."

In the autumn phase, the major problem of any poetry that takes as its goal the "outlines of being and its expressings" (CP, 424) is fully asserted. The problems are not concerned with the "outlines" (which Stevens effectively provided in his most carefully organized aesthetic statement, "Notes Toward a Supreme Fiction") but with the "expressings" of Being. While the poet did propose a theory of "language as revelation" in "Description Without Place" (CP, 339–46), which I have already discussed, the implicit theory that was announced concerned only the "possibility" of such a language. There was no attempt to create an actual poetry in which "Being would / Come true" (CP, 341). While "Credences of Summer" attempted to present the full vision in which the "rock of summer" (Being) is seen as "the truth," the complete confidence and serenity that "Credences" describes is lost in the later poems.

The central element of Stevens's poetic language both in theory and in practice is the metaphor. Though metaphor is called "an evasion" in the summer phase, it nevertheless functions to express the poet's vision in "Credences of Summer." The most important example of metaphor, "the rock of summer," was the center around which the rest of the poem revolved. As Stevens enters the autumn phase, metaphor itself becomes ambivalent. It is no doubt typical of poets who write poetry about poetry that, as Heidegger observes, their meditations on the poetic use of language are very nearly as important as any other subject.[26] These poets (Heidegger cites Hölderlin as an example) provide original uses and concepts of language that should be valued beyond their immediate aesthetic uses.

The relations between the question of Being (*Seinsfrage*) and language are fully treated by Heidegger in his essays on the essence of poetry. Heidegger chooses the poetry of Hölderlin as his example not because he is necessarily greater than Shakespeare, Goethe, Dante, or Homer, but "because Hölderlin's poetry was borne on by the poetic vocation to write expressly of the essence of poetry. For us Hölderlin is in a pre-eminent sense 'the poet of the poet.' "[27] For poets like Hölderlin and Stevens, the poetry of Being is the subject of the poems and the processes involved in creating this poetry are the crucial themes of many of the poems.

As Heidegger begins to discuss the question of the meaning of Being in *Sein und Zeit* and in later works, he emphasizes the difficulties of expressing the ideas that are essential to any kind of understanding of the question that is being asked. First, there is the problem of understanding the "ontological difference" that Heidegger cites frequently in both his early and later writings. Simply stated, the problem for the poet of Being is that Being itself is not an entity and thus cannot be spoken of as if it were. Yet Being can only appear in the presence of entities and is integrally related to the way in which things are made present. Hence, though Being itself is the most common and immediate of goals for a poet, it is, at the same time,

---

26. "Hölderlin and the Essence of Poetry," p. 271.
27. *Ibid.*

the most difficult concept to make sense of, since each
attempt to associate it with the things that it makes present
tends to make one think of it as if it were an entity (a thing
that exists much like other things). The tendency of ontologists and ontological poets is usually toward hypostatization, that is, treating the concept as if it were a substance.
Heidegger calls the difference between *Sein* and *das
Seiende* the "ontological difference." This difference is expressed as the division between the "ontological" (that
which concerns Being itself, i.e., *Sein*) and the "ontic" (that
which concerns the beings, i.e., the entities or things that
exist).[28] For Heidegger, every attempt to reveal the truth
of Being is at the same time a dissimulation of that truth.[29]
Every attempt to express Being, even for the privileged
speaker (the poet), is a dual movement toward and away
from the truth of the nature of Being. Each attempt to
name or identify Being, or, as Heidegger is sometimes
prone to call it, "the truth of the Being of things" is a
process of revealing and concealing. For Stevens, the same
concept is evoked in the questions about metaphor.
Metaphor both reveals and evades the nature of the experience of Being. Language, particularly poetic language, is posited by both Heidegger and Stevens as that
which makes or establishes the Being of the world, which
otherwise could not be known. But in the act of establishing, language tends to fix that which cannot be fixed. Stevens expresses this problem in "Two Versions of the Same
Poem" (CP, 353–54), both versions of which fall under the
parenthetical subtitle "That Which Cannot Be Fixed":
"Once more he turned to that which cannot be fixed. / By
the sea, insolid rock, stentor, and said: . . ."

---

28. *Sein und Zeit* (Halle, 1929), pp. 7–9; *Kant und das Problem der Metaphysik*
(Bonn, 1929; rev. ed., Frankfurt, 1951), pp. 17–19.
    29. *Vom Wesen der Wahrheit*, pp. 18–19, trans. R. F. C. Hull and Alan Crick as
"On the Essence of Truth," in *Existence and Being*, ed. Werner Brock (Chicago,
1949; paperback ed., 1967), pp. 292–324, esp. pp. 310–16.

These vigors make, thrice-triple-syllabled,

The difficult images of possible shapes,
That cannot now be fixed. Only there is

A beating and a beating in the centre of
The sea, a strength that tumbles everywhere,

Like more and more becoming less and less
Like space dividing its blue and by division

Being changed from space to the sailor's métier,
Or say from that which was conceived to that

Which was realized, like reason's constant ruin.
                                    (CP, 353–54)

There is something at the center "beating and beating," which can only be suggested by metaphorical changes because it is more than reason ("like reason's constant ruin"). The poet's word, in Heidegger's view, comes as close as any speech to approximating the nature of Being but, even though poetizing is a privileged process, the nature of the poet's medium is ambiguous.

Heidegger defines poetry (in an essay entitled *"Der Ursprung des Kunstwerkes"*)[30] as the highest of the arts and tends to think of poetry as that art which approaches the truth of Being most closely. Yet, in the final analysis, poetry must always remain indirect in its effects, dependent on more than the simple denotation of words to suggest the meaning of Being. Because poetry evokes various levels of meaning and suggests preconceptual awareness, it proposes modes of expression that are available to neither philosophical discourse nor ordinary language.[31]

---

30. *Holzwege*, pp. 7–68.
31. Although Helen Hennessy Vendler does not explain why this is so, the advantages of poetic language in expressing subtleties of thought are suggested when she writes that "the untoward modulations of tense [she is referring to verb tenses that Stevens frequently uses] are simply not available to the critic who tries to paraphrase Stevens in prose, and so an apprehension [expressed in the

The other arts are part of poetry: "Alle kunst ist als Ge-
schehenlassen der Ankunft der Wahrheit des Seienden als
eines solchen im Wesen Dichtung."[32] Language is the
highest art and has held, for Heidegger, a special place
ever since the initial analysis of *Dasein*'s modes of Being in
Sein und Zeit. One of the three essential modes of *Dasein*'s
Being-in-the-world was *Rede* ("speech or language")
which, along with *Befindlichkeit* (state of mind or mood)
and *Verstehen* (understanding), formed the three modes of
Dasein's Being-in-the world. These three modes are simul-
taneous and together they describe the essential ways in
which *Dasein* understood itself as "Being-in-the-world"
and Being-toward-Death (*In-der-Welt-sein* and *Sein-zum-
Tode*). In the later meditations on the relation of poetry
and Being, Heidegger reaffirms this stance when he writes
that poetic language functions as that which brings the
Being of the things that exist into the open or into a state
of openness: "Die Sprache bringt das Seiende als ein
Seiendes allererst ins Offene. . . . "[33] Thus poetic language
has a privileged role in Heidegger's ontology, since it
brings the Being of the things into the open so that it may
be made clear. The poetry of Being, in Heidegger's
analysis, "projects a light," by reason of which "it is possible
to declare the nature of the Being of the thing as the thing
is brought into the open. . . . "[34]

For Heidegger, then, in both the essay "Hölderlin and
the Essence of Poetry" and in the later essays collected in

---

poetry] becomes a statement [in the critic's language], an intuition becomes a
dogma." See "The Qualified Assertions of Wallace Stevens," in *The Act of the Mind*,
pp. 164–65.

32. "Der Ursprung des Kunstwerkes," in *Holzwege,* p. 59. In a free translation
this sentence is as follows: "All art, as the letting come to pass (letting-happen) of
the coming (revelation) of truth of the things that exist (entities or beings) as
such, is in essence poetry."

33. *Holzwege,* p. 60. In English: "Language brings the thing itself that exists
into the open [so that the Being of the thing can be revealed]."

34. *Holzwege,* p. 61. In the original this passage is as follows: "Dichtung ist ein
Entwerfen des Lichten und solches Sagen ist auch ein Entwerfen des Lichten,
darin angesagt wird, als was das Seinde ins Offene kommt. . . ."

Holzwege, the proper domain of poetry is language, and where the philosopher begins to discuss the relation between poetry and the question of Being, he decides that the essence of poetry can be grasped in the ontological function of language. Poetry is, for Heidegger, authentic language. "The essence of poetry is the establishment (origination) of Being through words."[35]

However, the authentic use of language does not set the poet free of the problems of expressing the nature of Being, because language as it is described in *Sein und Zeit* is never completely authentic but is constantly falling off into inauthentic discourse, which Heidegger calls *Gerede* ("prattle").[36] This falling off from originative language is an unavoidable aspect of human language and of *Dasein*'s existence, which is a process of fluctuation between authentic and inauthentic modes of existence. While the poet is considered a privileged user of language, he nevertheless is human and cannot avoid degrees of dissimulation in his poetry. Thus, the nature of the language at its most authentic level is still ambivalent, since it both reveals and conceals the truth of Being.

With this brief summary of Heidegger's view of poetic language and the ontological importance of poetry, my approach to Stevens's later poems about the poetry of Being is more easily understood. Stevens's questions about the efficacy of metaphor are reflections of the dual nature of language as a medium for revealing the truth of Being.[37] With Heidegger's description of the dual function of all poetic language, the nature of Stevens's meditations on metaphor as it both reveals and falsifies the poet's experience of Being becomes clear. Thus, in a poem that explicitly treats the subject of poetic language, "The Motive for Metaphor," the ambivalent attitude suggests the difficulties of expressing the truth of Being.

---

35. "Hölderlin and the Essence of Poetry," p. 281.
36. *Sein und Zeit,* pp. 160–70, 348–49.
37. *Vom Wesen der Wahrheit,* p. 18.

You like it under the trees in autumn,
Because everything is half dead.
The wind moves like a cripple among the leaves
And repeats words without meaning.

In the same way, you were happy in spring,
With the half colors of quarter-things,
The slightly brighter sky, the melting clouds,
The single bird, the obscure moon—

The obscure moon lighting an obscure world
Of things that would never be quite expressed,
Where you yourself were never quite yourself
And did not want nor have to be,

Desiring the exhilarations of changes:
The motive for metaphor, shrinking from
The weight of primary noon,
The ABC of being,

The ruddy temper, the hammer
Of red and blue, and hard sound—
Steel against intimation—the sharp flash,
The vital, arrogant, fatal, dominant X.

(CP, 288)

The poem begins with a reference to autumn, the season
between the fulfillment of summer and the void of winter.
During this period of the creative life, the world and the
mind are on the downward cycle, moving from summer to
winter, from fulfillment to nothingness. In the duration of
existence, this cycle normally represents the archetypal
movement of a man's life span, his moving toward death,
aware of his existence as *Sein-zum-Tode*. But for Stevens,
the seasons are psychic equivalents of the fictive cycles of
creation and decreation; the temporal periods of creative
activity serve as the underlying structure of the later
poems. The love of autumn is equated in this poem with
the love of spring, because both seasons are points in the
imagination's duration that are neither full nor empty. In
this part of the fictive duration, things are half-realized

("half-dead" and, implicitly, half-alive). Neither the total negation of winter nor the fulfillment of summer is present or possible. These two seasons are the periods during which the imagination evades the full revelation of Being. They suggest the motive for metaphor because both autumn and spring are seasons of observable change— nature itself is in a process of either growth or decay— and the exterior changes can be matched by the interior changes of metaphorical transformation.

The slow-paced rhythm of the opening stanzas suggests the gradual alterations that take place both inside and outside during this phase of creative activity. The first two stanzas state explicitly the equivalence of autumn and spring as the seasons of desire, when the force and vitality of both mind and world are at a midpoint, traveling in time toward another goal. Compared to the relatively absolute ends of summer and winter, the spring and autumn periods are distinguished by a lack of vitality and inspiration. The imagination moves in obscure and indirect ways characterized by the dissimulations of metaphor.

In the two periods described in this poem, the poet's vision is obscured and his ability to reveal either the apogee or the nadir of creativity is in doubt. The moon (Stevens's usual image for the imagination, which functions here in its normal symbolic capacity) is described as "lighting an obscure world / Of things that would never be quite expressed" (CP, 288). In short, these periods, as they are presented in many poems in *Transport to Summer* and *The Auroras of Autumn* are characteristically empty of the vital contact with Being that starts and completes each fictive duration, each new beginning of the imagination's seasonal year. Failure to realize clarity in the fictive world is equated with a failure to realize the self in seasons when "you yourself were never quite yourself / And did not want nor have to be" (CP, 288).

Since the autumn phase of the world and the mind is slow to be born and slow to die, the poet "desires the exhilaration of changes" that are produced by the metaphor-making process. It gives the poet a way of taking part in the changes that are observed around him, but it also provides a way of dissimulating any kind of vital contact. He can, through metaphor, avoid "the weight of primary noon / The ABC of being" (CP, 288). At the nadir and at the apogee (also midnight and noon respectively in Stevens's temporal scheme) the mind confronts the essential nothingness and the potential fulfillment of Being itself—the ABC's or elementary characteristics that were described in "Credences of Summer." But during other times (and I mean the word *times* in a literal as well as figurative sense, since the temporal quality of the creative experience of Being is stressed not only by the seasons but also by the quickened cadence of the poem as it reaches its conclusion) the mind can only wait, presuming that "It Must Change." Metaphor is the poet's way of partaking in this change, even though the ambivalent nature of metaphor may lead to an inauthentic use of language.[38]

As the motive for metaphor is announced, the lines become short phrases in imitation of the directness and quickening pace of experience in the "primary" duration. The contact with the center is characterized by hard sounds, discordant phrases, and a chopped rhythm.

> . . . the sharp flash,
> The vital, arrogant, fatal, dominant X.
> (CP, 288)

Each phrase emphasizes the quickened sense of life that comes from contact with Being either at the apex or the lowpoint of the creative cycle. Here, the mind ("intimation") comes in contact with the thing itself ("steel") and

---

38. For Heidegger, inauthentic use of language would mean that the language conceals or avoids the question of Being. All discourse that does not function toward revealing, making clear, or projecting *Dasein's* apprehension and understanding of Being is inauthentic. See *Sein und Zeit,* pp. 165–69.

the disclosure of Being takes the form of a frightening
experience of heightened intensity.

In this poem, the function of metaphor is to lead away
from this experience. It explicitly conceals rather than reveals. But each phrase that describes the contact with
Being acts metaphorically so that the words used, even
though the truth of Being and the poet's sense of Being
are to be avoided, still suggest indirectly the force that
might be confronted at "primary noon." The concord of
"red and blue" (Stevens's colors for reality and the imagination), the hammer that suggests the quick realization of
contact, and the "hard sound" of the "dominant X" all
suggest aspects of Being or the absolute quality of the
experience of Being that only metaphor can achieve.
Nowhere in the poem is the force named directly nor are
there any words except *being* itself that can suggest the full
truth of the experience of Being. Unnamed, an "X" that is
nominated as source and goal, Being itself is both
suggested and avoided by the metaphors of this poem.
The ambiguous activity of the metaphors is evidence of
Stevens's affinity with Heidegger. Thus, where Heidegger
writes that language is essentially both revelation and dissimulation of the truth of Being,[39] Stevens would seem to
be in accord. The nature of poetic language and the
difficulty of achieving the "expressings" of the poet's sense
of Being are part of the reason for the poet's later claims
that "the intricate evasions of as" and the "evasion by a
single metaphor" are a constant threat to the poetry of
Being. During the periods of spring and autumn, the
poet's sense of Being falters and he must generate
metaphors in order to keep going. To keep taking part in
the change that will bring a new beginning or a new end,
he must initiate a new start or a new fulfillment, both of
which will coincide at the moment when the fictive duration is completed.

---

39. *Vom Wesen der Wahrheit,* p. 17.

Another example of this state of mind is described in
"Crude Foyer," where the temporal position of the creative process is caught between the high point and low point
of the wavelike cycle. Again, the absence of vision denotes
a poverty of the imagination, which in this period is unable
to create a sense of the experience of Being from the past.
Spring and autumn are crisis points in the creative life,
where the poet loses confidence in his ability to begin the
creative cycle again. The failure of metaphor in these
periods connotes the failure of language to express whatever it was that was so important about the "moment of
imperishable bliss" of other parts of the fictive cycles.
These periods "in-between" beginning and end, even in
the fictive duration of the imagination's cycles, are not like
the winter phase (though there are certain similarities of
imagery). In winter (as in "No Possum, No Stop, No Tat-
ers" [CP, 293–94]), though "the field is frozen, the leaves
are dry" and "Bad is final in this light" (CP, 293), the
finality of the winter phase brings something new, a new
sense of the purity of vision. Hence, instead of depression
and despondency, "the savage hollow of winter sound"
(CP, 294) is a place and time where "in this bad . . . we
reach / The last purity of the knowledge of good" (CP,
294). In spring and autumn, the absence that is evoked
brings no final light. Hence, in "Crude Foyer," the poet
reaches a state similar to that in "The Motive For
Metaphor," where he suffers "an innocence of an absolute" that he calls "false happiness" (CP, 305). In this
period,

> . . . we know that we use
> Only the eye as faculty, that the mind
> Is the eye, and that this landscape of the mind
>
> Is a landscape only of the eye; and that
> We are ignorant men incapable
> Of the least, minor, vital metaphor, content,
> At last, there, when it turns out to be here.
>   (CP, 305)

The essential poverty of the human condition is evoked through the ignorance that in this case does not suggest innocence or lack of presuppositions as did the "ignorant eye" of "Notes Toward a Supreme Fiction." Rather, the poet reaches a point in pure thought where, like the Canon Aspirin, he is at the end of both thought and fact. Unlike Canon Aspirin, he fails to achieve the vision of harmony or the center. Rather, at the end of thought there lies ". . . A foyer of the spirit in a landscape of the mind, / In which we sit and wear humanity's bleak crown" (CP, 305). When the period of the creative cycle is out of phase, the poet realizes the poverty of human existence. The poem describes the basic condition of Heidegger's *Dasein* before it begins to project its possibilities for Being-in-the-World toward the future. Without confidence, the poet can proceed no further. Metaphor, in this period, would be a welcome start even though its dual function is fully recognized. The landscape of the mind is of no importance if the temporal rhythms of the creative process are out of phase. The "center" and the "amassing harmony" that were envisioned at the end of thought and fact in "Notes" and "Credences" are absent here. In this period, the extremes of self-doubt and the lowpoint of creative activity are recorded. But they form, nevertheless, part of the endless repetition and must be endured even if they are only "an occupation" (CP, 405). For to partake in change is to keep creating changes in the knowledge that the cycle will complete itself.

The seasons as figures for the cycles of imagination are rather well-recognized phenomena in the later poetry and it is not my point to belabor the seasons of spring and autumn.[40] But the fact is that none of the critics who speak of the seasons of the imagination or the "climates of Wal-

---

40. The best discussion of the seasons of Stevens's imagination is Richard A. Macksey's "The Climates of Wallace Stevens," in *The Act of the Mind*, pp. 185–223. However, Macksey treats only the winter phase and leaves the other three seasons almost without comment. A recent article on the functions of metaphor

lace Stevens" mentions the in-between periods in any context other than the traditional and rather outworn ideas of
spring and fall as the seasons of renewal and decay. In
Stevens's imagination, they are hardly so easily
categorized. Critics have pointed out the presence of the
seasonal sequences that are maintained throughout the
Collected Poems, but where the seasons before *Transport to
Summer* tended to signify the traditional poetic connotations, in these later poems the most precise indicator or
sign of the faltering imagination in these seasons is the
poet's professed attitude toward metaphor. Hence, when
the poet announces in "Metaphor as Degeneration" the
demise of metaphor, it sounds like the same process that
has been followed in such diverse poems as "Add This to
Rhetoric" (CP, 188), "Credences of Summer" (CP, 373),
and "Bouquet of Roses in Sunlight" (CP, 431). In each case
the poet's sense of what is experienced exceeds the capability of metaphor ("so sense exceeds all metaphor" [CP,
431]). But I might add that metaphor remains, in practice,
in spite of the theoretical pronouncements of these poems.
   In the poems of spring and autumn,

> . . . to speak of the whole world as metaphor
> Is still to stick to the contents of the mind
> And the desire to believe in metaphor.
>   (CP, 332)

Metaphor in this case is clearly false, for the believer in
metaphor must be aware "that what [he] believes is not
true" (CP, 332).
   If the problem for Stevens is the truth of metaphor,
then metaphor will always be tainted since, as Heidegger

---

in Stevens's poetry by Donald Sheehan uses each of the seasons as examples of
the ways in which Stevens attempts to resolve the conflict between imagination and
reality by the use of metaphor. However, Sheehan does not connect the seasons
with any kind of temporal pattern nor does he mention the two crucial metaphors
of the later poetry, the river and the rock, except in passing. Nonetheless, it is
the most complete study of metaphor yet published. See "Stevens' Theory of
Metaphor," *Papers on Language and Literature* 2 (Winter 1966): 57–66.

writes, the truth as revelation is always accompanied by the untruth of concealment.[41] The metaphor that is discussed in "The Pure Good of Theory" is not true, because it evades, just as the metaphor in "The Motive for Metaphor" evaded, the source of both the mind and the world. To treat the world and the mind as metaphor is to refuse to recognize either as it might be. Such a view approaches the extreme of solipsism. If this is the end product of all metaphor, then rightfully metaphor is "not true." Each metaphor (and by extension each poem) would begin in falsehood and proceed no further. The goal of the poetry of Being is missed, since metaphor as evasion implies a conscious dissimulation. As Northrop Frye points out, "clearly if metaphor is 'merely' this [the rhetoric of analogy between nature and the imagination], the use of metaphor could only accentuate what Stevens' poetry tries to annihilate, the sense of a contrast or great gulf fixed between subject and object, consciousness and existence."[42] If metaphor were simply evasion, every motive for metaphor would be a shrinking from the contact with Being.

In the winter phase, metaphor is absent to the extent that "the absence of the imagination had itself to be imagined" (CP, 503). In "The Plain Sense of Things," a poem of the winter phase of the imagination, the zero point of creativity is, just like every other phase or season, a period of imaginative activity that must be imagined in order to be known.

> After the leaves have fallen, we return
> To a plain sense of things. It was as if
> We had come to an end of the imagination,
> Inanimate in an inert savoir.
>   (CP, 502)

---

41. *Vom Wesen der Wahrheit,* p. 17.

42. "The Realistic Oriole: A Study of Wallace Stevens," *Hudson Review* 10 (Autumn 1957), 353–70. Reprinted in *Wallace Stevens: A Collection of Critical Essays,* ed. Marie Borroff, pp. 169–70.

But, as Kermode and others have pointed out, there is a great deal of difference between the "as if" of these lines and the assertion that some critics have seen.[43] The "as if" still insists upon the fictive nature of the poem in which "an" end of the imagination in winter is proposed. Nevertheless, while the imagination is always present, even if muted, the process of metaphor (which, we recall, is the essential poetic process of language) is absent ". . . for it is difficult even to choose the adjective / For this blank cold . . ." (CP, 502). Yet the adjective is chosen. In the winter phase, the metaphor, while absent in principle, still asserts its presence in the words of the poem that describe its absence.

The poet of Being desires more than the ambiguity of traditional metaphor, which both reveals and evades the truth of Being. As Stevens meditates the function of poetic language, he proposes two distinct possibilities in the later poetry. Both possibilities are variations upon traditional poetic symbols: the metaphors of the river and the rock.

The first proposal defines a new kind of metaphor, which will express the nature of Being as the poet experiences it. The definition begins in the early poems of *The Auroras of Autumn* at the end of a sequence of poems that treat the theme of time and the cycles of change in the autumn phase of the imagination's cycle. The central poem of this meditation, "The Auroras of Autumn" (CP, 411–21), provides a background for nearly all the meditations in this volume. In "The Auroras of Autumn," Stevens treats the theme of mutability and of the possible ways of accepting change and old age as part of existence. However, in "The Auroras of Autumn," none of the suggestions seems to give access to the poetry of Being. As in the earlier poems of autumn, the imagination is out of phase and thus the meditations of Being are carried out without the freshness of either the full vision of summer or the naked exposure

---

43. Kermode, pp. 118–19.

of winter. In a long meditation the speaker attempts to imagine what Being might be like. But he can only evoke "a time of innocence" in which vision or disclosure might take place. Without the immediate experience of vision, there is no confidence.

> If it is not a thing of time, nor of place
>
> Existing in the idea of it, alone,
> In the sense against calamity, it is not
> Less real. For the oldest and coldest philosopher
>
> There is or may be a time of innocence
> As pure principle. Its nature is its end,
> That it should be, and yet not be, a thing. . . .
>
> (CP, 418)

The poet proposes the possibility of a time of innocence in which the eye could see what had earlier (in "Notes Toward a Supreme Fiction") been called the "first idea" of the thing. But this idea remains only possible. The speaker does not assert that Being exists or even that it is disclosed. Rather, he carefully qualifies his statement to "may be," and thus the time of vision wherein disclosure might be possible is only a distant conditional period in autumn. In "A Primitive Like An Orb," the principle evoked "is and / It is not and therefore is" (CP, 440). In this case, it is and yet is not a thing. Heidegger's "ontological difference" is alluded to in these lines. Further equivocation does little to make clear what is discussed in this passage, and without Heidegger's description of the problems of expressing the sense of Being, the reader would be lost:

> It is like a thing of ether that exists
> Almost as predicate. But it exists,
> It exists, it is visible, it is, it is.
> (CP, 418)

In terms of straight description this is as close as the poet

can come to describing his sense of Being. Being is not a
thing of ether, only "like" a thing of ether. Being does not
exist as predicate but "almost" as predicate. Nevertheless,
after these qualifications, which are purposefully inserted
to give a sense of the subject without misleading the listener, the speaker still asserts the existence and visibility of
the unnamed "it" that the "oldest and coldest philosopher"
intuits in the time of innocence. The experience of Being
is described

> As if the innocent mother sang in the dark
> Of the room and on an accordion, half-heard,
> Created the time and place in which we breathed....
> (CP, 419)

But, in both cases, the attempt to express the nature of
Being fails. In these lines even naked assertion fails. The
speaker senses his failure for, at the end of "The Auroras
of Autumn," he makes fun of the poet's inability to express
the outlines of Being by calling the poet figure "the spectre
of the spheres" (CP, 420).

The poem that follows "The Auroras of Autumn,"
namely, "Large Red Man Reading," explicitly reaffirms
the goal of the poetry of Being by stating that goal as
plainly as possible. In "Large Red Man Reading" the
ghosts and spirits of past lives are envisioned as returning
to earth in order to hear the poet figure (a kind of ultimate
poet of the ultimate poem) read "from out of the purple
tabulae" (the book of the imagination)

> The outlines of being and its expressings, the
>   syllables of its law:
> *Poesis, poesis,* the literal characters, the vatic lines.
> (CP, 424)

Listening to the poet figure read the poetry of Being, these
spirits, who no longer can partake in Being in the world,
are described as "those who would have wept to step
barefoot into reality" (CP, 423) after hearing the "poem of

life" that the large red man reads. Immediately following this reaffirmation of the goal of the later poetry, a man is described in "This Solitude of Cataracts" meditating the new metaphor:

> He never felt twice the same about the flecked river,
> Which kept flowing and never the same way twice,
>   flowing
>
> Through many places, as if it stood still in one,
> Fixed like a lake on which the wild ducks fluttered,
>
> Ruffling its common reflections, thought-like
>   Monadnocks.
> There seemed to be an apostrophe that was not spoken.
>
> There was so much that was real that was not real at
>   all.
>   (CP, 424–25)

The river that is introduced suggests first the traditional use of the river as a metaphor for time. The fact that it never flowed the same way twice seems an allusion to the Heraclitean aphorism about stepping into the same river twice. Yet this river leaps out of its boundaries "flowing through many places" while appearing to stand still "in one" place. It both moves and stands still. The man who walks beside the river visualizes both the movement and the stasis of the river that flows in time and yet appears to be the same at each succeeding moment, "like a lake on which the wild ducks fluttered" (CP, 424). While the poem concludes with a full statement of the man's desire for permanence and stability, the metaphor of the river is used again in "The Countryman." Here the river is explicitly a river in Pennsylvania. However, unlike the real river, which is named, the river in this poem comes from time and not from a place. Its source is "the cap of midnight" (CP, 428). As the river image is developed, the poem presents a figure for the imagination, "a countryman" who "walks beside the river."

> He broods of neither cap nor cape,
> But only of your swarthy motion,
> But always of the swarthy water,
> Of which Swatara is the breathing,
>
> The name. He does not speak beside you
> He is there because he wants to be
> And because being there in the heavy hills
> And along the moving of the water—
>
> Being there is being in a place
> As of a character everywhere,
> The place of a swarthy presence moving,
> Slowly, to the look of a swarthy name.
>
> (CP, 428–29)

He broods about the dark motion of the river, which in the
traditional metaphor represents the flux of time. But, his
explicit broodings are of neither cap ("the cap of midnight" named as the source of the river) nor cape ("the
cape at which / you enter the swarthy sea," which is the final
goal of the river's course). The man broods then not of
beginning or end, but of the passing of the river, which is
symbolically the passing of time. The river then has become a metaphor, but it has not lost its identity for "the
name", though separated syntactically from Swatara, the
actual river, still refers to that river. The metaphor
suggests "a swarthy presence" in which "being there is
being in a place," a line that would sound like pure
Heidegger if translated into German (for example, *Da-
Sein ist in-der-Welt-sein*). But the full metaphor is not developed until the poet meditates the process of metaphor
explicitly in "Metaphor as Degeneration." The poet proposes that a new metaphor will suggest neither the immobil-
ity nor the synthesis of opposites that the old metaphors
implied. In Wimsatt's terms, the metaphor is a process
rather than a result; a movement rather than a stasis.[44] But

----

44. See W. K. Wimsatt, "Symbol and Metaphor," in *The Verbal Icon: Studies in
the Meaning of Poetry* (New York, 1954; paperback ed., 1962), pp. 119–32.

a better description of this kind of metaphor is provided
by the poet in "Metaphor as Degeneration":

> If there is a man white as marble
> Sits in a wood, in the greenest part,
> Brooding sounds of the images of death,
>
> So there is a man in black space
> Sits in nothing that we know,
> Brooding the sounds of river noises;
>
> And these images, these reverberations,
> And others, make certain how being
> Includes death and the imagination.
>
> The marble man remains himself in space.
> The man in the black wood descends unchanged.
> It is certain that the river
>
> Is not Swatara. The swarthy water
> That flows round the earth and through the skies,
> Twisting among the universal spaces,
>
> Is not Swatara. It is being.
> That is the flock-flecked river, the water,
> The blown sheen—or is it air?
>
> How, then, is metaphor degeneration,
> When Swatara becomes this undulant river
> And the river becomes the landless, waterless ocean?
>
> Here the black violets grow down to its banks
> And the memorial mosses hang their green
> Upon it, as it flows ahead.
>
> (CP, 444–45)

The poet's proposition is that a new kind of metaphor is
needed to express his sense of Being. Two distinct images
are presented in the first two stanzas, but their presence in
the poem is conditional. The syntactic structure of these
stanzas sets up an "if" clause that effectively qualifies both
images. Each is present on the condition that the other is
present. Perhaps a clearer way to explain this dependence
of images on each other is to recall the fourth canto of "It

Must Change" (CP, 392), where the interaction and interdependence of opposites was called "the origin of change."
Both images are metaphors, or, rather, are personifications that are treated as metaphors. The first figure, a
man, is a static metaphor for the imagination. He is associated with the permanence of marble and sits in a
clearly describable place doing the traditional work of the
imagination (brooding upon the meaning of death). The
second man is virtually without description for he is an
image of death. He is in "black space," and sits in a place
that is beyond the limits of knowledge. Both men are said
to be contemplating "sounds," but neither sound is something that one is likely to hear. The "images of death" and
the "river noises" (which are associated with Being in
stanza six) are both outside normal human perception.
Having described the two figures and having indirectly
established them as metaphors for the imagination and
death respectively, the poem then announces how the relationship of these images ("these reverberations") "makes
certain how being / Includes death and the imagination"
(CP, 444).

However, while the inclusiveness of Being is posited as a
certainty, neither of the metaphors for the parts of the
whole adequately suggests the nature of the whole. Synecdoche fails, just as both of the metaphors remain static. If
Being includes both of these metaphors, how can the
poem suggest this inclusiveness? The method that the
poem proposes is indicated when, in the first two lines of
the fourth stanza, the two men are presented again. But
this time both figures are slightly changed. While the
poem explicitly states that both men, in effect, remain the
same, the images that were originally associated with
either one or the other now become interchangeable. The
new kind of metaphor will contain this characteristic. Once
the process of change and interchange has been established, the poem can then propose the solution to the
problem of creating a metaphor for Being itself.

This solution is found in the image of "the swarthy water / That flows round the earth and through the skies, / Twisting among universal spaces" (CP, 444). Stevens implicitly rejects the old metaphors by choosing a complex image that does not remain fixed. As the poet contemplates his metaphor, it changes. It is first "water," then a "flock-flecked river" reflecting light in movement. Then it becomes simply transparent, making visible everything that it contains: "—or is it air?" (CP, 444). The answer to the question "How then is metaphor degeneration?" is twofold. First, a metaphor that suggests an all-inclusive, constantly changing referent must itself have those characteristics and thus must constantly appear to be degenerating into something else. Second, even though the metaphor might suggest the nature of Being, it also misrepresents the truth of Being (and, I might add, the traditional definition of metaphor). The speaker can only assert that "It is certain that the river / Is not Swatara . . . It is being" (CP, 444). But the nature of the metaphor that is constantly changing is a difficult concept to define. Hence, when the speaker repeats the original description of the river, he includes both the real river in Pennsylvania and the fictive river that acts as a metaphor. Rather than degenerating, the metaphor expands toward the all-inclusiveness of Being. To stop the expansion and remind the reader of the origin of change, the poet returns to the "here" of both present time and present space to suggest that not only does the river expand as Being expands, it also flows ahead in time. The final stanza evokes the finality of temporal flow, for it is upon the flow of the river that "memorial mosses hang their green" (CP, 445). What has happened to the archetypal metaphor of the river as time? Stevens has reversed it in such a way that the river is now a metaphor for Being and only its motion is time.[45]

---

45. For another interpretation of the river metaphor, see Frank Doggett, p. 71, who writes that both rivers (CP, 444, 533) are metaphors for time. His

In this way he can incorporate both the inclusiveness and the temporal basis of his subject in the poetry of Being, since his metaphor functions as an expansion in space and a movement in time. This metaphorical river becomes one answer to the poet's problem of how to express a sense of Being. It is not a substance and yet is integrally related to all substances. Each attempt to name it tends to hypostatize it, and yet it must be named in order to be revealed. Here, the river image is an image without an edge that blurs and changes shape as it is described. The poem takes the Heraclitean metaphor for time and changes it in such a way as to include both the idea of Being and the related concept of temporality.

Stevens repeats this metaphor several times in the later poetry to suggest the relation of Being and time. In "An Old Man Asleep," the first poem in *The Rock,* the final sequence in the *Collected Poems,* the poet's sense of Being retains its association with the river metaphor as the gradual changes of old age show that both the world and the self are slowed as if in sleep. Hence, the sense of Being itself slows so that it becomes "The river motion, the drowsy motion of the river R" (CP, 501).

In "The River of Rivers in Connecticut," the actual referent, such as Swatara in the other poems, is no longer vital to this metaphor. The sense of the metaphor expands so that it is no longer associated with any particular river, but "the river of rivers," the central river of which all rivers might become examples:

> There is a great river this side of Stygia,
> Before one comes to the first black cataracts
> And trees that lack the intelligence of trees.

---

confusion seems based on his refusal to believe the statement "It is Being" in "Metaphor as Degeneration" and his failure to distinguish between the motion of the river (which *is* a flowing in time) and the meaning of the river as an image (or, as I define it, a metaphor).

In that river, far this side of Stygia,
The mere flowing of the water is a gayety,
Flashing and flashing in the sun. On its banks,

No shadow walks. The river is fateful,
Like the last one. But there is no ferryman.
He could not bend against its propelling force.

It is not to be seen beneath the appearances
That tell of it. The steeple at Farmington
Stands glistening and Haddam shines and sways.

It is the third commonness with light and air,
A curriculum, a vigor, a local abstraction . . .
Call it once more, a river, an unnamed flowing,

Space filled, reflecting the seasons, the folk-lore
Of each of the senses; call it, again and again,
The river that flows nowhere, like a sea.
                                        (CP, 533)

This side of the traditional metaphor for death (the river Stygia) stands a new metaphor for Being. Such a river, though, is not visible except in the changes in light and motion of the things themselves. This concept of Being is closely parallel to Heidegger's contention that Being is always *das Sein des Seienden,* something that can only be revealed through the things that have it. Hence, the river "is not to be seen beneath the appearances / That tell of it" (CP, 533). In spite of the assertion that "the mere flowing of the water is a gayety, / Flashing and flashing in the sun" (CP, 533), the nature of this river makes its meaning difficult to conceive.

Each part of the description, however, corresponds to Heidegger's indirect ways of describing Being in his ontological *Denken des Seins.* Each of the qualities of Being is peculiarly abstract and apparently unnamable. Ordinary things seem to stand out ("glisten," "shine," and "sway" in stanza four) because of the river. Yet, Being itself is not to be observed, only identified by the indefinite pronoun "it" and its metaphorical relationships. However, there should be no question about the meaning of the metaphor after the discussion of "Metaphor as Degeneration." It is a curriculum (in the original Latin sense of the word a "running" or a "course") and a "vigor" (an energy, a power), yet, because it cannot be apprehended as a thing, it exists only in the mind as an abstraction. Being is as common and pervasive as light and air (and in Stevens's poetry of Being is frequently associated with illumination and invisibile movement of change, i.e., wind). Nevertheless, it must be characterized as "an unnamed flowing." The obvious relation of Being to space and time concepts (encompassing all space and grounded in time) is included when the poet refers to it as "space filled, reflecting the seasons" (CP, 533). A more interesting description (which, as the theory of "Description Without Place" claims, is revelation) of the nature of Being occurs in the compressed phrase: "the folk-lore / Of each of the senses" (CP, 533). This metaphor directs the reader toward a more complete understanding of Being as that which provides the intentional object of every human sense. Perception without Being would be, in Heidegger's and Stevens's views, impossible. Without Being there is nothing. Stevens at this point approaches Heidegger's view that the Being of the things that make up the field of *Dasein* is the essence or basis of any perception of these things. Being is that by virtue of which things appear and are present. The thing perceived must first "be" before its presence can be brought to the mind.

The poem characterizes the motion of Being as a Heraclitean flowing or flux, yet an undirected flowing that surrounds us "like a sea." The flowing is the *Zeitlichkeit* (temporality; the sense of time as a ground) of Being, a movement that was also observed in "Metaphor as Degeneration" and "The Countryman." The movement of the river then is in time, and not in space. Hence, the river "flows nowhere"(CP, 533). In this poem one of the metaphors for Being is completed. In these final poems Stevens develops a new kind of metaphor, which is demonstrated in the poetry rather than proposed as a possible theory.

In the later poetry, this second metaphor for Being takes on new shapes and meanings as it is developed first in the autumn phase and then fully formed in the final poems of the winter phase of the imagination. In autumn, the fully realized "rock of summer" that was the center of the vision in "Credences of Summer" changes into an unknowable "rock of autumn" (CP, 476). In the autumn phase, the uncertainties of existence and premonitions of a final end lead the poet to his darkest visions.

> The hiburnal dark that hung
> In primavera, the shadow of bare rock,
> Becomes the rock of autumn, glittering,
> Ponderable source of each imponderable. . . .
>
> (CP, 476)

In this passage(from "An Ordinary Evening in New Haven"), the poet re-creates the metaphor for Being, the "glittering, / Ponderable source." But in the autumn phase, the vision is muted and obscure. The radiance, color, and trumpeting that announced the "fully visible" rock of summer in "Credences of Summer" are no longer possible. Only "a shadow of bare rock" remains. The flashing of sapphires is replaced by a faint "glittering." As the previous discussion demonstrated, autumn (like spring, the "primavera") is the dark time of the poet's creative cycle. In this sense, the autumn phase is characterized by the traditional poetic motifs of decay and degeneration.

In the winter phase, a part of Stevens's cycles that has been thoroughly discussed by Richard A. Macksey, J. Hillis Miller, and Roy Harvey Pearce,[46] the prevalent images are

---

46. Each of these critics concentrates on only the winter phase and the associations with the concept of decreation. See Pearce, pp. 404–19; Miller, pp. 264–84; and Macksey, pp. 185–203.

of nothingness, barrenness, and an enduring cold. All of these associations suggest the endpoint of life and the absolute void of death. But just as the endpoint in summer was both an end and a new beginning, so the finality that is suggested in many of the winter poems signals not merely a total absence or final annihilation, but a rebirth as well. It is not the case, as Miller claims, that "the nothing is not nothing. It is. It is being" and that "the paradoxical appearance to man of being in the form of nothing is the true cause of the ambiguity of this poetry."[47] Miller was one of the first to recognize the importance of the ontological concerns of the later poetry, and while his perception of Stevens's final interest in Being provides a genuine contribution to Stevens criticism, he quite wrongly thinks that "Being is nothing." Although Stevens's use of the images of nothingness might suggest this kind of equation, the confusion that Miller initiates adds ambiguities to poems that need not be ambiguous. The function of nothingness (and the associated images of winter) is to set apart and make possible the appearance of Being. I think I can clarify this point by comparing Heidegger's account of the nothing(*das Nicht*) and nothingness in *Einführung in die Metaphysik* and "Was ist Metaphysik"[48] with Stevens's use of nothingness. Heidegger refers to the function of the nothing as that "absolute impossibility of Being, which makes possible the disclosure of the Being of the things that are."[49] For Heidegger, it is as if nothingness were the black void against which the presence of Being becomes knowable. It plays, in Heidegger's ontological meditations, a positive role in the sense that nothingness makes the dis-

47. Miller, p. 279.
48. *Einführung in die Metaphysik* (Tübingen, 1963), pp. 84–90. Translated by Ralph Manheim as *An Introduction to Metaphysics* (New Haven, 1959; paperback ed., New York, 1961), pp. 93–104; *Was ist Metaphysik* (Bonn, 1930), pp. 32–41. Translated by R. F. C. Hull and Allan Crick as *"What is Metaphysics?"* in *Existence and Being*, pp. 337–48. See also *Sein und Zeit*, pp. 185–87.
49. *Einführung in die Metaphysik*, p. 85.

closure of Being possible. But not because Being is nothing or because nothingness is the source or ground of
Being. For Heidegger, Nothing is no-thing. It is not think-
able and it can in no way be thought of as anything but an
opposite of Being. The fact that Being appears out of (as
in "out of the context of") nothingness is not intended to
equate or identify the two opposite concepts. Just as light
appears in a context of darkness, so Being appears in a
context of nothingness. One does not equate the total absence of light with light, and in a like way, Heidegger
insists, one does not equate the absence of Being with Being.[50]

For Stevens, the images of nothingness serve the same
kind of purpose. Hence, even at the extremes of decreation that are described in the winter phase of the imagination, the nothingness and barrenness presented serve to
make visible that which would be less easily seen in a more
cluttered scene. In much the same way as the blackness of
space makes possible the perception of the stars, the decreations that are completed in the winter phase (a phase
that includes midnight, the extreme of night) define the
extreme limits of both mind and world. For this reason,
the season of the mind that is evoked in the following
passage is not total nothingness.

> The last leaf that is going to fall has fallen.
> The robins are là-bas, the squirrels, in tree-caves,
> Huddle together in the knowledge of squirrels.
>
> The wind has blown the silence of summer away.
> It buzzes beyond the horizon or in the ground:
> In mud under ponds, where the sky used to be reflected.
>
> The barrenness that appears is an exposing.
> It is not part of what is absent, a halt
> For farewells, a sad hanging on for remembrances.

---

50. *Ibid.*, pp. 85–86.

It is a coming on and a coming forth.
The pines that were fans and fragrances emerge,
Staked solidly in a gusty grappling with rocks.

The glass of air becomes an element—
It was something imagined that has been washed away.
A clearness has returned. It stands restored.

It is not an empty clearness, a bottomless sight.
It is a visibility of thought,
In which hundreds of eyes, in one mind, see at once.

                                        (CP, 487–88)

The first stanzas begin slowly in a leisurely evocation of
winter. The scene described is empty of all life, so that
even "the silence of summer" buzzes unheard beyond the
possibility of sense perception. Having described the landscape, the speaker then asserts the affirmative nature of
the scene, the season, and the nothingness that is evoked
as a setting: "The barrenness that appears is an exposing."
Even in the dead of winter, something is present. It is
neither part of what is absent in the scene nor part of what
is absent from the mind in this phase of the creative cycle.
Both the mind of the observer and the mindlessness of the
scene (figured by the "knowledge of squirrels" in tree
caves) are emptied of memory, preconception, and exterior effects. Only what is present (and clearly so) can be
exposed. At the zero point of decreation, "an exposing"
takes place. The difficulty of describing what is exposed is
repeated when the speaker calls it "a coming on and a
coming forth." Like the empty consciousness that beholds
"Nothing that is not there and the nothing that is" in a very
early version of the same experience (in "The Snow Man"
[CP, 91]), the "exposing" that appears out of nothingness
is neither completely of the mind nor completely of the
scene. The two seem fused as they are caught in a similar
phase of the seasonal cycle. Natural objects take on a new
relation to the observer (the pines begin a "gusty grappling
with rocks"). What had always been invisible, the air itself,

becomes metaphorically "an element" that is visible. But the revelation that takes place does not expose a nothingness that is positive, as C. Roland Wagner would have it.[51] Rather, the source of creativity is revealed in the vision of winter. "It is not an empty clearness, a bottomless sight," because it brings the mind and the world together at the limits of both. Heidegger's description of the function of the nothing that reveals Being by a kind of contrast provides a way of identifying what is revealed in this passage and why it cannot be equated with any particular thing or solid. Stevens adds a more explicit explanation for the preciseness and yet vagueness of this vision when he writes the conclusion to "An Ordinary Evening in New Haven" (in the following section of the poem):

> It is not in the premise that reality
> Is a solid. It may be a shade that traverses
> A dust, a force that traverses a shade.
>   (CP, 489)

The search for an adequate expression of the poet's sense of Being leads to these kinds of statements, which say a great deal about the kind of revelation that he is trying to express, but which, of necessity, must remain curiously obscure. If reality is not the solid world of physical facts and objects, what is it? Heidegger's statements about the problems of expressing the truth of Being suggest the ways in which Stevens, in this final passage of an important late poem, is as precise as he can be without misshaping the truth of his experience of Being. "It may," he writes, be like light traversing finite particles. Or, it may be the force that makes the light visible in its movement. Whichever it is, it is that by virtue of which both the light and the dust are made present. This is nearly as much as the poet can say, since these poems "Are the edgings and

---

51. C. Roland Wagner, "The Idea of Nothingness in Wallace Stevens," *Accent* 12 (Spring 1952): 11–21.

inchings of final form, / The swarming activities of the formulae / Of statement, directly and indirectly getting at . . ." (CP, 488).

In the poems of *The Rock,* the title of the last section of *The Collected Poems,* the poetry of Being reaches its final statement. The lessons of the poet of Being are most fully concentrated in the title poem of the last section.[52] The poem begins with the reflections of an old man on his past. In the first section, "Seventy Years Later," the ancient poet speaks of his doubts about the reality and value of his existence. As he meditates in a deceptively casual iambic pentameter, he recalls not just the experiences of his life, but, more important, the expressions of his existence in the poetry that he had written. "The sounds of the guitar" and "the words spoken" no longer seem to be vital. The meetings with the "interior paramour" (whether she is the "naked nameless dame," the "mundo," or the unnamed "paramour") that were recorded in "Yellow Afternoon," "The Hand as a Being," and in the "Prologue" to "Notes Toward a Supreme Fiction" are questioned along with the sufficiency of his poems. He refers to the past expressions of the disclosure of Being

As if nothingness contained a métier,
A vital assumption, an impermanence
In its permanent cold, an illusion so desired

That the green leaves came and covered the high rock,
That the lilacs came and bloomed, like a blindness cleaned,
Exclaiming bright sight, as it was satisfied,

In a birth of sight.

(CP, 526)

---

52. For other discussions of "The Rock," see especially Mills, pp. 107–09; Marjorie Perloff, "Irony in Wallace Stevens's The Rock," *American Literature* 36 (November 1964): 32–42; Mildred Hartsock, "*Wallace Stevens and 'The Rock,'*" *Personalist* 42 (Winter 1961): 66–76; Kermode, pp. 122–26; Riddel, pp. 248–51; Doggett, pp. 171–72; Pearce, pp. 409–12; and Baird, pp. 43, 88, 100–103 and *passim.*

Each of the poems of vision is described in this passage.
Was the vision an illusion? Was the poetry of Being only an
empty search for a "nothingness that contained a métier?"
Was the impermanent "vital assumption" simply a way to
keep writing, to keep occupied? These implied questions
are not answered. The poet feels "as if" that were the case,
and yet he can remember "the blindness cleaned" in the
previous cycles of creative activity. He can recall still that
sight "was satisfied, / In a birth of sight." Hence, where the
major portion of the first section seems fully tinged with
the melancholy of an old man approaching his end, the
last three lines suggest the way in which the poetry of
Being is the truth of Being-in-the-world.

> The blooming and the musk
> Were being alive, an incessant being alive,
> A particular of being, that gross universe.
>   (CP, 526)

The conditional verbs and phrases of the whole poem are
turned toward affirmation in these lines. They assert again
the value of the fictions that fulfilled ("incessant being
alive") continually the Being of the poet. Each poem was "a
particular of being," a small part of the whole of Being. In
serving as a part of the truth of Being ("that gross universe"), the poet achieved his goal.

In the second section, "The Poem as Icon," the poet
reassesses the function of the poem as it is related to the
rock of winter:

> It is not enough to cover the rock with leaves.
> We must be cured of it by a cure of the ground
> Or a cure of ourselves, that is equal to a cure
>
> Of the ground, a cure beyond forgetfulness.
>   (CP, 526)

The "cure of the ground" is not, as Roy Harvey Pearce
writes, the cure of a disease, as if the whole idea of a

ground (a base or ultimate source) were a sickness.[53]
Rather, the poet searches for the source that will cure the
poet in his old age (I take the term "cure" to mean both
something that will bring health and something that will
preserve, as in "a cure" for bacon). Since the center or
source that is represented by the rock of Being is both
within the mind and outside, the cure can be either "of the
ground" or "of ourselves." The poems ("leaves") that cover
the rock will not suffice. The poet implies that the rock
must be both covered and uncovered, revealed and hidden by the poems ("fictions of the leaves" CP, 526).

> And yet the leaves, if they broke into bud,
> If they broke into bloom, if they bore fruit,
>
> If we ate the incipient colorings
> Of their fresh culls might be a cure of the ground.
> (CP, 526)

The proposition here is that if the poetry ("the fiction of
the leaves") fulfills its potential, then the poems that we
make to cover up the truth of Being (the rock) might at the
same time reveal that same truth. While the symbols and
metaphors may seem a little confusing at this point, the
relations between images are explained when the speaker
brings them all together.

> The fiction of the leaves is the icon
>
> Of the poem, the figuration of blessedness,
> And the icon is the man. The pearled chaplet of spring,
> The magnum wreath of summer, time's autumn snood,
>
> Its copy of the sun, these cover the rock.
> These leaves are the poem, the icon and the man.
> These are a cure of the ground and of ourselves,
>
> In the predicate that there is nothing else.
> (CP, 526–27)

---

53. Pearce, "The Last Lesson of the Master," in *The Act of the Mind*, p. 123.

Hence, if the poems ripen in phase with the natural cycles, like the fruit that serves as a metaphor for the products of the imagination, then the explicit relation between fiction, leaves, icon, poem, and man is made clear by the series of equations that tend to unify all the disparate elements. The meaning of this tendency toward unity is clarified by the underlying unity provided by the rock itself. Since the poet's creations are metaphorically leaves, icons, and literally poems, there should be no problem in understanding that part of the series. But how does the icon become the man? This metaphorical relationship is illustrated by the entire cycle of the imagination which, in this final vision, tends toward a profound unity. Each of the seasons is represented by circular images (chaplet, wreath, and snood) that include each of the others. As the later poems develop a new vision of the functions of the cycles of de-creation and creation, the cycles of winter and summer are shown to be similar in the sense that both are the seasons of fulfilled desire. Stevens comes to a full statement of the necessity of a poetry of Being as he asserts that the leaves "are a cure of the ground" (a basic or fundamental cure) that will reveal the truth of the rock and yet will provide the pleasures that were projected in the final sections of "It Must Give Pleasure." As a more complete explanation of how the poetry of Being will accomplish both the revelation of the truth of Being and provide the pleasure of fulfillment, the speaker refers back to the cycles of the creative pattern:

> They bud and bloom and bear their fruit without change.
> They are more than leaves that cover the barren rock
>
> They bud the whitest eye, the pallidest sprout,
> New senses in the engenderings of sense,
> The desire to be at the end of distances,
>
> The body quickened and the mind in root.
> They bloom as a man loves, as he lives in love.
> They bear their fruit so that the year is known.

> As if its understanding was brown skin,
> The honey in its pulp, the final found,
> The plenty of the year and of the world.
>
> In this plenty, the poem makes meanings of the rock,
> Of such mixed motion and such imagery
> That its barrenness becomes a thousand things
>
> And so exists no more. This is the cure
> Of leaves and of the ground and of ourselves.
> His words are both the icon and the man.
>
> (CP, 527)

The pleasure is to be taken in each completed creation, for each creation (like the leaves) does more than simply cover the barren rock of winter, the symbol of minimal disclosure of Being; it blooms, and becomes a self-sufficient truth in itself. The poems reveal new senses, a quickened body, and a satisfied mind (in root).

As in "Credences of Summer," the full understanding of the metaphor of the rock leads to a full understanding of the possibilities of poetry, which will provide the "plenty of the year and of the world" as it brings both together within the cycle of the imagination. For the poem "makes meanings of the rock" by expanding the possibilities for fulfillment and for Being in the world. Only through poetry can the rock of Being be made fully apparent and thus only poetry can make fruitful, hence abolish the "barrenness" of the rock. Poetry becomes that which will both preserve and give health to the world, Being itself, and man. It is in this role that the words of the poet are the "icon" (both in the sense of image and as sacred personage), for they both establish and preserve Being.

To understand the implications of such a poetry, the full meaning of the rock is stated in the final section. Each of the different ways in which the rock is described affirms the interpretation, which is never made explicit. The rock is Being. It is both "the gray particular of man's life" and "the stone from which he rises, up—and—ho, / The step to the bleaker depths of his descents . . ." (CP, 528). It thus is at the beginning and at the end, present at the heights of summer (the rises) and at the depths of winter. It "is the habitation of the whole, / Its strength and measure" (CP, 528). As the "starting point of the human and the end" it fits Heidegger's definitions in each respect. For it is in Being that "space itself is contained, the gate / To the enclosure, day, the things illumined / By day, night and that which night illumines" (CP, 528).

Thus, in the last great "night-hymn" to the metaphor for Being, Stevens closes "the gate to the enclosure," having both projected and fulfilled the possibility of the unity of Being in the revelation of poetry. The final poems, written after the publication of the *Collected Poems,* affirm the direction of Stevens's last poems.[54] The full possibilities of a poetry of Being had been reached to the extent that he had communicated his vision. But as all the critics of the later poetry have agreed, "it is a difficult apperception, this gorging good" (CP, 440). The complete understanding of the development of the late poetry of Stevens depends upon a realization on the reader's part that the success of the final vision (in simple terms) is a direct result of the kind of aspirations that Stevens set for himself. Perhaps it is true in the last analysis of the poems of Being that

> We do not prove the existence of the poem.
> It is something seen and known in lesser poems.
> It is the huge, high harmony that sounds
> A little and a little, suddenly,
> By means of a separate sense.
>
> (CP, 440)

Like its subject matter, the "essential poem at the center of things" that will fully reveal the truth of Being is a goal that is only reached by a full attunement to the nature of the vision that is expressed. Thus, while "one poem proves

---

54. These poems are collected in *OP,* 92–118.

another and the whole" (CP, 441), in the sense that each poem adds a new dimension to the whole of Being, the whole of Being may be accessible only to the "clairvoyant men"

> that need no proof:
> The lover, the believer and the poet.
> Their words are chosen out of their desire,
> The joy of language, when it is themselves.
> With these they celebrate the central poem,
> The fulfillment of fulfillments, in opulent,
> Last terms, the largest, bulging still with more.
>   (CP, 441)

While the poet could never feel that he had completed his self-defined "unofficial view of being" (NA, 41), he at least grew confident in the last poems that what he had completed was an honest record of his attempts to outline and express a poetry of Being. The poems are difficult and sometimes obscure to most readers, but the reasons for the apparent difficulty and obscurity are not simply the willfulness and intentional obfuscations of the poet. Quite the reverse is true, for the later poems are attempts to render as clearly as possible the poet's sense of something that is difficult to express in concrete or literal terms. As the poet realized in "The Planet on the Table" (CP, 532–33) and "Not Ideas About the Thing, But the Thing Itself" (CP, 534), the last poems of *The Collected Poems,* each of his poems had been "the cry of its occasion, part / Of the res itself and not about it" (CP, 473), and each had made up a part of a larger whole. There was no proving the whole, because it was the whole of Being. That would have been the subject of the celebrated "essential poem at the centre of things . . ." (CP, 440), which the poet calls "a poem / Of the whole, the essential compact of the parts, / The roundness that pulls tight the ring . . ." (CP, 442). Just as the rock of Being in "Credences of Summer" represented the completed experience of fulfilled Being, so the vision of the whole of Being in "A Primitive Like An

Orb" would be the final "source of trumpeting seraphs in the eye, / A source of pleasant outbursts in the ear" (CP, 442).

Thus, while the parts of the whole suggest the nature of the whole, they remain incomplete. Part of the mood of acceptance that is present in the final poems of both *The Collected Poems* and *Opus Posthumous* is a result of the poet's realization of the limitations of being human. The poems that one *might* have written *might* have been interesting, but Pearce is wrong in implying that Stevens failed to take a last step and wrong in thinking that perhaps the answer to the riddle of the later Stevens might have been in those unwritten poems.[55]

Thus, while the comparisons with Heidegger's analysis of the nature of Being and the function of poetry help make clear the kinds of problems that Stevens treats in the later poetry, it is finally the poetry and not the philosophy that expresses the full sense of Being as being fully human. Heidegger provides the critic a way of approaching the poetry of Stevens and a theory of the ontological function of poetry, both of which are helpful in discussing the development of the poet and the meanings of his poems. But the conclusion of every critic must rest finally with the poems themselves. The explanations of how and to what degree the poems express the poet's sense of Being depend ultimately on the poems and not on the philosophy. It is perhaps only at the end of such a study that one reaches a full understanding of Heidegger's elevated concept of the poet's role in the study of Being. I suggest that Stevens is as deserving of Heidegger's plaudits as Hölderlin and Rilke, for like both of these German poets, Stevens is the poet of the poetry of Being.

---

55. See "The Last Lesson of the Master," in *The Act of the Mind*, pp. 121, 137–42.

Selected Bibliography

Adorno, T. W. "Husserl and the Problem of Idealism." *Journal of Philosophy* 37 (1940): 5–18.

Alleman, Beda. *Hölderlin und Heidegger.* Zürich: Atlantis, 1956.

Bachelard, Gaston. *The Poetics of Space.* Translated by Marie Jolas. New York: The Orion Press, 1964.

Bachelard, Suzanne. *A Study of Husserl's "Formal and Transcendental Logic."* Translated by L. E. Embree. Evanston, Ill.: Northwestern University Press, 1968.

Baker, Howard. "Add This to Rhetoric." *The Harvard Advocate* 127 (December 1940): 16–18.

Baird, James. *The Dome and the Rock: Structure in the Poetry of Wallace Stevens.* Baltimore, Md.: The Johns Hopkins Press, 1968.

———. "Transvaluation in the Poetry of Wallace Stevens." *"Tennessee Studies in Literature, Special Number; Studies in Honor of John C. Hodges and Alwin Thaler.* Knoxville, Tenn., 1961, pp. 163–73.

Beaufret, Jean. "Heidegger et le problème de la vérité." *Fontaine* 63 (1947): 146–74.

Beck, Maximillian. "The Last Phase of Husserl's Phenomenology." *Philosophy and Phenomenological Research* 1 (1941): 479–91.

Benamou, Michel. "Beyond Emerald or Amethyst." *Dartmouth College Library Bulletin.* n.s. 4 (December 1961): 60–66.

———. "Wallace Stevens and the Symbolist Imagination." *Journal of English Literary History* 31 (March 1964): 35–63. Reprinted in *The Act of the Mind: Essays on the Poetry of Wallace Stevens,* edited by Roy Harvey Pearce and J. Hillis Miller. Baltimore: The Johns Hopkins Press, 1965, pp. 92–120.

———. *Wallace Stevens and the Symbolist Imagination.* Princeton, N.J.: The Princeton University Press, 1972.

———. "The Structures of Wallace Stevens' Imagination." *Mundus Artium* 1 (Winter 1967): 73–84.

Berger, Gaston. *Le Cogito dans la philosophie de Husserl.* Paris: Aubier, 1941.

Bertholf, Robert J. "The Vast Ventriloquism: Wordsworth and Wallace Stevens." Ph.D. Dissertation, University of Oregon, 1968.

Bevis, William. "Metaphor in Stevens." *Shenandoah* 15 (Winter 1964): 35–48.

Bewley, Marius. "The Poetry of Wallace Stevens." *Partisan Review* 16 (September 1949): 895–915. Reprinted in *The Achievement of Wallace Stevens,* edited by Ashley Brown and Robert S. Haller. New York: J. B. Lippincott Company, 1963, pp. 141–61.

Biemel, Walter. *Le Concept de monde chez Heidegger.* Louvain: Nauwelaerts, 1950.

Birault, Henri. "Existence et vérité d'après Heidegger." *Revue de Métaphysique et de la Morale* 56 (1950): 35–87.

Black, Max. *Models and Metaphors: Studies in Language and Philosophy.* Ithaca, N. Y.: Cornell University Press, 1962.

Blackmur, R. P. "Examples of Wallace Stevens." *Hound & Horn* 2 (January–March 1932): 223–55. Reprinted in his *Form and Value in Modern Poetry.* Garden City, N. Y.: Doubleday & Company, Inc., 1957, pp. 183–212; also reprinted in *The Achievement of Wallace Stevens,* edited by Ashley Brown and Robert S. Haller. New York: J. B. Lippincott Company, 1963, pp. 52–80.

———. "An Abstraction Blooded." *Partisan Review* 10 (May–June 1943): 297–301. Reprinted under the title "Wallace Stevens: An Abstraction Blooded," in his *Form and*

Value in Modern Poetry. Garden City, N. Y.: Doubleday & Company, 1957, pp. 213–18.

———. "The Substance that Prevails." *The Kenyon Review* 17 (Winter 1955): 95–110.

Bloom, Harold. "Notes Toward a Supreme Fiction: A Commentary." In *Wallace Stevens: A Collection of Critical Essays,* edited by Marie Borroff. Englewood Cliffs, N.J.: Prentice-Hall, Inc., 1963, pp. 76–95.

———. "The Central Man: Emerson, Whitman, Wallace Stevens." *Massachusetts Review* 7 (Winter 1966): 23–42.

Brand, Gerd. *Welt, Ich, und Zeit.* The Hague: Martinus Nijhoff, 1955.

Brown, Ashley and Haller, Robert S., eds. *The Achievement of Wallace Stevens.* New York: J. B. Lippincott Company, 1962.

Brown, Merle E. "Concordia Discors in the Poetry of Wallace Stevens." *American Literature* 34 (May 1962): 246–69.

———. *Wallace Stevens: The Poem as Act.* Detroit, Mich.: Wayne State University Press, 1970.

Browne, Robert M. "Grammar and Rhetoric in Criticism." *Texas Studies in Literature and Language* 3 (Spring 1961): 144–57.

Bryer, Jackson, and Riddel, Joseph N. "A Checklist of Stevens Criticism." *Twentieth Century Literature* 8 (October 1962–January 1963): 124–42.

Buchwald, Emile. "Wallace Stevens: The Delicate Eye of the Mind." *American Quarterly* 14 (Summer 1962): 185–96.

Buddeberg, Else. *Heidegger und die Dichtung: Hölderlin, Rilke.* Stuttgart: J. B. Metzlersche, 1953.

——— *Denken und Dichten des Seins: Heidegger und Rilke.* Stuttgart: J. B. Metzlersche, 1956.

Buhr, Marjorie. "The Impossible Possible Philosopher's Man: Wallace Stevens." *The Carrell* 6 (June 1965): 7–13.

Burney, William. *Wallace Stevens.* New York: Twayne, 1968.

Burnshaw, Stanley. "Turmoil on the Middle Ground." *New Masses* 17 (October 1, 1935): 42.

———. "Wallace Stevens and the Statue." *The Sewanee Review* 69 (July–September 1961): 355–66.

Buttel, Robert. *The Making of Harmonium.* Princeton, N. J.: The Princeton University Press, 1967.

Cambon, Glauco. "Nothingness as Catalyst: An Analysis of Three Poems by Ungaretti, Rilke and Stevens." *Comparative Literature Studies,* Spec. Advance Issue, 1963, pp. 91–99.

————. "Wallace Stevens: 'Notes Toward a Supreme Fiction,' " in his *The Inclusive Flame: Studies in Modern American Poetry.* Bloomington, Ind.: Indiana University Press, 1965; paperback edition, 1965, pp. 79–119.

Cairns, Dorion. "Results of Husserl's Investigations." *Journal of Philosophy* 36 (1941): 479–91.

Chapelle, Albert. *L'ontologie phénoménologique de Heidegger.* Paris-Bruxelles: Editions Universitaires, 1962.

Davie, Donald. "The Auroras of Autumn." *Perspective* 7 (Autumn 1954): 125–36. Reprinted in *The Achievement of Wallace Stevens,* edited by Ashley Brown and Robert S. Haller. New York: J. B. Lippincott Company, 1963, pp. 166–78.

————. "Notes on the Later Poems of Stevens." *Shenandoah* 7 (Summer 1956): 40–41.

Delius, Harald. "Descriptive Interpretation." *Philosophy and Phenomenological Research* 13 (1953): 305–23.

Dembo, L. S. "Wallace Stevens: Meta-men and Para-things," in his *Conceptions of Reality in Modern American Poetry.* Berkeley and Los Angeles: University of California Press, 1966, pp. 81–107.

De Waelhens, Alphonse. *La Philosophie de Martin Heidegger.* Louvain: Institut Supérieur de Philosophie, 1942.

————. *Phénoménologie et vérité: Essai sur l'évolution de l'idée de vérité chez Husserl et Heidegger.* Paris: Presses Universitaires, 1953.

Doggett, Frank. *Stevens' Poetry of Thought.* Baltimore: the Johns Hopkins Press, 1966; paperback edition, 1966.

Dondeyne, Albert. "La différence ontologique chez M. Heidegger." *Revue Philosophique de Louvain* 56 (1958): 35–62, 251–293.

Donoghue, Denis. "Wallace Stevens," in his *Connoisseurs of Chaos: Ideas of Order in Modern American Poetry.* New York: The Macmillan Company, 1965, pp. 190–215.

Dufrenne, Mikel. *The Notion of A Priori*. Translated by Edward S. Casy. Evanston, Ill.: Northwestern University Press, 1966.

Earle, William. "Wahl on Heidegger on Being." *Philosophical Review* 67 (1958): 85–90.

Eberhardt, Richard. "Emerson and Wallace Stevens." *The Literary Review* 7 (Autumn 1963): 51–71.

Edie, James M. "Transcendental Phenomenology and Existentialism." *Philosophy and Phenomenological Research* 25 (1964–65): 52–63. Reprinted in *Phenomenology: The Philosophy of Edmund Husserl and Its Interpretation*, edited by Joseph J. Kockelmans. New York: Anchor Books, 1967.

Ehrenpreis, Irvin, ed. *Wallace Stevens: A Critical Anthology*. Harmondsworth, Eng.: Penguin Books, 1972.

Eliade, Mircea. *Cosmos and History: The Myth of the Eternal Return*. Translated by Willard R. Trask. New York: Pantheon Books, 1954; paperback edition, New York: Harper and Row, 1951.

———. *Myth and Reality*. Translated by Willard R. Trask. New York: Harper and Row, 1963.

———. *Patterns in Comparative Religion*. Translated by Willard R. Trask. New York: Harper and Row, 1958.

———. *The Sacred and the Profane: The Nature of Religion*. Translated by Willard R. Trask. New York: Harcourt, Brace and World, 1959; paperback edition, 1959.

Enck, John J. *Wallace Stevens: Images and Judgments*. Carbondale, Ill.: Southern Illinois University Press, 1964.

Farber, Marvin. *The Aims of Phenomenology: The Motives, Methods, and Impact of Husserl's Thought*. New York: Harper and Row, 1966.

———. *The Foundation of Phenomenology: Edmund Husserl and the Quest for a Rigorous Science of Philosophy*. Cambridge, Mass.: Harvard University Press, 1943.

———. "Heidegger on the Essence of Truth." *Philosophy and Phenomenological Research* 18 (1958): 523–32.

———. "The Ideal of a Presuppositionless Philosophy," in *Philosophical Essays in Memory of Edmund Husserl*, edited by Marvin Farber. Cambridge, Mass.: Harvard University Press, 1940. Reprinted in *Phenomenology: The Philosophy of*

Edmund Husserl and Its Interpretations, edited by Joseph J. Kockelmans. New York: Anchor Books, 1967.

Finch, John. "North and South in Stevens' American." *The Harvard Advocate* 127 (December 1940): 23–26.

Fink, Eugen. "Operative Begriffe in Husserls Phänomenologie." *Zeitschrift für philosophische Forschung* 11 (1957): 321–37.

————. *Studien zur Phänomenologie: 1930–1939.* The Hague: Nijhoff, 1966.

Frank, Joseph. *The Widening Gyre: Crisis and Mastery in Modern Literature.* New Brunswick, N.J.: Rutgers University Press, 1963.

Freedman, Ralph. "Wallace Stevens and Rainer Maria Rilke: Two Versions of a Poetic," *The Poet as Critic,* edited by Frederick P. W. McDowell. Evanston, Ill.: Northwestern University Press, 1967, pp. 60–80.

Frings, Manfred S., ed. *Heidegger and the Quest for Truth.* Chicago: Quadrangle Books, 1968.

Frye, Northrop. "The Realistic Oriole: A Study of Wallace Stevens." *Hudson Review* 10 (Autumn, 1957): 353–70. Reprinted in his *Fables of Identity: Studies in Poetic Mythology.* New York: Harcourt, Brace & World, Inc., 1963, pp. 230–55; also reprinted in *Wallace Stevens: A Collection of Critical Essays,* edited by Marie Borroff. Englewood Cliffs, N.J.: Prentice-Hall, 1963, pp. 161–176.

Fuchs, Daniel. *The Comic Spirit of Wallace Stevens.* Durham, N.C.: Duke University Press, 1963.

————. "Wallace Stevens and Santayana," in *Patterns of Commitment in American Literature,* edited by Marston LaFrance. Toronto: University of Toronto Press, 1967, pp. 135–64.

Fulton, James Street. "Husserl's Significance for the Theory of Truth." *Monist* 45 (1945): 264–306.

Funke, Gerhard. *Zur Transzendentalen Phänomenologie.* Bonn: Bouvier, 1957.

Gibson, W. R. Boyce. "The Problem of Real and Ideal in the Phenomenology of Husserl." *Mind* 34 (1925): 311–33.

Granel, Gérard. *Le Sens du temps et de la perception chez E. Husserl.* Paris: Gallimard, 1968.

Gray, J. Glenn. "Heidegger's 'Being,'" *Journal of Philosophy* 49 (1952): 415–22.

———. "Heidegger's Course from Human Existence to Nature." *Journal of Philosophy* 56 (1957): 197–207.

Grene, Marjorie. *Martin Heidegger.* New York: Hilary, 1957.

Hamilton, Kenneth G. "Edmund Husserl's Contribution to Philosophy." *Journal of Philosophy* 21 (1939): 225–32.

Hartsock, Mildred E. "Image and Idea in the Poetry of Stevens." *Twentieth Century Literature* 7 (April 1961): 10–21.

———. "Wallace Stevens and the 'Rock.'" *Personalist* 42 (Winter 1961): 66–76

Heidegger, Martin. "The Age of the World View." Translated by Marjorie Grene. *Measure* 2 (1951): 269–84.

———. *Being and Time.* Translated by John Macquarrie and Edward Robinson. London: SCM, 1962.

———. "Brief über den 'Humanismus,'" in *Platons Lehre von der Wahrheit.* Bern: Francke, 1947, pp. 53–119.

———. *Discourse on Thinking,* Translated by J. Anderson and E. E. Freund. New York: Harper and Row, 1966.

———. *Einführung in die Metaphysik.* Tübingen: Niemeyer, 1953.

———. *Erläuterung zu Hölderlins Dichtung.* 2nd ed. Frankfurt: Klostermann, 1951.

———. *Essays in Metaphysics: Identity and Difference.* Translated by K. F. Leidecker. New York: Philosophical Library, 1960.

———. *The Essence of Reasons.* Translated by Terrence Malick. Evanston, Ill.: Northwestern University Press, 1969.

———. *De L'Essence de la Vérité.* Translated by Alphonse De Waelhens. Louvain: Institut Supérieur de Philosophie, 1948.

———. *Gelassenheit.* Pfullingen: Neske, 1959.

———. "Hölderlin and the Essence of Poetry." Translated by Douglas Scott, in *Existence and Being,* edited by Werner Brock. Chicago: Regnery, 1949; paperback edition, 1967, pp. 270–91.

———. "Hölderlins Himmel und Erde," in *Hölderlin Jahrbuch.* Tübingen: Mohr, 1960, pp. 17–39.

———. *Holzwege*. Frankfurt: Klostermann, 1950.

———. *Identität und Differenz*. Pfullingen: Neske, 1957.

———. *Introduction to Metaphysics*. Translated by Ralph Mannheim. New Haven: Yale University Press, 1958; paperback edition, New York: Anchor Books, 1961.

———. *Kant and the Problem of Metaphysics*. Translated by James Churchill. Bloomington, Ind.: Indiana University Press, 1962; paperback edition, 1965.

———. *Kant et le problème de la métaphysique*. With Introduction and translated by A. De Waelhens and Walter Biemel. Paris: Presses Universitaires, 1953.

———. *Kant und das Problem der Metaphysik*. 2nd ed. Frankfurt: Klostermann, 1951.

———. "The Origin of a Work of Art." Translated by A. Hofstaedter, in *Philosophies of Art and Beauty*. New York: Random House, 1965, pp. 647–701.

———. "On the Essence of Truth." Translated by R. F. C. Hull and Alan Crick, in *Existence and Being*, edited by Werner Brock. Chicago: Regnery, 1949; paperback edition, 1967, pp. 292–324.

———. *The Question of Being*. Translated by W. Kluback and J. Wild. New York: Twayne, 1959.

———. "Remembrance of the Poet." Translated by Douglas Scott, in *Existence and Being*, edited by Werner Brock. Chicago: Regnery, 1949; paperback edition, 1967, pp. 233–69.

———. *Zur Seinsfrage*. Frankfurt, Klostermann, 1956.

———. *Sein und Zeit*. Halle a. d. s.: Niemeyer, 1929.

———. *Unterwegs zur Sprache*. Pfullingen: Neske, 1959.

———. *Zu einem Vers von Mörike*. Zürich: Atlantis, 1951.

———. *Vorträge und Aufsätze*. Pfullingen: Neske, 1954.

———. *Was Heisst Denken*. Tübingen: Niemeyer, 1954.

———. *Was ist Metaphysik?* 5th ed. [Introduction and Epilogue added.] Frankfurt: Klostermann, 1949.

———. *What is a Thing?* Translated by W. B. Barton, Jr., and Vera Dutsch. Chicago: Regnery, 1967.

————. *What is Called Thinking?* Translated by Fred D. Wieck and J. Glenn Gray. New York: Harper and Row, 1968.

————. "What is Metaphysics?" Translated by R. F. C. Hull and Alan Crick, in *Existence and Being,* edited by Werner Brock. Chicago: Regnery, 1949; paperback edition, 1967, pp. 325–61.

————. *Vom Wesen des Grundes.* 4th ed. Frankfurt: Klostermann, 1955.

————. *Vom Wesen der Wahrheit.* Frankfurt: Klostermann, 1943.

Heringman, Bernard. "The Poetry of Synthesis." *Perspective* 7 (Autumn 1954), 167–75.

Husserl, Edmund. *Cartesianische Meditationen und Pariser Vorträge.* Edited by S. Strasser. (*Husserliana,* Band I.) The Hague: Martinus Nijhoff, 1950.

————. *Cartesian Meditations.* Translated by Dorion Cairns. The Hague: Martinus Nijhoff, 1960; paperback edition, 1964.

————. *The Crisis of European Sciences and Transcendental Phenomenology: An Introduction to Phenomenological Philosophy.* Translated by David Carr. Evanston, Ill.: Northwestern University Press, 1970.

————. *Erste Philosophie (1923–24), Part II, Theorie der phänomenologischen Reduktion.* Edited with introduction by Rudolf Boehm. The Hague: Nijhoff, 1959.

————. *Experience and Judgment.* Translated by James S. Churchill and Karl Ameriks. Evanston, Ill.: Northwestern University Press, 1973.

————. *Formal and Transcendental Logic.* Translated by Dorion Cairns. The Hague: Martinus Nijhoff, 1969.

————. *Die Idee der Phänomenologie: Fünf Vorlesungen.* Edited by Walter Biemel. (*Husserliana,* Band II.) The Hague: Martinus Nijhoff, 1950.

————. *The Idea of Phenomenology.* Translated by William P. Alston and George Nakhnikian. The Hague: Martinus Nijhoff, 1964.

————. *Ideen zu einer reinen Phänomenologie und phänomenologischen Philosophie.* 3 vols. Edited by Walter Biemel and Marly

Biemel. (*Husserliana,* Bands, III, IV, and V.) The Hague: Martinus Nijhoff, 1950–52.

———— . *Ideas: General Introduction to Pure Phenomenology.* Translated by W. R. Boyce Gibson. London: Allen and Unwin, 1931.

———— . "Philosophie als strenge Wissenshaft." *Logos* 1 (1910–11): 289–341.

Jarrell, Randall. "Reflections on Wallace Stevens." *Partisan Review* 18 (May-June 1951): 335–44. Reprinted in his *Poetry and the Age.* New York: Alfred A. Knopf, 1953; paperback edition, New York: Vintage Books, 1951, pp. 121–34.

———— . "The Collected Poems of Wallace Stevens." *Yale Review,* n. s. 44 (March 1955): 340–53. Reprinted in *The Achievement of Wallace Stevens,* edited by Ashley Brown and Robert S. Haller. New York: J. B. Lippincott Company, 1963, pp. 179–92.

Kaufmann, W. F. "The Value of Heidegger's Analysis of Existence for Literary Criticism." *Modern Language Notes* 47 (1933): 487–91.

Kermode, Frank. *Wallace Stevens.* Edinburgh: Oliver and Boyd Ltd., 1960; paperback edition, New York: Grove Press, 1960.

———— . "The Words of the World: On Wallace Stevens." *Encounter* 14 (April 1960): 45–50.

———— . " 'Notes Toward a Supreme Fiction': A Commentary." *Annali dell Istituto Universitario Orientale: Sezione Germanica* 4 (Naples, 1961): 173–201.

———— . *The Sense of An Ending: Studies in the Theory of Fiction.* Oxford: Oxford University Press, 1966; paperback edition, 1968.

Kessler, Edward. *Images of Wallace Stevens.* New Brunswick, N. J.: Rutgers University Press, 1972.

King, Magda. *Heidegger's Philosophy: A Guide to His Basic Thought.* New York: MacMillan, 1964; paperback edition, Dell Publishing Co., 1966.

Kocklemans, Joseph J. *A First Introduction to Husserl's Phenomenology.* Pittsburgh, Pa.: Duquesne University Press, 1967.

———. *Martin Heidegger: A First Introduction to His Philosophy.* Pittsburgh, Pa.: Duquesne University Press, 1965.

———, ed. *Phenomenology: The Philosophy of Edmund Husserl and Its Interpretation.* New York: Anchor Books, 1967.

Landgrebe, Ludwig. *Phänomenologie und Metaphysik.* Hamburg: Schröder, 1949.

Langbaum, Robert. "The New Nature Poetry." *American Scholar* 28 (Summer 1959): 323–40.

Langen, Thomas. *The Meaning of Heidegger: A Critical Study of an Existentialist Phenomenology.* New York: Columbia University Press, 1959; paperback edition, 1961.

Lauer, Quentin. *Phénoménologie de Husserl: Essai sur la genèse de l'intentionnalité.* Paris: Presses Universitaires, 1955.

———. *The Triumph of Subjectivity: An Introduction to Transcendental Phenomenology.* New York: Fordham University Press, 1958.

Lentricchia, Frank. *The Gaiety of Language: An Essay on the Radical Poetics of W. B. Yeats and Wallace Stevens.* Berkeley and Los Angeles: University of California, 1968.

Levi, Albert William. *Literature, Philosophy and the Imagination.* Bloomington, Ind.: Indiana University Press, 1962.

Levinas, Emmanuel. *En découvrant l'existence avec Husserl et Heidegger.* Paris: Vrin, 1949.

Litz, A. Walton. *Introspective Voyager: The Poetic Development of Wallace Stevens.* New York: Oxford University Press, 1972.

Löwith, Karl. *Heidegger: Denker in dürftiger Zeit.* Frankfurt: Fischer, 1953.

Macksey, Richard A. "The Climates of Wallace Stevens," in *The Act of the Mind: Essays on the Poetry of Wallace Stevens,* edited by Roy Harvey Pearce and J. Hillis Miller. Baltimore, Md.: The Johns Hopkins Press, 1965, pp. 185–223.

Martz, Louis L. "Wallace Stevens: The Romance of the Precise." *Yale Poetry Review* 2 (August 1946): 13–20.

———. "Wallace Stevens: The World as Meditation." *Yale Review,* n.s. 47 (Summer 1958): 517–36. Reprinted in his *The Poem of the Mind: Essays on Poetry/English and American.* New

York: Oxford University Press, 1966, pp. 200–223; also reprinted in *Wallace Stevens: A Collection of Critical Essays,* edited by Marie Borroff. Englewood Cliffs, N.J.: Prentice-Hall, 1963, pp. 133–50; also reprinted in *The Achievement of Wallace Stevens,* edited by Ashley Brown and Robert S. Haller. New York: J. B. Lippincott Company, 1963, pp. 211–31.

————. "The World of Wallace Stevens." *Modern American Poetry,* Focus Five, edited by B. Rajan. London: Dennis Dobson Ltd., 1950. Reprinted under the title "Wallace Stevens: The Skeptical Music," in his *The Poem of the Mind: Essays on Poetry/English and American.* New York: Oxford University Press, 1966, pp. 183–99.

McFadden, George. "Probing for an Integration: Color Symbolism in Wallace Stevens." *Modern Philology* 57 (February 1961): 186–93.

McNamara, Peter L., ed. *Critics on Wallace Stevens.* Coral Gables, Fla. , University of Miami Press, 1972.

Merlan, Philip. "Time Consciousness in Husserl and Heidegger." *Philosophy and Phenomenological Research* 8 (1947): 25–53.

Merleau-Ponty, Maurice. *Phénoménologie de la perception.* Paris: Gallimard, 1945.

————. *Phenomenology of Perception.* Translated by Colin Smith. London: Routledge & Kegan Paul, 1962.

Miller, J. Hillis. "Wallace Stevens' Poetry of Being." *Journal of English Literary History* 31 (March 1964): 86–105. Reprinted in *The Act of the Mind: Essays on the Poetry of Wallace Stevens,* edited by Roy Harvey Pearce and J. Hillis Miller. Baltimore: The Johns Hopkins Press, 1965, pp. 143–62.

————. "Wallace Stevens," in his *Poets of Reality: Six Twentieth-Century Writers.* Cambridge, Mass.: Harvard University Press, 1965, pp. 217–84.

Mills, Ralph J., Jr. "Wallace Stevens: The Image of the Rock." *Accent,* 18 (Spring 1958): 75–89. Reprinted in *Wallace Stevens: A Collection of Critical Essays,* edited by Marie Borroff. Englewood Cliffs, N. J.: Prentice-Hall, Inc., 1963, pp. 96–110.

Morse, Samuel French. "The Motive for Metaphor—Wallace Stevens: His Poetry and Practice." *Origin,* no. 5 (Spring 1952), pp. 3–65.

————. " 'Letters d'un Soldat.' " *Dartmouth College Library Bulletin,* n.s. 4 (December 1961): 44–50.

————. "The Native Element." *The Kenyon Review* 20 (Summer 1958): 446–65. Reprinted in *The Achievement of Wallace Stevens,* edited by Ashley Brown and Robert S. Haller. New York: J. B. Lippincott Company, 1963, pp. 193–210.

————. "Wallace Stevens, Bergson, Pater." *Journal of English Literary History* 31 (March 1964): 1–34. Reprinted in *The Act of the Mind: Essays on the Poetry of Wallace Stevens,* edited by Roy Harvey Pearce and J. Hillis Miller. Baltimore, Md.: The Johns Hopkins Press, 1965, pp. 58–91.

————. *Wallace Stevens: Poetry as Life.* New York: Pegasus, 1970.

————. "Wallace Stevens: Some Ideas About the Thing Itself." *Boston University Studies in English* 2 (Spring 1965): 55–64.

Nassar, Eugene Paul. *Wallace Stevens: An Anatomy of Figuration.* Philadelphia, Pa.: University of Pennsylvania Press, 1965.

Natanson, Maurice. *Edmund Husserl: Philosopher of Infinite Tasks.* Evanston, Ill.: Northwestern University Press, 1973.

Owen, David. " 'The Glass of Water.' " *Perspective* 7 (Autumn 1954): 175–83.

Otto, Rudolf. *The Idea of the Holy.* Translated by B. L. Bracey. London: n.p., 1923.

————. *Mysticism East and West: A Comparative Analysis of the Nature of Mysticism.* Translated by B. L. Bracey and R. C. Payne. New York: Macmillan, 1932; paperback edition, Collier Books, 1962.

Pack, Robert. *Wallace Stevens: An Approach to his Poetry and Thought.* New Brunswick, N. J.: Rutgers University Press, 1958.

Pearce, Roy Harvey. *The Continuity of American Poetry.* Princeton, N. J.: Princeton University Press, 1961; paperback edition, 1965.

————. "Wallace Stevens: The Life of the Imagination." *Publications of the Modern Language Association* 66 (September 1951):

561–82. Reprinted in *Wallace Stevens: A Collection of Critical Essays,* edited by Marie Borroff. Englewood Cliffs, N. J.: Prentice-Hall, Inc., 1963, pp. 111–32.

_____ . "Wallace Stevens: The Last Lesson of the Master." *Journal of English Literary History* 31 (March 1964): 64–86. Reprinted in *The Act of the Mind: Essays on the Poetry of Wallace Stevens,* edited by Roy Harvey Pearce and J. Hillis Miller. Baltimore, Md.: The Johns Hopkins Press, 1965, pp. 121–42.

_____ , and Miller, J. Hillis, eds. *The Act of the Mind: Essays on the Poetry of Wallace Stevens.* Baltimore, Md.: The Johns Hopkins Press, 1965.

Peirce, Charles Sanders. *The Collected Papers of Charles Sanders Perice.* Edited by Charles Hartshorne and Paul Weiss. Cambridge, Mass.: Harvard University Press, 1931.

Perloff, Marjorie. "Irony in Wallace Stevens' *The Rock.*" *American Literature* 36 (November 1964): 327–42.

Pöggeler, Otto. *Der Denkweg Martin Heideggers.* Pfullingen: Neske, 1963.

_____ . "Sein als Ereignis." *Zeitschrift für philosophische Forschung.* 13 (1959): 597–632.

Poggioli, Renato, trans. *Wallace Stevens: Mattino Domenicale Ed Altre Poesie.* Torino, Italy: Giulio Einaudi, 1954.

Poulet, Georges. *Studies in Human Time.* Translated by Elliott Coleman. Baltimore: The Johns Hopkins Press, 1956.

_____ . *The Metamorphoses of the Circle.* Translated by Carley Dawson and Elliott Coleman. Baltimore: The Johns Hopkins Press, 1966.

Quinn, Sister M. Bernetta. "Metamorphosis in Wallace Stevens." *The Sewanee Review* 60 (Spring 1952): 230–52. Reprinted in her *The Metamorphic Tradition in Modern Poetry.* New Brunswick, N. J.: Rutgers University Press, 1955, pp. 49–58; also reprinted in *Wallace Stevens: A Collection of Critical Essays,* edited by Marie Borroff. Englewood Cliffs, N. J.: Prentice-Hall, Inc., 1963, pp. 54–70.

Richard, Jean-Pierre. *Littérature et sensation.* Paris: Editions de Seuil, 1954.

Richardson, William J. *Heidegger: Through Phenomenology to Thought.* The Hague: Martinus Nijhoff, 1967.

Ricoeur, Paul. *Husserl: An Analysis of His Phenomenology.* Translated by Edward G. Ballard and Lester E. Embree. Evanston, Ill.: Northwestern University Press, 1967.

Riddel, Joseph H. "The Contours of Stevens' Criticism." *Journal of English Literary History* 31 (March 1964): 106–38. Reprinted in *The Act of the Mind: Essays on the Poetry of Wallace Stevens,* edited by Roy Harvey Pearce and J. Hillis Miller. Baltimore: The Johns Hopkins Press, 1965, pp. 243–76.

———. *The Clairvoyant Eye: The Poetry and Poetics of Wallace Stevens.* Baton Rouge, La.: Louisiana State University Press, 1965.

———. "Wallace Stevens—'It Must be Human,' " *The English Journal* 56 (April 1967): 525–34.

———. "Blue Voyager." *Salmagundi* 2, no. 2 (1967–68): 61–74.

Ryle, Gilbert. [A Review of Heidegger's *Sein und Zeit*]. *Mind* 38 (1929): 355–70.

Santayana, George. *Interpretations of Poetry and Religion.* New York: Harper Torchbook, 1957.

Schmidt, Richard. "Husserl's Transcendental-Phenomenological Reduction." *Philosophy and Phenomenological Research* 20 (1959): 238–45. Reprinted in *Phenomenology: The Philosophy of Edmund Husserl and Its Interpretation,* edited by Joseph J. Kockelmans. Garden City, N. Y.: Anchor Books, 1967, pp. 58–67.

Schrader, George. "Heidegger's Ontology of Human Existence." *Review of Metaphysics* 10 (1956): 35–56.

Schrag, Calvin O. "Phenomenology, Ontology, and History in the Philosophy of Martin Heidegger." *Revue Internationale de Philosophie* 12 (1958): 117–32. Reprinted in *Phenomenology: The Philosophy of Edmund Husserl and Its Interpretation,* edited by Joseph J. Kockelmans. Garden City, N. J.: Anchor Books, 1967, pp. 277–93.

Seidel, George Joseph. *Martin Heidegger and the Pre-Socratics: An Introduction to His Thought.* Lincoln, Neb.: University of Nebraska Press, 1964.

Sheehan, Donald. "Wallace Stevens' Theory of Metaphor." *Papers on Language and Literature* 2 (Winter 1966): 57–66.

———."Wallace Stevens in the 30's: Gaudy Bosh and Gesture's Whim" in *The Thirties: Fiction, Poetry, Drama,* edited by Warren French. Deland, Fla.: Everett Edwards, Inc., 1967, pp. 147–67.

Sokolowski, Robert. *The Formation of Husserl's Concept of Constitution.* The Hague: Martinus Nijhoff, 1964.

Spiegelberg, Herbert. *The Phenomenological Movement: A Historical Introduction.* 2 vols. The Hague: Martinus Nijhoff, 1960.

Stallknecht, Newton P. "Absence in Reality: A Study in The Epistemology of the Blue Guitar." *The Kenyon Review* 21 (Autumn 1959): 545–62.

Stern, Herbert J. *Wallace Stevens: Art of Uncertainty.* Ann Arbor, Mich.: The University of Michigan Press, 1966.

Strasser, Stephen. *Phenomenology and the Human Sciences.* Pittsburgh, Pa.: Duquesne University Press, 1963.

Sukenick, Ronald. *Wallace Stevens: Musing the Obscure.* New York: New York University Press, 1967; paperback edition, 1967.

Vaihinger, Hans. *The Philosophy of "As If."* translated by C. K. Ogden. London: Kegan Paul, Trench, Trubner and Co., Ltd., 1924.

Vendler, Helen Hennessey. *On Extended Wings.* Cambridge, Mass.: Harvard University Press, 1969.

Versenyi, Laszlo. *Heidegger, Being, and Truth.* New Haven and London: Yale University Press, 1965.

Vycinas, Vincent. *Earth and Gods: An Introduction to the Philosophy of Martin Heidegger.* The Hague: Martinus Nijhoff, 1961.

Wagner, C. Roland. "A Central Poetry." *Hudson Review* 5 (Spring 1952): 144–48. Reprinted in *Wallace Stevens: A Collection of Critical Essays,* edited by Marie Borroff. Englewood Cliffs, N. J.: Prentice-Hall, Inc., 1963, pp. 71–75.

———. "The Idea of Nothingness in Wallace Stevens." *Accent* 12 (Spring 1952): 111–21.

Wahl, Jean. *Phénoménologie—Existence.* Paris: Arthaud, 1947.

_____ . *Vers la fin de l'ontologie: Etude sur l'introduction dans la métaphysique par Heidegger.* Paris: Société d'Enseignement Supérieur, 1956.

_____ . *Les philosophes de l'existence.* Paris: Librairie Armand Colin, 1959.

_____ . *Philosophies of Existence: An Introduction to The Basic Thought of Kierkegaard, Heidegger, Jaspers, Marcel, Sartre.* Translated by F. M. Lory. New York: Schocken Books, 1969.

Watts, Harold H. "Wallace Stevens and the Rock of Summer." *The Kenyon Review* 14 (Winter 1952): 122–40.

Weatherhead, A. Kingsley. *The Edge of the Image: Marianne Moore, William Carlos Williams, and Some Other Poets.* Seattle and London: University of Washington Press, 1967.

Weil, Simone. *La Pesanteur et la grace.* Paris: Plon, 1947.

Weiss, Helene. "The Greek Conception of Time and Being in the Light of Heidegger's Philosophy." *Philosophy and Phenomenological Research* 2 (1942): 173–87.

Welch, E. Parl. *The Philosophy of Edmund Husserl: The Origin and Development of Phenomenology.* New York: Columbia University Press, 1965.

Wells, Henry W. *Introduction to Wallace Stevens.* Bloomington, Ind.: Indiana University Press, 1964.

Will, Frederic. "Heidegger and the Gods of Poetry." *The Personalist* 43 (1962): 157–67. Reprinted in his *Literature Inside Out: Ten Speculative Essays.* Cleveland, Ohio: The Press of Western Reserve University, 1966, pp. 25–35.

Winters, Yvor. *On Modern Poets.* New York: Meridian Books, Inc., 1959.

Wyschogrod, Michael. *Kierkegaard and Heidegger: The Ontology of Existence.* London: Kegan Paul, 1954.

Index of Subjects and Titles

Act of the Mind, The, 17n, 20–22, and passim
Annali dell'Istituto Universitario Orientale: Sezione Germanica, 139n

Baird, James, 17n, 19, 22n, 86, 99, 109–10n, 128n, 134 and passim
Being, 20, 20n, 21–22 and passim
Benamou, Michel, 104n
Bergson, Henri, 187
Bertholf, Robert J., 87n, 199n, 225n, 228n
Blackmur, R. P., 139n, 140, 195
Bloom, Harold, 139n, 167n, 175, 185, 196n, 199n, 201–2
Borroff, Marie, 30n
Brown, Merle, 70n, 139
Bryer, Jackson, 19n
Buhr, Marjorie, 22
Burney, William, 101, 103n, 131
Burnshaw, Stanley, 59–60n
Buttel, Robert, 29n

Cambon, Glauco, 22, 35, 158n, 167n
Chapelle, Albert, 116n, 165n
Char, René, 13–14
Chocorua, 223

Church, Henry, 138–39n, 141
Clairvoyant Eye, The, 17n, 18n, 29n and passim
Coleridge, S. T., 44, 96
Comic Spirit of Wallace Stevens, The, 29n, 30n, 43n, 88n, 91n, 106n, 110, 120–21, 136, 146n, and passim
Complementarity, Theory of, 178–79n
Connoisseurs of Chaos: Ideas of Order in Modern American Poetry, 106
Continuity of American Poetry, The, 17n, 26n, 188n, 261n
Crane, Hart, 192
Crispin, 37–38

Decreation, 26n, 29–30, passim
Descartes, René, 116, 124, 169–72
Description: phenomenological, 30–37 and passim; Stevens's theory of, 157–66
De Waelhens, Alphonse, 165n
Doggett, Frank, 17n, 18, 70n, 73n, 89, 104n, 127, 131, 151n, 170n, 174n and passim
Dome and the Rock, The, 19, 22n, 86n, 99, 109–10n, 134 and passim

293

Eidos (and Eidetic), 96–97, 98
Eliade, Mircea, 111n, 160n, 184n, 196n, 202, 211
Eliot, T. S., 192
Enck, John J., 121
Epistemology, 31–58, 86–114
Existence and Being, 148–49, 150n, 163n, 215n, 221n, 237–38, 241
Existent (*das Seiend*), 20n, 114n and passim

Fancy (*die Phantasie*), 96; Husserl on, 75n
Fiction (*die Fiktion*), 75n; Stevens on theory of, 67–68, 73–75; Stevens on Supreme Fiction, 139–212
Finch, John, 37n
Fraisse, Paul, 180n
Freud, Sigmund, 195
Frye, Northrup, 162n, 249
Fuchs, Daniel, 29–30n, 43n, 88n, 91n, 106n, 110, 120–21, 136, 146n and passim

Gaiety of Language, The, 29n, 50–51n, 54n
Goethe, Johann Wolfgang von, 159n, 237

Hammond, Mac, 70n
Hartsock, Mildred, 214n
Heidegger, Martin, 10–11, 22–28, 114 and passim; attunement (*Befindlichkeit*), 116, 116–17n, 118–19, 207; authenticity (*Eigenlichkeit*), 143–44, 159n, 207, 244–45; Being (*Sein*), 20n and passim; beings (*die Seiende*), 114n; Being-in-the-World (In-der-Welt-sein), 116 and passim; Being-toward-Death (*Sein-zum-Tode*), 190–91, 209, 211–12, 233–34; *Dasein*, 20n, 22, 114n, 115 and passim; nothing (*das Nicht*), 204, 262–63; ontology, 22–25, 156; phenomenology (*die Phänomenologie*), 84, 145–46n; poets and poetry (*Dichter und Dichtung*), 155–66, 239–42; projection (*Entwurfenheit*), 164–66, 171; possibility (*Möglichkeit*), 158–59, 165–66; relation to Husserl, 10–11, 145n; repetition (*Wiederholung*), 182–83; self-knowledge (*sich erkennen und sich können*), 144–45; speech (*Rede*), 240–42; (*Sprach*), 155–66, 239–40; temporality and time (*Zeitlichkeit und die Zeit*), 22, 24–29, esp. 181–83, 211–12, 256–60; transparency (*die Durchsichtigkeit*), 143–44
Heidegger, Martin: works of:
"Brief über den'Humanismus,' " 163n, 230n
Einführung in die Metaphysik (*Introduction to Metaphysics*), 262–63
Erläuterungen zu Hölderlins Dichtung, 148–49, 150n, 163n, 215n, 221n, 237–38, 241
"Hölderlin und das Wesen der Dichtung" ("Holderlin and the Essence of Poetry"), 148–49, 150n, 163n, 215n, 237–38, 247
Holzwege, 215n, 230n, 239–41n
Kant und das Problem der Metaphysik (*Kant and the Problem of Metaphysics*), 238
Platons Lehre von der Wahrheit ("Plato's Doctrine of Truth"), 163n, 230n
Sein und Zeit (*Being and Time*), 114n, 116, 117, 117n, 119, 122, 132n, 143n, 144n, 145–46n, 156n, 157n, 159n, 162–63n, 165n, 166n, 171–72n, 181–82n, 215n, 223n, 244n and passim
Vorträge und Aufsätze, 230–31
Was ist Metaphysik? ("What is Metaphysics?"), 262
Vom Wesen der Wahrheit ("On the Essence of Truth"), 228n, 238n, 241n, 245n, 249n
Heraclitus (Heraclitan), 258, 260

Heringman, Bernard, 188n
Hölderlin, J. C. F., 237, 273
Husserl, Edmund, 10–11, 23, 25 and passim; adequacy, 90, 96–97n; consciousness (*Bewusstsein*), 86–87; Epochē (ἐποχή), 92–93, 104n, 107, 112; Eidetic inquiry (*Eidos*), 96–97; Fictions (*die Fiktion*), 75n; first philosophy (*erste Philosophie*), 90; intentionality (*Intentionalität*), 33–34; logic (*Logik*), 32; natural standpoint (*natürlichen Einstellung*), 80–81; phenomenology (*die Phänomenologie*), 30–37 and passim; reductions (*die Reduktionen*), 34–37, 92–95; suppositions (*die Voraussetzungen*), 31–35; things themselves (*die Sachen selbst*), 86–87; transcendental subjectivity (*die transzendent Subjektivität*), 92–94
Husserl, Edmund: works of:
Cartesianische Meditationen und Pariser Vorträge (*Cartesian Meditations*), 23, 92n (also *Les Méditations Cartésiennes*), 23
Die Idee der Phänomenologie (*The Idea of Phenomenology*), 33–34
Ideen zu einer reinen Phänomenologie und phänomenologischen Philosophie (*Ideas: General Introduction to Pure Phenomenology*), 31–34, 75, 75n, 81, 82n, 92, 92n, 94n, 96–97
"Philosophie als strenge Wissenshaft," 31n, 33n

Imagination, 71–72, 95, 95n, passim
Inclusive Flame, The, 22, 35, 158n, 167n

Jarrell, Randall, 18n, 214

Kant, Immanuel, 158, 174
Keats, John, 42, 236
Kermode, Frank, 85, 151n, 178–79n, 185n, 210, 228n
Kocklemans, Joseph J., 33n, 34, 94n

Landgrebe, Ludwig, 94n
Language: as description, 157–66; as ambiguous, 160–67 and passim; Heidegger on language, 155–66, 238–41
Lentricchia, Peter, 29n, 50–51n, 54
Löwith, Karl, 165n

McFadden, George, 134n, 235n
Macksey, Richard A., 17n, 22, 35–36, 247n, 261
Making of Harmonium, The, 29n
Martz, William, 30n, 51n, 214, 231
Mattino Domenicale ed Altre Poesie, 60n
Marx, Werner, 116n, 165n
Miller, J. Hillis, 20–22, 66n, 123, 123n, 261n, 262 and passim
Mills, Ralph J., 215n
Morse, Samuel French, 18n, 24n, 112n
Mysticism: in Stevens, 9–10, 142–43; in Rudolf Otto, 142

Nassar, Eugene Paul, 91n, 135n, 148n, 170n, 203n, 207n, 219–20n, 235n
Nemerov, Howard, 214n
Nietzsche, F. W., 176, 176n

O'Conner, William Van, 189
Oley, Pennsylvania, 224–25
Ontology: Heidegger on, 22–25, 157 and passim; and poetry, 155–56
Otto, Rudolph, 142

Pack, Robert, 214n
Pearce, Roy Harvey, 114n, 139n, 188n, 214n, 261n, 267–68
Phantasie, die: in Husserl, 74–75
Pnenomenology: Husserl's, 30–37 and passim; Heidegger's, 84, 145–46
Philosophy: and poetry, 17–28 and passim
Pieper, Josef, 228n
Plato, 31–32

Poetry (Stevens's): of Being, 113–15
and passim; of the act of the mind,
87–113; of process, 29–84
Poets of Reality, 20–22, 66, 123, 261n
Poggioli, Renato, 60n
Poulet, Georges, 180n

Richardson, William J., 116n, 165n,
182n
Riddel, Joseph N., 17n, 18n, 19n, 50n,
55, 88, 151n, 155, 168n, 187, 203
and passim
Rilke, Rainer Maria, 272–73

Santayana, George, 9, 10
Shakespeare, William, 83, 217, 235
Shaping Spirit, The, 189
Sheehan, Donald, 247–48n
Shelley, Percey Bysshe, 189–90, 193–
94
Stallknecht, Newton P., 60n
Stern, Herbert, 29n
Stevens, Holly, 14, 24n
Stevens, Wallace: on change, 178–94;
on decreation (and creation), 26n,
107–8 and passim; development in
the poetry of, 10–11, 21–28 and
passim; fictions, 67–68, 73–75 and
passim; imagination, 71–72, 95, 95n
and passim; language, 157–66;
metaphor, 162, 239–59; nothingness, 260–66; personae, 141, 160,
177n, 234–35; as philosophical
poet, 17–28, 30–31, 90–91, 195–
96; as the poet of Being, 115–22,
124–25, 132–37, 178–94, 208–12;
poetry of disclosure, 115–19;
poetry of process, 85–88; possibility,
158–59; repetition, 10, 208–12; on
time, 165n, 179–94, 209, 216–36,
260–61
Stevens, Wallace: works of:
"Academic Discourse in Havanna,"
41–50

"Adagia," passim
"Add This to Rhetoric," 99, 248
"American Sublime," The, 50
"An Old Man Asleep," 258
"Angel Surrounded by Paysans," 5
"Asides on the Oboe," 133
Auroras of Autumn, The, 19, 213,
250–73
"Auroras of Autumn, The," 250–
52
"Bouquet of Roses in Sunlight," 248
"Candle a Saint, The," 128–29
"Chocorua to its Neighbor," 177n,
223
Collected Poems of Wallace Stevens, The,
11, 14, 22n and passim
"Collect of Philosophy, A," 18n
"Comedian as the Letter C, The,"
37, 38
"Contrary Theses (II)," 129–32
"Countryman, The," 253–54
"Credences of Summer," 10, 31,
216–36 and passim
"Crude Foyer," 246–47
"Dance of the Macabre Mice," 49
"Description Without Place," 155–
66, 236
"Esthétique du Mal," 187, 195
"Evening Without Angels," 49
"Extracts from Addresses to the
Academy of Fine Ideas," 137,
154, 207
"Farewell to Florida," 37–41
"Glass of Water, The," 95–99
"Hand as a Being, The," 133–35
Harmonium, 24, 29–31
"Homunculus et la Belle Etoile,"
31–32
"Idea of Order at Key West, The,"
25, 50–57
Ideas of Order, 25, 29–32, 33 and
passim
"Imagination as Value," The, 95
"Invective Against Swans," 43, 43n

"Landscape With Boat," 106–12
"Large Red Man Reading," 159, 171, 252–53
"Latest Freed Man, The," 113, 115–23, 154
Letters of Wallace Stevens (ed. Holly Stevens), 24, 64, 66, 73, 138–39n, 167, 170n, 173, 176, 198
"Man on the Dump, The," 100–105
"Man with the Blue Guitar, The," 25, 48, 57, 59–84
"Meditation Celestial & Terrestrial," 50
"Metaphor as Degeneration," 254–58
"Motive for Metaphor, The," 246–47
Necessary Angel, The, 18, 95, 155
"Noble Rider and the Sound of Words, The," 27n, 28n, 150, 155
"No Possum, No Stop, No Tatters," 246
"Not Ideas About the Thing but the Thing Itself," 86, 272–73
Notes Toward a Supreme Fiction, 27, 138
"Notes Toward a Supreme Fiction," 27, 138–212, 222n and passim
"O Florida, Venereal Soil," 40
"Of Bright & Blue Birds & the Gala Sun," 135–37, 154
"Of Modern Poetry," 87–89
"On the Road Home," 103–5
Opus Posthumous (ed. Samuel French Morse), 23, 271n, 272–73
"Ordinary Evening in New Haven, An," 9, 261–66
Owl's Clover, 59, 59n
Parts of a World, 27, 85, 86–114, 116–37
"Plain Sense of Things, The," 249–50
"Planet on the Table, The," 272
"Poems of our Climate, The," 90–95

"Primitive Like an Orb, A," 251, 271–73
"Prologues to What is Possible," 166
"Pure Good of Theory, The," 248–49
"River of Rivers in Connecticut, The," 258–60
Rock, The, 20
"Rock, The," 214 and passim, esp. 266–72
"Sad Strains of a Gay Waltz," 48–49
"Sailing After Lunch," 49
"Sea Surface Full of Clouds," 40, 78
"Sense of the Sleight-of-Hand Man, The," 124–25, 134
"Six Significant Landscapes," 32
"Snow Man, The," 40, 264
"Study of Two Pears," 99
"Sunday Morning," 40–41, 112, 191, 211
"Thirteen Ways of Looking at a Blackbird," 78
"This Solitude of Cataracts," 253–54
"To an Old Philosopher in Rome," 9
Transport to Summer, 19, 138–237, 238–50
"Two or Three Ideas," 30n
"Two Versions of the Same Poem," 238–39
"Yellow Afternoon," 125–34
Stevens' Poetry of Thought, 17n, 18, 70, 73n and passim
Sukenick, Ronald, 66n, 67n, 69n, 77n, 170n, 173n, 190n, 205–6n, 214n, 227n
Symbolism: Stevens and the symbolist aesthetic, 104

Time (and temporality): in Heidegger, 22–29, 181–83, 211–12, 256–60; in Husserl, 87, 93; in Stevens, 179–94, 209, 216–38

Valéry, Paul, 192
Vendler, Helen Henessey, 49, 54n, 158, 239–40n

Wagner, C. Roland, 132n, 265
Wahl, Jean, 10, 23
Wallace Stevens (Burney), 101, 103n, 131
Wallace Stevens (Kermode), 85
Wallace Stevens: A Collection of Critical Essays, 30 and passim
Wallace Stevens: An Anatomy of Figura-
tion (Nassar), 91n, 135n, 148n, 170n, 203n, 207n, 219–20n
Wallace Stevens: Art of Uncertainty (Stern), 29n
Wallace Stevens: Musing the Obscure (Sukenick), 66n, 67n, 69n, 77n, 170n, 173n and passim
Wallace Stevens: The Symbolist Imagina-tion (Benamou), 104
Wells, Henry, 51n, 216
Williams, William Carlos, 86, 193
Wimsatt, W. K., 254, 254n
Winters, Yvor, 214